D1323391

Revolutionary Nativism

Revolutionary Nativism

Fascism and Culture in China, 1925–1937 » MAGGIE CLINTON

Duke University Press   Durham and London   2017

Cover designed by Matthew Tauch
Text designed by Courtney Leigh Baker
Typeset in Whitman and Trade Gothic by Westchester Publishing Services

Library of Congress Cataloging-in-Publication Data
Names: Clinton, Maggie, [date] author.
Title: Revolutionary nativism : fascism and culture in China, 1925–1937 /
Maggie Clinton.
Description: Durham : Duke University Press, 2017. |
Includes bibliographical references and index.
Identifiers:
LCCN 2016043541 (print)
LCCN 2016046041 (ebook)
ISBN 9780822363620 (hardcover : alk. paper)
ISBN 9780822363774 (pbk. : alk. paper)
ISBN 9780822373032 (e-book)
Subjects: LCSH: Zhongguo guo min dang. | China—History—1928–1937. |
China—Politics and government—1912–1949. | Politics and culture—China. |
Fascism—China. | Nationalism—China.
Classification: LCC DS777.48.C59 2017 (print) | LCC DS777.48 (ebook) |
DDC 320.53/3095109043—dc23
LC record available at https://lccn.loc.gov/2016043541

Cover art: Illustration from Qiantu (the Future) 1, no. 8, 1933.

FOR ROGER

Contents

Acknowledgments

This book began at New York University, where it was nurtured by a wealth of brilliant mentors and friends. I thank first and foremost Rebecca Karl for her acumen and sustained encouragement. Manu Goswami and Harry Harootunian offered critical insights at every step; Mary Nolan and Andrew Sartori generously helped me refine the project's claims. Faculty including Yukiko Hanawa, Moss Roberts, Kristin Ross, Joanna Waley-Cohen, and Xudong Zhang imparted key ideas. My extended cohort, including William Armshaw, Kristin Bayer, Wei-chi Chen, Sasha Disko, Leigh Claire La Berge, Priya Lal, John Pat Leary, Natasha Lightfoot, Shane Minkin, Osamu Nakano, Michael Palm, Sherene Seikaly, Naomi Schiller, Zach Schwartz-Weinstein, Quinn Slobodian, and Qian Zhu, offered lasting inspiration as well as sharp feedback on the project as it developed.

Colleagues at Middlebury College have likewise been tremendously generous and supportive. I am particularly grateful to Ian Barrow, Rebecca Bennette, Natasha Chang, Nicholas Clifford, Rachael Joo, Joyce Mao, Kathy Morse, Jamie McCallum, Alexis Peri, Yumna Siddiqi, Sarah Stroup, Jessica Teets, Rebecca Tiger, Jacob Tropp, Edward Vazquez, Max Ward, and Don Wyatt. Middlebury students, in their capacities as research assistants and interlocutors, have also helped me write a better book: Allison Bernard, Chime Dolma, Jonathan Fall, Denise Hoffman, Jihad Hajjouji, Steven Luo, Khine Su, Ye Tian, and Winnie Yeung deserve special thanks. By helping me navigate the Middlebury landscape, Claire Wilkinson and Renee Brown also greatly facilitated the writing process.

Questions raised and comments offered in various conference, workshop, and research settings over the years have aided this project in innumerable ways. I especially thank Angie Baecker, Nadya Bair, Doris Bergen, Jia-ching Chen, Wei-chi Chen, Parks Coble, Robert Cole, Alexander F. Day, Mirela David, Dai Jinhua, Geoff Eley, Joshua Fogel, Takashi Fujitani, Jane Hayward, Michael Gibbs Hill, Reto Hofmann, Fabio Lanza, Li Chi-ping, Jane Liau, Andy Liu, Luo Zhitian, Ken Kawashima, Mark McConaghy, Edward McCord, Viren Murthy, Christopher Nugent, Janet Poole, Andre Schmid, Richard Jean So, Joan Judge, Julia Adeney Thomas, Brian Tsui, Ke-wen Wang, Max Ward, Yiching Wu, Qian Zhu, and the late Ramon Myers. Manu Goswami and Greg Grandin have been continuously inspiring, and Rebecca Karl has remained a source of unfailing enthusiasm. Kristin Mulready-Stone gave helpful suggestions for revising the manuscript as a whole. Claire Jarvis, Naomi Fry, Sasha Disko (who also provided this book's German translations), and the rest of our dispersed writing group made these revisions feel like a more collective endeavor, and ongoing conversations with Brian Tsui prompted me to reconsider the project's scope as the revisions went along. Naomi Schiller and Max Ward valiantly read many drafts and answered countless questions; their camaraderie throughout has been invaluable.

Librarians at the National Library of China (Beijing), the Peking University Library, the National Central Library (Taiwan), Stanford's East Asia Library, the Hoover Institution Library and Archives, the Harvard-Yenching Library, and the Middlebury College library provided invaluable assistance. I especially thank Rachel Manning, interlibrary loan coordinator at Middlebury College, for tirelessly sourcing materials for me to consult here in rural Vermont, as well as Middlebury research librarian Brenda Ellis for her patience with all manner of questions.

This project has been generously facilitated by a Mellon/ACLS Dissertation Completion Fellowship, Fulbright IIE, the Blakemore-Freeman Foundation, the New York University Graduate School of Arts and Sciences, the Center for Chinese Studies at the National Central Library in Taiwan, and by Middlebury College. Encouragement has also come from the Clintons, Whites, Pundits, Winters, Bayer-Selas, Chen-hsi Wong, and H. C. Fall Willeboordse. I am most grateful to Roger White for his constant companionship and willingness to talk through all aspects of the project over a seemingly endless number of years, and also for our amazing daughter Helena, who arrived just as this book was coming together as a book. Helena's caregivers at the College Street Children's Center, and especially Alyshia

Murphy and Vivian Yuan Pien, deserve special praise for affording me the time to write.

Finally, I thank Ken Wissoker for his sustained support for the project, Elizabeth Ault for her timely interventions, Mark Mastromarino for preparing the index, and the two anonymous manuscript readers for Duke University Press for their exceedingly generous and exacting feedback. I could not have hoped for more thoughtful interlocutors. The book's shortcomings are of course my own.

Introduction

[The Three Principles of the People] have inherited the morality and essential spirit of ancient China—that of Emperors Yao and Shun, of Kings Wen and Wu, of the Duke of Zhou and Confucius—they employ the native spirit of the Chinese race to lead the revolution and revive the nation.—CHIANG KAI-SHEK, March 1933

From June 1925 until October 1926, a general strike brought work in Hong Kong to a halt, while consumers in the Canton delta boycotted commodities imported via the British colony. The strike-boycott, materially supported by Canton's Soviet-backed United Front government and directed against colonial authorities in Hong Kong, followed a crescendo of anti-imperialist and labor actions throughout mainland China in the early 1920s. Launched in response to the 1925 May 30th Incident, in which British-commanded policemen had killed and wounded Chinese demonstrators in Shanghai's International Settlement, the Hong Kong–Canton strike-boycott signaled not only the sharp escalation of popular anti-imperialism but also the increased power of organized labor.[1] To contemporary observers, its protracted temporal duration and extensive geographical coordination across British colonial and Chinese national space suggested the dawn of a new era of anti-imperialist agitation. Canton's novel experiment in revolutionary organization—in which the Moscow-based Communist International directed an alliance between the Chinese Nationalist Party (Guomindang, GMD) and members of the Chinese Communist Party (CCP)—had rendered southern China a magnet for anti-imperialist, anticapitalist, and feminist revolutionaries from across China and around the world, earning Canton the nickname Moscow East.[2] The strike-boycott, as well as Soviet training of soldiers at the newly founded Whampoa Military Academy, signaled that Canton's United Front was emerging as a disciplined fighting force. Less than a decade after the Russian Revolution, Communists had set roots in an important node of global imperialism, shifting the local meanings of revolutionary politics and prompting new forms of reaction within Chinese society and the metropolitan world.

Imperialist responses to the 1923–27 United Front were swift and violent, involving parades of foreign gunboats in Canton harbor, deadly attacks by colonial police forces on Chinese demonstrators, and ultimately the provision of arms to Chiang Kai-shek's Nationalist forces to bring the United Front to an official end.[3] Reactions by Chinese merchants to the United Front's intersecting nationalist and class-based goals were more measured, but still vacillated between suspicion and hostility.[4] For many in the GMD, Chinese Communist participation in the United Front prompted fear of the potential derailing of a long-germinating nationalist project focused on developing Chinese industry and infrastructure under the guidance of a powerful state—future aspirations that were predicated on eradicating regional warlords and on liberating the nation from imperialist intervention. The untimely death in March 1925 of Nationalist Party leader Sun Yat-sen rendered the revolution's trajectory even more uncertain. Anti-Communist groups quickly coalesced within the party, but their increasingly vocal opposition to Communism did not dull their own revolutionary aspirations.[5] Instead, a range of longtime party activists as well as a cohort of young military cadets amplified their claims upon its course. Now schooled in Soviet methods of agitation and witness to the seductions of modern life, these revolutionaries renewed their commitment to remaking the Chinese sociopolitical landscape and to forcibly overcoming whatever obstacles appeared to stand in their way. Political pluralism increasingly seemed a luxury that even established imperialist powers could ill afford, and lockstep national unity a necessary precondition for China's revolution to advance at all.

In 1925, the veteran Nationalist activist and translator of Marxist theory Dai Jitao favorably likened Sun Yat-sen's developmental program to "aborting the fetus of a recently impregnated capitalism."[6] Dai's language indexed a growing ambivalence among the GMD right wing regarding the social consequences of the industrial development that they championed, evincing at once a desire to introduce capitalist production methods evenly across China's vast territory and a fear of their socially anarchic effects. Dai intimated here that Sun's program could rid the Chinese social body of unwanted offspring while still nurturing its productive capacities, in the way that abortion ideally terminates a pregnancy without rendering the woman's body sterile. Dai's concerns were soon amplified by a host of Nationalist strategists who became increasingly convinced that the unified nation, not the proletariat or peasantry, was the proper agent of a properly Chinese revolution. These men, trained at military and technical schools in China, Europe, the United States, the USSR, and Japan, began to champion "native culture" (*guyou wenhua*) as the glue binding this revolutionary nation together. Discomfited by the seemingly unpatriotic thrust of the New Culture and May Fourth movements—which in the 1910s had attacked Confucianism as responsible for China's apparent failure to modernize—they found in Sun Yat-sen's writings a revolutionary program that instead vouchsafed this heritage. There was nothing incompatible between Confucianism and industrial modernity, Sun had stressed. The Nationalist leader had gone so far as to align New Culture / May Fourth critics of Confucianism with China's "oppression by foreign nations," while identifying his own GMD as a defender of China's "native morality" and therefore with "Chinese people" who held these morals dear.[7] After Chiang Kai-shek violently severed the GMD's United Front ties to the Communist Party in 1927, Sun's most virulently nationalistic supporters followed Dai Jitao in insisting that reviving China's native Confucian culture was key to national rebirth in a militantly corporatist form. Confucian culture, as these supporters interpreted it, mandated the kinds of social hierarchies that were natural to China, the kinds of work ethics and consumption practices that were collectively beneficial, and the kinds of people who did and did not belong within the national fold.

This book is a study of the sharp rightward turn taken by revolutionary nationalist groups that operated under the umbrella of the GMD during the 1920s and 1930s. It focuses on the characteristics of the polity that groups known as the CC Clique and the Blue Shirts strove to cement, and why the officers and engineers who led them regarded culture as integral to this project. I use the term *fascism* to describe their politics for several reasons. First, it signals that they were not conservative, predemocratic, or merely authoritarian. Their hostility to liberal democracy was as informed by modern political and economic theories as was their violent hatred of Communism. It was, moreover, inseparably entwined with aspirations to permanently resolve tensions of modern life that scholars have long since demonstrated gripped major cities like Shanghai and Canton. These plans foregrounded disciplining, under the sign of a Confucian culture now re-cast as a guarantor of hierarchical efficiency, newly classed and gendered social actors. Second, the term *fascism* allows us to grasp the simultaneously revolutionary and counterrevolutionary dynamics of the political solutions that Blue Shirt and CC Clique militants offered, and hence an opportunity to better understand the historical conditions under which fascism emerges and coalesces. This book does not consider the regime that the GMD estab-lished in Nanjing following Chiang Kai-shek's 1927 coup d'état to have been a fascist state, or the GMD in its entirety to have become a fascist party dur-ing the 1927–37 Nanjing Decade. It is instead a study of fascist organizations that attained considerable power but failed to fully capture a state or to in turn secure hegemony among a predominantly agrarian and nonindustrial population. It is specifically concerned with the modernism of Blue Shirt and CC Clique aspirations, the violence that they justified to realize them, and the enduring legacies of their efforts to link Confucianism to an anti-liberal, anti-Communist program of state-led industrial development.

Making sense of the violent nexus of revolutionary and counterrevolu-tionary politics that appeared within GMD ranks after Sun Yat-sen's death requires drawing from conceptual rubrics developed to explain manifesta-tions of fascism in Europe and Japan. Yet these rubrics must also be modi-fied to account for China's colonized circumstances as well as the dramatic unevenness of its socioeconomic landscape, in which ways of life in coastal cities were often more akin to those of the metropolitan world than to those of the national interior to which Chinese fascists laid claim.[8] It is moreover necessary to acknowledge how GMD desires for industrial development and national sovereignty were articulated in the shadow of imperialist racism and ongoing rivalry for access to China's markets and resources. They were seeking to resolve a protracted crisis of political hegemony, one largely induced by imperialist disruptions to an enduring dynastic system. This book builds upon scholarship that has understood fascism as an extreme manifestation of nationalism and therefore regards anticolonial national-isms as potentially as susceptible to fascist radicalization as their metro-politan counterparts.[9] Conditions in coastal China and the world writ large were volatile and antagonistic in ways that prompted Sun Yat-sen's most ardent devotees to amplify their conviction that the Chinese nation was bound together by an ancient cultural force. They intensified nationalism's Janus-faced historical imaginary—which projects the national community both forward and backward in time—by distilling Confucianism into a transhistorical "national spirit" (*minzu jingshen*) capable of reenchanting an industrializing world.[10] The synergy between this enduring spirit and Sun's program, they believed, could resolve China's postdynastic sociopolitical crises, recoup masculine authority, restore the nation to its rightful position of world leadership, and more generally allow for everything and nothing about the nation to change simultaneously.

Representing the Future and Its Past

In 1933, several issues of the Shanghai monthly periodical *Qiantu* (the *Future*), published by a fascist organization known to Chinese and foreign publics as the Blue Shirts, ran a vibrantly colored, abstract cover image of an archer atop an ancient chariot (fig. 1.1).[11] The archer, depicted in red against a graphic blue, gray, and white background, drives his chariot beneath a blazing red sun. His arrow is trained on the masthead characters *Qiantu*, which are printed in a geometric font with circles and triangles in the place of dot strokes. Archery and charioteering—two of the six arts required for mastery by scholars during the ancient Zhou Dynasty (1046–256 BCE)—are represented here in a modernist idiom.[12] The image conjures a lapsed Confucian scholarly ideal conjoining physical and mental agility, and suggests the forceful leap required in the present to connect China's militarily formidable past with a radiant new future. Depicting means of violence in an abstract, aesthetically pleasing fashion, the cover evinces a simultaneous yearning for both the ancient past and a modern future. China's national rebirth appears here as an anticonservative "thrust towards a *new* type of society," building "rhetorically on the cultural achievements attributed to the former, more 'glorious' or healthy eras" rather than suggesting a desire to return to the dynastic past as such.[13] Indeed, the cover image highlighted the tangled expressions of nostalgia and expectation contained in pages of the *Future* during its six-year run from 1933 to 1938. There, the two-faced temporal glances that are typical of all nationalist movements assumed particularly mythic and contradictory dimensions, as contributors reckoned with the violence that imperialism had wrought against China's dynastic ways of life, the causes of China's present turmoil, and the fact that a range of political actors contested their authority to craft China's future. While drawing inspiration from traditions associated with the nation's dominant ethnic group, the Han, contributors to the *Future* stressed the

FIGURE I.1 » *Qiantu* (the *Future*) 1, no. 8 (1933).

imperative to begin history anew by overcoming China's fallen present and building a modern society superior to the unstable, class warfare–ridden conditions into which the West had descended since World War I.

In May 1933, as the *Future* expanded its circulation, a Shanghai-based, popular front coalition of distinguished writers and activists including Song Qingling (widow of Sun Yat-sen), Lu Xun, and the American journalist Agnes Smedley submitted a letter to Shanghai's German legation condemning the violence that the Nazis had unleashed upon Germany since seizing power that March. Collectively signed by the China League for Civil Rights (Zhongguo minquan baozhang tongmeng), the letter cataloged Nazi crimes and condemned the "terror which is crippling the social, intellectual and cultural life of Germany."[14] The league's statement of solidarity with victims of a government then tied to the Nanjing regime described its own mission as one which "fights against the Terror in China, fights for the civil and human rights of the Chinese people, and which allies itself with progressive forces throughout the world."[15] The league's self-consciously internationalist ethos, the links that it drew between Nazi and Nationalist terror, and the fact that it managed to publish this statement in the mainstream Shanghai daily *Shenbao*, quickly caught the organization in Blue Shirt crosshairs. Barely a month after the letter was submitted, one of the league's founding members was assassinated by Blue Shirt–run secret services. Some sixteen months later, Blue Shirts killed the managing editor of the *Shenbao*.[16] These murders were committed not merely to silence critics of the Nanjing regime and to intimidate the press into line but as part of a larger agenda to facilitate China's national rebirth.

The White Terror perpetrated during the Nanjing Decade—the ten-year span from 1927 to 1937 when the Nationalists ruled China from the city of Nanjing—was sustained by the operational and intellectual labor of the Blue Shirts and another fascist faction known as the CC Clique. Both groups worked assiduously to narrow the parameters of national belonging, to expand the range of people subject to state discipline, and to lay claim to leadership of the Chinese revolution. Analyses of the White Terror typically focus on its victims, particularly elite writers and organizers like Ding Ling and Qu Qiubai, as well as the assassinated Civil Rights League founder Yang Xingfo (Yang Quan) and the prominent *Shenbao* newspaperman Shi Liangcai. The stories of these victims are vital to understanding the course of China's revolutions, but so too are the perspectives of the men who terrorized them. There are no victims without victimizers, at least as far as political violence is concerned. The victimizers in this case left a voluminous public paper trail rationalizing their actions. Although media participation at first seems at odds with Blue Shirt and CC Clique proclivities for clandestine operations, it was in fact consistent with their desires to be heard and appreciated by the public but not accountable to it in ways of which they disapproved. Here, they illuminated the contours of a nation that they believed themselves to be regenerating and why it should inspire self-sacrificial devotion. It was through these vectors, in particular their forays into publishing, that they worked to secure popular consent and foster the same kind of nationalism that they themselves so passionately felt.

In China's vibrant interwar "mediasphere[s]," the Blue Shirts and CC Clique positioned themselves as political vanguards through skillful deployment of revolutionary rhetoric and modernist aesthetics.[17] Art deco and other popular styles of graphic abstraction that scholars have hitherto associated with interwar Shanghai's commercial publishers and left-wing progressives were also embraced by the far right wing of the GMD, whose reputation for cultural conservatism is belied by their enthusiasm for modernist imagery, industrial progress, and technologies of mass communication. Their extensive array of publications, which included newspapers, magazines, pamphlets, books, and pictorials, forged links between the rural front lines on which they battled Communist soldiers, the city streets on which they terrorized liberals and leftists, and the rhetorical battlefields of China's 1920s and 1930s culture wars.[18] Here, they staked a public claim to emergent revolutionary rhetoric and symbolism, communicating that they were more capable than any other organized political group of delivering upon modernity's promises and that they could also prevent the nation from being divested of its unique qualities amid the development process. Read in light of the Blue Shirts' and CC Clique's behind-the-scenes activities, this paper trail reveals how perpetrators of the White Terror articulated national-regenerative fantasies akin to those of fascist movements elsewhere in the world while seeking to resolve locally specific crises.[19]

This paper trail does so via its content as well as its conditions of production and circulation. The fact that the newspapers, magazines, and so on of GMD fascists had to compete in an already-saturated marketplace signaled how far the Nationalist government was from realizing the kind of total control that they desired. Despite their distaste for the very idea of an uncontrolled press and its subjection to market forces, Blue Shirts took out advertisements for their flagship magazine the *Future* in the back of the

Shenbao less than two years before they killed Shi Liangcai, and as they used the pages of their own magazines to rail against the dissenting voices represented there.[20] The limited and fractured sovereignty of the state that they served meant that they had to compete for readers with the sizeable volume of Chinese- and foreign-language material available in China's major cities, including that produced and imported via the colonial concessions. Circulating one's ideas via print media may have been a favored practice of Chinese political activists since at least the late nineteenth century—gaining new force during the May Fourth Movement and reframed through the lens of propaganda during the United Front—but fascists balked at the idea that they should have to vie for popular attention or market approbation.[21] They did not just support censorship but advocated total state control of everything produced and consumed within national borders; they also favored violent direct action against men and women who dissented. The fact that dissenting voices continued to proliferate through the 1930s had the effect of confirming for GMD fascists the nefarious presence of the subversive forces, and hence the rightfulness of their recourse to violence to force people into line. In other words, Blue Shirt and CC Clique activists regarded the continued proliferation of opposing forces as evidence that Chinese society needed ever greater unity and discipline. That citizens of Nationalist China continued to have other political options to which they could turn—of the kind that were successfully foreclosed by fascists in Germany, Italy, and Japan, but could not be in China as long as the unequal treaties remained in effect and vast areas of the country remained beyond Nationalist jurisdiction—made them clamor all the more stridently for cultural control and lockstep national cohesion.

The vanguardism asserted by the Blue Shirts and CC Clique in the pages of their publications shared a politico-intellectual genealogy with that of their Communist rivals, but it is important to recognize from the outset ways in which their agendas diverged and hence the terms over which right and left fought. In place of class struggle fascists emphasized interclass harmony; in place of exploited classes they highlighted an exploited national community; and in place of solidaristic internationalism they stressed unified national struggle within a Darwinist world order.[22] This is not to suggest that there were not overlaps and intersections between the ideas of China's left and right, especially as these positions were crystallizing during the 1920s and as the Nationalists after 1927 struggled to distinguish in legal and practical terms what was revolutionary versus counterrevolutionary.[23]

It is also the case that leftists and rightists were mutually influenced by the New Culture and May Fourth movements as well as by the rhetoric and dynamics of the United Front. As GMD rightists insisted with escalating virulence that the national collective, not a particular class, was the rightful agent of China's revolution, they invoked Confucian culture as the grounds of this nation's cohesion through time and space, gathering the bewildering diversity of people living within China's territorial borders past and present together under a single sign. And in styling their political agenda as antifeudal and anticonservative, they unmoored this culture from specific historical referents, distilling it into an ancient national spirit that could animate a forward-looking, modernizing program of industrial and infrastructural development.

The Nation as Revolutionary Subject

A key element of post–United Front political struggles was the power to define the goals of revolution and to name its primary protagonists. From the mid-1920s onward, right-wing activists within the GMD had insisted that the true subject of revolution was a harmoniously cooperative national body, bound together by culture, acting in concert against a range of internal and external threats. These struggles emerged not from a state of relative social stability, but from the charged conjuncture of an ongoing postdynastic reordering of Chinese society and a volatile world poised between two cataclysmic wars. Arno Mayer has suggested that "students of crisis politics need multi-angled and adjustable lenses with which to examine such unsettled situations. These lenses must be able to focus on the narrow synchronic and the broad diachronic aspects of explosive conjunctures as well as on the intersections between them."[24] In this light, the GMD right wing's narrowing in on Confucianism as the cultural glue that lent the national subject its coherence can be seen in diachronic context as a reaction against 1910s New Culture and May Fourth Movement critiques of China's dynastic past, in addition to a more general rethinking of that past in the wake of imperialism. At the same time, their militant defense of the national-particular was in synchronic step with worldwide forces of counterrevolution against the internationalist ethos of Communism as well as liberal cosmopolitanisms. Following the 1927 party purge, when Communists were violently expelled from the Soviet-backed alliance, both the CCP and the GMD branded each other counterrevolutionary.[25] Militants in the GMD remained committed to an idea of revolution waged in the name of the nation, and increasingly fought both for and against capitalism, seeking to foster capitalist productive methods throughout China while also taming the social alienations, transformed gender relations, and class tensions that capitalism inevitably generates.[26] Confucianism's stress on social harmony, these party militants maintained, surmounted capitalism's instabilities, and it also sanctioned violence against people who appeared to subvert national cohesion via internationalist, cosmopolitan, or generally degenerate activities.

In the wake of Sun Yat-sen's 1925 death, longtime GMD activists as well as newer recruits moved quickly to define the late leader's legacy and to assert their own power.[27] As Soviet advisers and Chinese Communists watched apprehensively, Whampoa Military Academy cadets formed Sun Yat-senism Study Societies (Sunwenzhuyi xuehui) with branches at universities as far away as Beijing, while anti-Communist party leaders drafted a new party agenda in that city's Western Hills.[28] Collectively, these men commenced the project of identifying why Sun's program was uniquely suited to Chinese social conditions, and conversely why Communism, among other possible political paths, was fundamentally anathema. The GMD would spearhead this theoretical, military, and political project for the remainder of the twentieth century—during the postwar period on Taiwan anchoring and assisting the United States' containment wars from Southeast Asia to Central America.[29] At its point of departure in the mid-1920s, this project was undertaken by militant nationalists seeking centralized state power to launch a sweeping range of modernizing programs that required the thoroughgoing transformation of popular subjectivities and ways of being. It germinated in dialogue with other anticolonial nationalisms across Asia and around the world, as well as with a newly emerging global form of counterrevolutionary reaction. This new form pitted itself against internationalism and cosmopolitanism, eschewed political liberalism and laissez-faire capitalism, valorized the nation and masculine prowess, and distinguished itself from conservatism by its revolutionary militancy and the all-encompassing nature of the change that it sought.

The Comintern agent M. N. Roy, who organized in China during the United Front, pointedly criticized Sun Yat-sen's thought as casting "the ominous shadow of fascism."[30] The fact that Chinese Communists also paid homage to Sun led political scientist A. J. Gregor to dismiss Roy's fascism observation as nonsensical, adding that the "Blue Shirts, like Chiang

Kai-shek and the [GMD], remained resolutely committed to the doctrines of Sun Yat-sen. They were developmental nationalists, absorbed in the economic development and the military defense of the national community" rather than fascistic in any identifiable way.[31] The scholar Maria Hsia Chang similarly argued that "whatever 'fascism' or 'totalitarianism' there might have been among the convictions held by both Sun and the members of the Renaissance Society can be better understood as a functional and contingent response made by developmental nationalists to the urgent problems of an economically backward and politically threatened community."[32] *Revolutionary Nativism* turns such claims around by arguing that, in 1920s and 1930s China, the "contingent response" of these "developmental nationalists" to defend a "backward" and "politically threatened community" was a fascist one.[33] Efforts to rigorously specify the political dynamics and internal complexities of the Nanjing regime, and likewise to avoid caricaturing Chiang Kai-shek and his supporters as they had been for decades in the People's Republic of China, has led some mainland scholars to avoid the term *fascism* entirely.[34] However, the imperative for historical specificity and to avoid unhelpful name calling need not prevent us from identifying political commonalities across different regions of the globe, especially as it is now taken for granted how tightly entwined many parts of Republican China were with the industrialized, metropolitan world. The scholarly rush to identify signs of the modern throughout China in the first half of the twentieth century should render the appearance of this eminently modern ideology there as well ultimately unsurprising.

As historian Margherita Zanasi has shown with respect to the GMD left wing, nothing precludes a developmental nationalism from assuming a fascist form.[35] This does not mean that the Nationalists' or even Sun Yat-sen's personal desire to see China become a cohesive, industrially and infrastructurally developed nation was intrinsically fascistic. It does mean, however, that Sun's ideas were neither static nor transhistorical. They were interpreted and striven for under specific circumstances. To realize the goal of a strong and industrially developed nation-state in the post–United Front period, the Nationalists engaged a formidable range of domestic and international opposition. From the mid-1920s onward, many within the GMD chose to redouble the force with which they pushed back against such opposition, decidedly crossing a nebulous threshold that Mayer identified between "containment" and "counterrevolution."[36] But it is equally true that many within the GMD continued to push forward their revolutionary aspirations with a newly intensified commitment.[37] They sought and found sanction for their actions in Sun's writings, driving Sun's hesitations about class struggle, his belief in national consanguinity, and his interest in reviving China's "native morality" to the extremes permitted and encouraged by a world on the cusp of World War II.

This book approaches GMD politics as an unfolding dynamic rather than as a fixed set of propositions. Such an approach allows us to see anticolonial, developmental nationalisms as historical and hence responsive to the forms of opposition against which they are articulated. Understanding interwar fascism as a nexus of revolutionary and counterrevolutionary politics—a politics that was anticonservative, antiliberal, anti-Communist, antifeminist, and historically rooted—also allows us to see how it was generated from within China's postdynastic landscape rather than imported from Europe or Japan.[38] Chinese fascists were indeed close followers of global events, and many of them studied or traveled abroad in the USSR, western Europe, Japan, and the United States. Their news media constantly reported on happenings from Madrid to Manila, and they were certainly inspired by fascist developments in Germany, Italy, and Japan. However, they were inspired by these developments because they resonated with beliefs already held and because they offered more successful examples of things that they wanted to achieve. Blue Shirt and CC Clique disinterest in precisely replicating metropolitan fascist ideologies in China, or in using imported terminology to describe their own political agenda, was consistent with their nationalism and with the nationalistic thrust of all interwar fascisms.[39] If we characterize Chinese fascists as mere imitators of Europeans or Japanese, we miss the ways in which they engaged with problems of imperialism. They understood China's global predicament to be quite different from that of metropolitan countries, tellingly identifying simultaneously with the agents and victims of metropolitan fascist aggressions. They for instance admired Italian corporatism but were also troubled by Italy's 1935 invasion of Ethiopia, as the latter's status as a nominally independent, nonwhite nation hemmed in by formal colonies appeared to mirror China's own with respect to Japan.[40] They were, moreover, aware of Nazi racism, just as they were aware of the racism that underpins all colonial projects.[41] But this awareness prevented them neither from desiring that China could assert its national will in the manner that Nazi Germany, Fascist Italy, and Imperial Japan were then doing, nor from advancing a nativist conception of the nation that strictly delimited who belonged and who did not. Examining fascism's local roots helps us to avoid treating capitalist development as if it were a natural historical course, or attributing the violence employed by the GMD to achieve their developmental ambitions to foreign-inspired fashions or lingering feudal dispositions. We can instead focus attention on the ways in which GMD militants redefined native traditions in a post–May Fourth, post–United Front context and worked to render unthinkable other possible arrangements of social and productive relations.

Over the course of the 1920s and 1930s, right-radicalized Nationalists progressively reread Sun Yat-sen's thought as a modern-day expression of ancient Confucian values. As historian Brian Tsui has underscored, such readings gained traction during the United Front via the writings of Dai Jitao, who channeled Sun's ideas in an overtly anti-Communist, Confucian-culturalist direction.[42] Although Sun himself was a product of colonial modernity—born in the post–Opium War Canton delta, educated in Hawaii and Hong Kong, and an inveterate globe-traveling revolutionary who acknowledged inspirations from Henry George to Henry Ford—Dai emphasized only the indigenous roots of Sun's thought, blanketing his eclectic global influences under a shroud of lapsed Confucian wisdom.[43] Dai Jitao thereby catalyzed the naturalization of associations between Confucianism and a form of economic development coming to be known globally as corporatism, and also laid groundwork for interpreting challenges to Confucianism as nationally subversive acts.

In the chapters that follow, I trace this Confucian-culturalist, or what I call nativist, turn through the complex factional alliances and personal ties that constituted the GMD right wing from the mid-1920s until the 1937 Japanese invasion of coastal China. By nativist, I mean the identification of Confucianism as the exclusive core of Chinese cultural and national belonging, as well as attendant efforts to cast other revolutionary projects or forms of political opposition as harmful to that culture and hence to the nation itself. Chiang Kai-shek stood at the apex of the GMD right wing and was devotedly supported by the two factions—the CC Clique and the Blue Shirts—on which this book focuses. Dai Jitao's ideas are discernible in the writings of both factions and in those of Chiang Kai-shek even as these men made nativist ideas their own and amplified them in varying ways. Personal ties—including those based on home provinces, familial friendships, marriages, and shared military and educational experiences—are important to this story. They often informed political allegiances and vice versa within the Nationalist Party structure during its early years. Chiang Kai-shek, for instance, first met Dai Jitao while studying abroad in Japan in 1909 through the introduction of Chiang's fellow Zhejiang provincial, veteran revolutionary Chen Qimei. Later, Chiang not only adopted Dai Jitao's nativist reading of Sun Yat-sen but also literally adopted a son that Dai had fathered with his Japanese mistress—a fact that renders Dai's 1925 rhetorical analogy between Sun's program and aborted fetuses, as well as his escalating moral sanctimoniousness, all the more worthy of analysis.[44] Before Chen Qimei's assassination in 1916, he had acted as a mentor to Chiang Kai-shek, while Chiang in turn became close with Chen Qimei's nephews Chen Guofu and Chen Lifu. The brothers would go on to found the CC Clique in 1927 and work closely with Dai Jitao throughout the 1930s.[45]

During the 1923–27 United Front period, as Chiang Kai-shek climbed the ranks of the National Revolutionary Army and assumed a leadership role at Canton's Whampoa Military Academy, Chen Guofu worked as a recruiter for Whampoa cadets. In this capacity, Chen Guofu encouraged his younger brother Chen Lifu to return from studying engineering in the United States; the younger Chen traveled to Canton in 1925 and soon became Chiang Kai-shek's personal secretary. That same year, young Whampoa cadets formed Sun Yat-senism study societies under the spell of Dai Jitao's reinterpretation of Sun to rival the academy's Communist cadet organization.[46] Members of these Sunist societies, including He Zhonghan, would soon form the Blue Shirts, and they in turn saw their operations financed in part by a bank chaired by Chen Guofu.[47] The life trajectories of the men who composed the GMD right wing thereby first intersected in United Front Canton, where they learned the powers of Soviet-style organization, military discipline, and agitational propaganda.

It was also in Canton that they grew inspired to theoretically and tactically contribute to Chiang Kai-shek's violent severing of the United Front in spring 1927, in the midst of the antiwarlord military campaigns up from Canton known as the Northern Expedition. The first few months of the White Terror involved the murder of three thousand to four thousand Communist Party members and thirty thousand of its presumed supporters, the imprisonment of twenty-five thousand others and the injuring of forty thousand more.[48] The events of spring 1927 were quickly interpreted by Communists and anticolonial nationalists around the world as a pivotal juncture not just in Chinese but in world revolutionary history: Chiang's coup became a component of power struggles between Stalin and Trotsky in the USSR, and it cast an ominous shadow over the future course of anticolonial struggles, particularly in Asia, where conflicts between Nationalist and Communist parties soon anchored major hot wars of the Cold War.[49] The nation in whose name they waged this violence was conceptualized largely in response to core debates of the 1910s New Culture and May Fourth movements, and with the aim of creating a hierarchical nation modeled by turns on a rationalized military and an efficient capitalist firm.

Cultural Revolution from the Right

While it at first seems surprising that men who trained as soldiers and engineers took an avid interest in cultural matters, this becomes less curious when we consider the activist milieus from which they emerged and how they understood culture to operate in the world. Their desire to simultaneously revive ancient Confucian values and to thoroughly revolutionize Chinese culture also becomes more intelligible. The 1910s New Culture and May Fourth movements that framed the school-age years of Nanjing Decade fascists had sourced many of China's postdynastic sociopolitical troubles to the patriarchal, authoritarian, and collectivist traditions of Confucianism, maintaining that upending these traditions at the level of writing and scholarship, as well as at the level of everyday thinking and practice, were preconditions for building modern institutions grounded in science and democracy.[50] Despite the range of political and epistemological standpoints that contributed to these movements, they also encompassed what Lydia Liu identified as a "gray area" of "undisputed knowledge" that enabled debates between contending participants to be possible in the first place.[51] This included a general agreement that culture (*wenhua*) no longer merely denoted a state of personal-artistic cultivation as it had during the dynastic era, but now also carried ethnographic meanings.[52] It moreover involved a consensus that Confucianism composed the core of China's national culture. Critiquing Confucianism qua Chinese culture quickly became axiomatic among leftists, especially among those who joined the Communist Party after 1921 and soon migrated south to Canton to join the United Front. At the same time, defending Confucianism quickly became central to the GMD's political project, especially to the young soldier and student recruits who also came of age during the New Culture and May Fourth movements and converged, like their Communist counterparts, in Canton after 1923.[53] If "May Fourth iconoclasm is itself a political and ideological construct that tells us more about the definition of twentieth-century Chinese modernity than the nature of 'traditional' society," Nationalists who became fascists in the late 1920s and 1930s can be understood as rebutting and inverting May Fourth's presentist picture of the Confucian past.[54] The material that May Fourth thinkers grappled with has been identified by historian Luo Zhitian as an "inheritance within rupture"; ideas and practices that had already been intensely reconsidered amid the sociopolitical upheaval that attended the collapse of the Qing by 1911.[55]

The GMD's turn to Confucianism during the Nanjing Decade has appeared to some as evidence of an enduring despotism. To others, most notably Joseph Levenson, it seemed a kind of "counterfeit of culturalistic confidence" in a tradition whose proper place was now the museum, as if those who championed aspects of Confucianism after 1911 rationally knew better but emotionally could not let go of something whose historical moment had demonstrably passed.[56] With the hindsight of postcolonial criticism, we can see that Nationalist defense of indigenous traditions was largely in sync with elite anticolonial nationalisms elsewhere in the world, more so than was the iconoclastic rejection of them by Chinese Communists. Though Nationalist invocations of spirit did not precisely correspond with those of, for instance, elite Indian nationalists concerned to demarcate noncolonized spheres of meaning and action, the comparison certainly highlights a common reaction against imperialist dispossessions, one that is obscured by Levenson's account.[57] Levenson nevertheless helpfully called attention to nationalism's affective dimensions, pointing us to the ways in which fascists understand themselves to love the nation more than anyone and actively supply themselves with reasons to kill and die for it. The GMD militants on which this book focuses were enraged by the damage wrought to a Confucian inheritance by imperialists from the nineteenth century onward, who had looted its material manifestations and placed them in their own museums while also condemning this inheritance as unscientific, inadequately rational, and generally incompatible with modernity. There is no reason to doubt that their interest in Confucianism stemmed at least in part from the fact that it named a set of shared experiences and beliefs that they had known in some form all their lives.[58] The problem taken up by this book is not whether their beliefs were genuine—as that is impossible to gauge in any case—but how and why they interpreted and defended Confucianism as the exclusive core of Chinese national belonging. The aspects of this richly nuanced politico-intellectual heritage that they promoted explicitly buttressed the remaking of Chinese society in a rationalized, efficient, and hierarchical fashion. They suppressed or ignored all other schools of dynastic thought in a way that sanitized the historical record and had potentially dire implications for the ethnically and religiously diverse populations within the territory that they claimed as China. And unlike conservative New Confucian philosophers of the same era, they were not interested in openly working through the relationship between historical ideas and modern social dynamics, but rather in asserting their perennial capacity to police the national boundary.

As subalternist critics have interrogated the social dimensions and elisions of the gestures of historical retrieval made by elite anticolonial nationalists, it is important to examine who stood to gain from those made by men like Chen Lifu, Dai Jitao, Chiang Kai-shek, and He Zhonghan. Later in the twentieth century, the Martinique-born Marxist Frantz Fanon would scathingly suggest that "the culture that the intellectual leans towards is often no more than a stock of particularisms. He wishes to attach himself to the people, but instead only catches hold of their outer garments."[59] To Fanon, the "national culture" championed by anticolonial elites was typically a patchwork of superficial gestures of cross-class solidarity, offering little of material benefit to the people invoked. Many aspects of the cultural-revolutionary project of GMD fascists during the 1930s—especially their constant invocations of the Confucian bonds of propriety, righteousness, integrity, and humility—rang like a "stock of particularisms." Still, their self-understanding as national vanguards—simultaneously at one with the masses and leaders thereof—meant that they were attempting a closer connection. As much as they desired to reclaim an indigenous patrimony of which the country was still being divested, they sought to fuse the nation's people into a single cooperative mass. Sometimes conceptualized as a machine, sometimes as an army, and sometimes as a living organism, all worthy parts of this mass were deemed vital to the successful functioning of the whole. Culture gave it shape, delimited its boundaries, and authorized a kind of hierarchically stratified sameness.

When CC Clique leader Chen Lifu called for "a revolution of culture," he was considering in all seriousness how to thoroughly transform national ways of life and restore its ancient glory simultaneously.[60] This revolutionary restorationism markedly differed from the cultural revolutionary aspirations of their Communist opponents, whose anti-Confucianism they now pilloried as an imperialistic and violently misguided legacy of the May Fourth Movement. This revolutionary-restorationist dynamic also distinguished Chen Lifu's agenda (along with that of the rest of the CC Clique and the Blue Shirts) from a conservative one. By invoking Confucianism as a transhistorical national spirit, rather than as a historically and textually rooted set of beliefs and practices, this heritage was freed up to animate a state-led program of material and industrial development, encouraging behaviors that would have been unrecognizable to anyone living in centuries past. The purported constancy of this spirit allowed them to simultaneously claim that they were revolutionizing the national landscape while also vouchsafing that everything would remain as it had always been. Under GMD guidance, the nation would become once again a place of comfort and familiarity, and its people would enjoy express trains, electrical grids, machine-powered factories, and militantly defended borders.

Working closely with Chiang Kai-shek's diaries, historian Yang Tianshi has noted how Chiang had been swept up in the reformist fervor of the May Fourth Movement. Yet whereas the dominant May Fourth ethos was strongly critical of traditional Chinese culture, "Chiang Kai-shek was different; although he had internalized the new thought, he was not interested in abandoning classical learning." Yang detected a shift around 1926 in Chiang's reading interests, which turned sharply toward classical texts.[61] By 1933 Chiang would openly exclaim that Sun Yat-sen's Three Principles of the People "have inherited the morality and essential spirit of ancient China— that of Emperors Yao and Shun, of Kings Wen and Wu, of the Duke of Zhou and Confucius—they employ the native spirit of the Chinese race to lead the revolution and revive the nation."[62] Here, Chiang was reiterating passages written by Dai Jitao in 1920s Canton, as well as historical sentiments repeatedly expressed in Blue Shirt and CC Clique writings during the 1930s. By drawing a direct line from China's prehistoric sage-emperors to its twentieth-century revolution, Chiang's words indexed an intensification of the Janus-faced glances toward both past and future evident in Sun's Yat-sen's, and indeed all, nationalisms. The chapters that follow attempt to untangle why the restoration of tradition was construed as both necessary and revolutionary.

Although Chiang Kai-shek publicly denied the existence of the Blue Shirts (the CC Clique was, by contrast, a relatively known government entity), his patronage of both groups as well as their loyalty to him has been amply documented. Chiang was their leader but their influence was clearly mutual. They relied on each other for power, position, and ideological motivation. Nevertheless, as a state leader with a growing international reputation, Chiang was also becoming many things to many people. As Japanese imperialist designs on China became increasingly territorial, Japanese intelligence services attempted to paint Chiang as a radical nationalist with fascist squads at his disposal and hence as a threat to Japanese interests in China.[63] At the same time, Chiang's Christian, Wellesley College–educated wife Song Meiling was actively painting a picture of Chiang to English-speaking audiences as a democratically inclined general who was doing his best to save his country from Communism and to navigate stormy domestic and international waters—laying groundwork for groups soon known in the United States as the "China Lobby."[64] *Revolutionary Nativism* finds the picture of Chiang as a leader with fascist affiliations to be closer to reality than were the sanitized images circulated to the American public by Song and the *Time-Life* empire of Henry Luce. The proximity of Generalissimo Chiang Kai-shek's own revolutionary ideals and counterrevolutionary actions during the Nanjing Decade to those of the Blue Shirts and CC Clique, as well as his reliance upon these groups for his own political ascent, force us to reckon with his fascist inclinations.[65] However, it is necessary to also recognize the kinds of political compromises that Chiang made to secure his own longevity. He disbanded the Blue Shirts (or at least repurposed them) in 1938 for the sake of again allying with the Chinese Communist Party against Japanese imperialism during the Second United Front, and he went on to lead the GMD for the rest of a turbulent half century. His myriad alliances lent his politics an opportunistic quality. Chiang's public acquiescence to Japanese appeasement policies during the 1930s, moreover, was undoubtedly among the reasons why fascistic nationalism failed to gain a wider public purchase in China, as the Generalissimo effectively thwarted the CC Clique and Blue Shirts from tapping into popular anti-Japanese sentiments and directing them sharply rightward. Chiang, like any leader who aspires to dictatorship, was not a self-made subject. By foregrounding the voices of men with whom he surrounded himself during the Canton and Nanjing periods, and how they conceptualized the relationship between culture and revolution, this book aims to shed new light on a brief but pivotal span of Chinese and world revolutionary history.

Plan of the Book

Revolutionary Nativism analyzes the years between 1925 and 1937 through multiple, overlapping lenses. Chapter 1 charts how the anti-Communist groups that coalesced within the Nationalist Party during the 1923–27 First

United Front transformed into fascist organizations known as the Blue Shirts and CC Clique during the 1927–37 Nanjing Decade. I identify ways in which their evolving ideas of national development reflected the military and technocratic milieus in which they were schooled, and how their covert White Terror operations assumed a very public face via their mass media interventions. These interventions, which embraced modernist aesthetics as well as modern technologies like radio and film, allow us to see how GMD fascists fashioned themselves as anticonservative political vanguards.

Chapter 2, "Spirit Is Eternal: Cultural Revolution from the Right," picks up chapter 1's thread by spotlighting tensions between fascists' modernizing aspirations and their desire to revive ancient Confucian values. I trace how their political position was forged in reaction to the dominant ethos of the 1910s New Culture and May Fourth movements and took inspiration from Sun Yat-sen's affirmation in United Front Canton that Confucianism and industrial modernity were in fact fully compatible. Confucian culture came to be seen as what bound the national revolutionary subject together, and this culture assumed increasingly mythic qualities as it was recast as a national spirit in a manner that helped to differentiate their political orientation from a "feudal" or conservative one. Far from an idle intellectual exercise, their spiritual turn had violent real-world consequences. I address these consequences in chapter 3, which traces the role of nativist discourse in Nationalist military counterinsurgency campaigns of the early 1930s— the starkest example of the Nationalists' counterrevolutionary furor. Here, I highlight the ways in which the Blue Shirts who took charge of political training within the Nationalist military cast Communism as fundamentally alien to China's national spirit. This characterization in turn justified campaigns to exterminate Communists and to incarcerate low-level followers deemed rehabilitable in political prisons called repentance camps (*fanxingyuan*). By figuring Communists as Moscow-directed sexual deviants who threatened time-honored Confucian ways of being and as bandits who lived off the labor of others, Nationalists positioned themselves as familiar, wholesome, productive, and modern. In the repentance camps, inmates ostensibly learned how to become productive members of an orderly Confucian society, while citizens beyond camp walls were instructed to police their own behavior in ways that demonstrated they did not belong inside them.

Chapter 4, "Fixing the Everyday: The New Life Movement and Taylorized Modernity," reexamines the New Life Movement (NLM) launched by the

Nationalists in 1934, focusing on the ways in which it sought to fix everyday life in a twofold sense. First, it examines how the fascists who spearheaded the movement touted rationalized Confucian precepts to foster the national unity that they believed necessary for industrial productivity and military preparedness. Building on Arif Dirlik's assessment of the NLM as counterrevolutionary, it traces the patriarchal, antidemocratic implications of the NLM's perspective on society, which was that of officers and managers who wanted people to act like soldiers in a national army or cogs in a giant social machine.[66] This chapter further looks at how the NLM sought to fix everyday life in a second sense by invoking Confucian values to slot people into legible social roles and eliminate the omnipresent possibility of resistance, inscribing feudalistic social hierarchies into the heart of a modernizing society. Departing from the ideals of social reciprocity intrinsic to dynastic strains of Confucian thought, NLM Confucianism stressed top-down chains of command and the unquestioning loyalty of social inferiors to superiors. The NLM thereby sought to create subjects who would accept state propaganda in intended ways and efficiently enact whatever was asked of them. The movement crystallized fascist ideas of cultural revolution and constituted the Sinophone world's first effort to affirm Confucian values as the bedrock of an alternative form of modernity.

Chapter 5, "Literature and Arts for the Nation," examines how the Blue Shirts and CC Clique worked to create "nationalist literature and arts" (*minzu wenyi*) and how they correspondingly justified kidnapping and murdering left-wing cultural elites as a means of speeding the revolution along. Through readings of Chen Lifu's 1933 tract *The Chinese Film Industry* and CC Clique spy chief Xu Enceng's narrative of his detention of the female Communist writer Ding Ling, this chapter reveals how celebrations of native culture prioritized efficiency—from the interpellating capacities of film to the perceived expediency of kidnapping writers to force them into the Nationalist camp. It is in their prescriptions for nationalist literature and arts that fascism's tendency to be what Roger Griffin called "populist in intent and rhetoric, yet elitist in practice" was especially apparent.[67] The book ends with a brief conclusion sketching reasons for fascism's failure to gain wider purchase in Nanjing Decade China, as well as the postwar afterlives of this period's revolutionary nativism.

1 » HIDING IN PLAIN SIGHT

Fascist Factions during the Nanjing Decade

When Chiang Kai-shek's troops abruptly expunged Chinese Communists from their Soviet-backed United Front alliance in April 1927, Shanghai's famed department stores, cabarets, and cinemas appeared as backdrops for a combat dynamic that had been erupting in cities like Munich, Barcelona, Tokyo, and Turin. Just as quickly, these physical markers of China's colonial predicament were revealed to be integral parts of the struggle that had led to the Shanghai bloodbath in the first place. The men who orchestrated the purge and the ensuing White Terror publicly expressed their enthrallment with the wonders of the industrial age—from cars to factories to the late art deco curves of streamline moderne—and their intent to extract these wonders from their present imperialist, degenerate, and socially divisive trappings. Marshaling cutting-edge communications technologies from radio to film, and circulating their revolutionary aspirations via print media that embraced modernist aesthetics, the GMD perpetrators of the White Terror continually emphasized the world-historical newness of the nonbourgeois, non-Communist, and uniquely Chinese revolutionary course that they were charting. This course, they believed, would generate a nationally harmonious form of industrial modernity that circumvented the crises then faced by metropolitan democracies, and defend China's ancient cultural particularity against the twinned universalizing threats of Communism and liberal imperialism.

This chapter traces how interwar fascism constituted a nexus of revolutionary and counterrevolutionary politics that became manifest in China when developmental nationalists, reacting violently against real and imagined threats, anointed themselves vanguards of the future. Their agenda was revolutionary in its aspiration to introduce capitalist forms of production evenly throughout China's vast territory (while understanding themselves as anticapitalist) and in its assumption that doing so required the total transformation of Chinese social life. Yet it was also counterrevolutionary in its conviction that labor, feminist, civil rights, and internationalist movements were legitimately tamed or crushed by whatever means necessary. The main perpetrators of the GMD White Terror—men affiliated with its Blue Shirt and CC Clique factions during the Nanjing Decade—did not envision returning China to a time before factories, films, or republican politics. Instead, they sought to construct a state with the power to harness modern social and technological forms and to police the nation's cultural boundaries. Despite the claims made by these GMD factions that they were following a uniquely Chinese revolutionary course prescribed by Sun Yatsen, their national regenerative fantasies were akin to those of other interwar fascist movements, as was their conviction that they were charting a path beyond Communism and liberalism.

Interwar historical actors and contemporary scholars have long debated whether fascism should be regarded as revolutionary or counterrevolutionary. Marxian commentators in particular, taking the Third Communist International's (Comintern) assessment of fascism as a last gasp of monopoly capitalism as a point of departure, have emphasized that whatever revolution fascists claimed to be fomenting merely reaffirmed existing capitalist property relations, this time disguised with Marxist iconography. In 1933, Ernst Bloch wrote of how Nazis first "stole the colour red, stirred things up with it. . . . Then they stole the street, the pressure it exerts. . . . All in all they pretended to be merely workers and nothing else. . . . And finally they pretend to think of nothing except what will change things." Bloch emphasized that the Nazi was "not content with torturing and killing workers.

He not only wants to smash the red front but also strips the jewelry off the supposed corpse."[1] Fascists thereby violently appropriated from Marxism its signs and symbols as well as its organizational arena and mass appeal. These trappings could not disguise fascism's lack of transformative substance, however, or how its repression and co-optation of workers' movements merely reiterated extant capitalist terms. Yet, as Roger Griffin has succinctly argued, the claim that fascism was merely counterrevolutionary "betrays an inability on the part of some scholars to accept that some of [fascism's] idealists were (and still are) genuinely looking for an alternative to liberalism, communism, conservatism, and capitalism as the formula for resolving the problems of the modern age."[2] When fascist aspirations to create a new social order are taken seriously, their transformative desires—from rescripting sexual relations to murdering the entirety of the world's Jewish population—stand out starkly.[3] To stress only fascism's counterrevolutionary dimensions fails to account for such world-transformative impulses, especially the pronounced desire in China for industrial development and how thoroughly this would alter the general character of social life. To stress only its revolutionary aspects, meanwhile, neglects the terror it waged against egalitarian and internationalist movements.

The social character of GMD conceptions of revolution certainly differed from that of the Communists.[4] It is nevertheless difficult not to concede their contextual radicalism, especially if we assume that much of China's hinterland was not subsumed by industrial capitalism at the time the United Front got under way. Sun Yat-sen's 1921 hymn to industrialization without social conflict, *The International Development of China*, for instance, mapped the wonderments of the machine age onto former Qing territory, reimagining terrain from Tibet to Manchuria as a tightly interlocked web of deepwater ports, railroad lines, and heavy-industrial centers. Sun's cornucopian understanding of China's "unlimited supplies of raw materials and cheap labor" figured China's industrial development as capable of resolving not just local problems but those of the world writ large.[5] As reiterated in his 1924 Canton lectures on the "Three Principles of the People," Sun did not expect China to enter a historical stage through which the West and Japan had already passed, but rather did expect that the state-directed transformation of its rural property relations and urban production methods would generate a new kind of social order, one unsusceptible to global crises and domestic antagonisms. If the Nationalists' revolutionary record in the post-1927 period once appeared "abortive"—prematurely truncated not just by Japan's 1937 invasion but by the Nationalists' own corruption and incompetence—Nationalist achievements in developing state, economic, and legal infrastructures and in reclaiming rights from imperialist powers are now well documented.[6] So, too, are the party's tenuous relations with both rural landed elites and urban capitalists.[7] These successes and relations suggest the potency of the third way that party militants were attempting to chart. However truncated GMD labors may have been, its constant invocation of the term *revolution (geming)* during the Nanjing Decade was not merely empty rhetoric.

At the same time, the revolutionary aspirations of these GMD militants cannot be separated from their efforts to crush all forces of opposition. These efforts did not inevitably flow from Sun Yat-sen's developmental program. Rather, they were exerted by men who grew convinced that realizing their own interpretation of Sun's vision—and thereby resolving the nation's protracted crises—required dictatorial rule and justified state terror. During the 1923–27 Soviet-brokered period of cooperation between the GMD and the Chinese Communist Party, the GMD was reorganized along democratic centralist lines. It gained a disciplined party-army and its rhetoric became infused with the language of propaganda, masses, and mobilization.[8] Party militants began to amplify a decades-germinating nationalist discourse that rejected the application of metropolitan class categories to Chinese circumstances, and cast the unified nation, bound together by Confucian culture, as the true agent of China's revolution. Soviet-style organization, Sunist ideas of elite-led development, and Confucian paternalism mutually imbued them with a sense of their own vanguardist authority vis-à-vis "the masses." After the GMD captured the state in 1927, the militants who constituted the party's Blue Shirt and CC Clique factions gained intermittent windows of opportunity to translate into practice their visions of remaking the nation in a maximally efficient and militantly hierarchical fashion. They exercised power largely through clandestine organizations that were by definition beyond public reproach while also actively participating in China's media circles, where they battled to eliminate all contending voices. Here, they marshaled modernist visual and linguistic signs to demonstrate their claims upon the future and the rightfulness of their own revolutionary leadership.

In the early twentieth century, desire for development knew few political boundaries. V. I. Lenin was as entranced by Henry Ford as was Le Corbusier.[9] Mohandas K. Gandhi's anti-industrialism was a relative outlier in the global spectrum of anticolonial thought. Nevertheless, it must still be recognized that notions of development harbored highly varied ideas about who was entitled to make planning decisions, who would reap the benefits of promised progress, what kinds of people would perform manual and caregiving labor, how these forms of labor were to be socially valued, and what kinds of force could be used to convince the unconvinced. Whose knowledge mattered? What kinds of expertise? Who should have the authority to manage farms and factories, to regulate women's bodies, and to set the parameters of the working day? After 1927, powerful groups within the GMD became increasingly adamant that the party-state, charged with ushering the national masses into modernity, would be the ultimate arbiter of all such questions. In the remainder of this chapter I sketch the key organizations and figures on which this book focuses, highlighting how their beliefs and practices compel us to understand them as fascist.

In and Out of the Shadows: The Formation of the CC Clique and Blue Shirts

In 1929, Dai Jitao, a longtime associate of Sun Yat-sen, paid a visit to Sun's widow Song Qingling at her home in Shanghai's French concession. At the time, Dai was closely affiliated with the CC Clique and had just begun a nearly two-decade tenure as president of the Nationalist government's Examination Branch.[10] Having served as the Whampoa Military Academy's propaganda director during the United Front period, and otherwise actively involved in crafting the Nationalists' image as the true inheritor of Sun Yat-sen's legacy (the specifics of which I discuss in chapter 2), Dai could barely suppress his irritation that Song refused to have anything to do with the new Nanjing regime. She had not only opted to settle in a colonial concession area beyond the sovereign jurisdiction of the Nationalist state, but she was increasingly allying with Nanjing's public critics. According to Song's record of the encounter, Dai visited largely to chastise her for drafting an unauthorized anti-imperialist telegram and for failing to publicly support the Nanjing regime. During the visit, Dai and Song challenged each other's interpretations of Sun's thought.[11] Song charged Dai and the regime that he served with distorting and usurping Sun's ideas, particularly by perpetually deferring the promised transition to popular rule, which in her view reproduced the imperialist canard that the Chinese were "behind by several hundred years, that we do not understand law or order, and so we are not able to govern ourselves."[12] Dai conversely charged Song with impatiently misunderstanding the temporality of Sun's revolutionary vision—which Dai estimated would take several hundred years rather than a single lifetime—and with willfully ignoring the material progress already evident in Nanjing, including the construction of a grand new boulevard named after Sun himself.[13] Song's activism, Dai insisted, constituted an "attack on the government" that damaged China's image at a moment of acute international danger. It moreover aided and abetted the Communists, who were "guided by Moscow, and committing murder and arson all across China."[14]

This tense exchange between Song Qingling and Dai Jitao contained dynamics at the heart of GMD fascism in the years leading up to Japan's invasion of China in 1937. Dai's accusation that Song did not understand the true nature of Sun's revolutionary vision, that her dissent endangered the safety of the republic, and that her actions aligned her with a foreign-directed Communist conspiracy constituted charges that fascists reiterated against their real and imagined enemies throughout the Nanjing Decade. Dai's insistence that he (and his GMD allies) possessed a knowledge of Sun's revolutionary vision that even Sun's widow did not comprehend was emblematic of their self-ascribed vanguardism as well as the new state's patriarchal posturing vis-à-vis its ostensibly wayward citizens. Whereas, Dai maintained, Nanjing had been hard at work pursuing a revolutionary course to provide for the nation's material welfare, women like Song carried on as if they knew what was best for themselves or for the nation as a whole. Dai's additional claim that Song's telegram endangered the nation at a time of international crisis, and that it abetted Communism, bespoke a logic that collapsed varying forms of political action into a catchall Communist menace. Because the Nanjing regime had already announced a Provisional List of Counterrevolutionary Crimes that made it a capital offense to form associations or to enter into alliances with foreigners perceived as subversive to the state, Dai's suggestion that Song's signature abetted a Moscow-directed Communist conspiracy contained the threat of capital punishment.[15] In this way, Dai's 1929 visit to Song encapsulated an unfolding dynamic between men working to consolidate their own power within the government and a society that they by turns conceived as insubordinate, or as what Sun Yat-sen had termed *buzhibujue*—"ignorant and unconscious."[16]

Song Qingling's privileged position as Sun's widow meant that she was relatively insulated from the violence that the state had meted out since 1927. During the first few years of the White Terror, targets of state violence were less frequently left-liberal elites like Song (though they would become targets by the early 1930s) than Communist organizers and urban workers. By 1929 the White Terror had already largely succeeded in pushing Communists out of the cities or so deeply underground that they were cut off from their now-decimated urban labor movement base.[17] Historian Ming K. Chan has explained how, after April 1927, China's labor movement was quickly crushed and co-opted.[18] Unions were "'reorganized' and placed under tight control by the [GMD] authorities, and labor leaders and union members suspected of leftist affiliation were frequently arrested and executed wholesale." The power that unions had won during the early 1920s was greatly diminished as "outright repression by force and legal restriction continued after 1927 on a much larger and more systematic scale," and once left-leaning and Communist unions continued to operate but became "yellow unions run by labor bosses or secret society figures and often living under the shadow of employers."[19] This repression was directly linked to what Chan called the "diehard party cadres of the CC Clique."[20] Members of this clique, including Dai Jitao, Chen Lifu, and Chen Guofu, had a wide range of expertise, from Marxist theory to engineering. They also shared a passion for constructing a national future that would be neither liberal nor Communist.

THE CC CLIQUE

The existence of cliques and factions within the GMD has long been identified as a major cause of the state's overall weakness during the Nanjing Decade.[21] Power struggles between differing party coalitions, whose memberships were often fluid, continued from the 1927 location of the new state in Nanjing until Wang Jingwei and other members of the party's left wing joined the Japanese occupation regime in 1940. The right wing–left wing split was a major but far from exclusive division within the GMD. Groups aligned with Chiang Kai-shek are often called the right wing, while groups aligned with Wang Jingwei the left wing as a result of their differing degrees of willingness to cooperate with Communists during the United Front. After Chiang's 1927 party purge, however, which forced the left wing to reconsider its allegiances, the Wang faction's "left wing" moniker became relatively meaningless even as strategic differences between left and right continued.[22] As Margherita Zanasi has shown, when Wang Jingwei and Chiang Kai-shek formed a coalition government between 1932 and 1935 (during which time Chiang pursued anti-Communist military campaigns in the countryside), Wang's faction in Nanjing implemented corporatist economic development strategies that should be seen as fascistic in their own right, eroding whatever left-wing credibility they had had.[23] Chiang Kai-shek's dominance within party and state structures was not reasonably secured until Wang Jingwei officially resigned in 1935; Chiang's ascent was greatly indebted to the labors of his CC Clique and Whampoa Clique–turned–Blue Shirt supporters.

Like the party's right wing–left wing split, power rivalries among Chiang's supporters were endemic, and their continual refusal to cooperate with one another as well as Chiang's tendency to pit them against each other surely hampered the regime's overall functioning. Yet here especially, differences that fueled turf wars between the military men that constituted the core of the Blue Shirts, and the civilian bureaucrats who made up the CC Clique, were not as significant as they themselves imagined them to be.[24] These groups had more in common ideologically than historians have acknowledged or that the actors in question were willing to admit. Both groups worked assiduously to craft an image of themselves as revolutionary vanguards more radical than the rest of the GMD, of Chiang Kai-shek as the nation's rightful dictator, and of the GMD as leading a revolution true to the Confucian developmentalism of Sun Yat-sen.[25] Convergences between their militaristic and technocratic worldviews—grounded in the entwined processes of rationalization that had transformed the military and business-bureaucratic milieus in which their worldviews took shape—moreover resulted in a shared conviction that the nation desperately needed a strong state to impose upon it hierarchy, efficiency, and discipline.

The name CC Clique (CC xi) is thought to have derived either from the last name of the brothers Chen Lifu and Chen Guofu, who founded and led it, or from shorthand for Central Club. Whatever the case, the Chen brothers stood at its helm and devoted their labors to promoting their own and Chiang Kai-shek's political power, with the broader aim of remolding state and nation on the model of an efficiently managed firm. According to Hung-Mao Tien, after Chen Lifu joined the United Front in Canton, "he and his brother [Guofu] and several fellow compatriots laid down long-term plans to promote their political influence."[26] In late 1926 they formed a group called the Zhejiang Society of Revolutionary Comrades—named for the province from which they and Chiang Kai-shek hailed—and in June 1927 officially formed the CC Clique, which absorbed members of various anti-Communist groups.[27] Their government influence expanded rapidly, with forty delegates represented at the 1929 Third Party Congress, and with

Chen Lifu, Dai Jitao, Chen Guofu, and Chiang Kai-shek all continuing as members of the Central Executive Committee, the state's highest decision-making body.[28] By the 1935 Fifth Party Congress, the CC Clique controlled a third of the Central Executive Committee and otherwise claimed some ten thousand members. The CC Clique's power base was initially rooted in their control of the party's Organization Department, which was headed by Chen Guofu from 1926 to 1932 and Chen Lifu thereafter. This department's influence stemmed from its authority to review and assign "high-level and middle-level personnel to various party branches in governments, the military, youth organizations, and trade-union agencies, and supervised their performance."[29] With a similar eye toward shaping the direction of the party itself, the CC Clique also created a Central Political Academy to recruit and train young cadres, which historian Guannan Li has assessed as "the decisive force that secured the rise and the dominance of the CC Clique."[30]

At Chiang Kai-shek's behest, Chen Lifu established a Bureau of Investigation under the auspices of the Organization Department.[31] This bureau's twofold purpose was to infiltrate Communist circles and to spy on Chiang's opponents within the party. Chen Lifu later recalled that initially, "[I] felt that my personality was not suited for it, nor did I have any relevant knowledge or experience since I had trained professionally as an engineer, and hence had a mind for things rather than people."[32] With Dai Jitao's reassurances, however, Chen took up the work and staffed his department with trusted associates, mostly "people who had studied engineering, natural and social sciences in the United States," rather than personnel with a specific understanding of how bureaus such as the American FBI or the Soviet Cheka operated. Among them was Xu Enceng, who had studied electrical engineering in the United States. The bureau's efficient organization reportedly enabled it to capture some sixteen thousand Communists shortly after its founding.[33] Though Chen's network soon overlapped with the intelligence services that Chiang Kai-shek instructed the Blue Shirt Dai Li to establish, its operations nevertheless constituted cornerstones of the White Terror.

The men at the helm of the CC Clique hailed primarily from Zhejiang Province; the Chen brothers were from a Wuxing gentry family that had long been active in Republican politics. The elder Chen, Guofu, was born in 1892. He had been introduced at an early age to revolutionary activity by his uncle Chen Qimei, a close ally of Sun Yat-sen. Chen Guofu attended various schools as a child, including a 1905 stretch in Changsha, Hunan, where a boycott of American commodities (prompted by outrage over ongoing Chinese exclusion laws in the United States) reportedly left a deep nationalistic impression.[34] He went on to study at military academies, formally joining Sun Yat-sen's revolutionary organization, the Tongmenghui, in 1912.[35] After Chen Qimei's 1916 assassination, Chen Guofu returned home to Wuxing where he studied Chinese medicine, telepathy, and oratory.[36] In 1920 he moved to Shanghai where he, along with Chiang Kai-shek and Dai Jitao, established a stock and commodity exchange to raise money for Sun's revolutionary movement then based in Canton.[37] When, in 1924, Sun Yat-sen appointed Chiang Kai-shek head of the Whampoa Military Academy, Chen Guofu became a recruiter of cadets and procurer of supplies.[38]

While Chen Guofu deepened his knowledge of commodities markets and revolutionary organizing, his younger brother, Lifu, developed an expertise in mine engineering. Born in Zhejiang in 1900, Chen Lifu received an early education in the Confucian classics before moving on to modern schools. After completing an undergraduate degree in mine engineering at Tianjin's Beiyang University in 1923, he moved to the United States to study for a master's degree at the University of Pittsburgh. Western Pennsylvania was by then a well-established center of U.S. coal and petroleum extraction as well as a key production site for iron and steel.[39] The location was thus ideal for nurturing Chen Lifu's burgeoning fascination with industrial development and resource management. Chen later recalled that he came to appreciate Sun Yat-sen's ideas while in Pennsylvania writing his master's thesis on mechanizing China's coal industry, learning to admire Sun's "original and brilliant concepts for building highways and railways, constructing three coastal ports, and establishing new industries, all to create a new China."[40] After finishing his degree, Chen Lifu traveled around the United States in a Ford motorcar purchased by future CC Clique member Xu Enceng (who had been in Pittsburgh doing practical training with the electrical and broadcasting firm Westinghouse) and another Chinese student at the Colorado School of Mines.[41] Their road trip included a stop in Detroit to tour a Ford factory, from which Chen left impressed by its "speed of production and high efficiency."[42] Chen then returned to Scranton, Pennsylvania, where he worked in a coal mine inspecting tunnel ventilation. In the pits, Chen was a target of the anti-intellectualism as well as the anti-Chinese racism of fellow mine workers.[43] Outside the mines, he received invitations to lecture at Scranton-area churches on classical Confucian texts. Chen recalled accepting these invitations with the assumption, "As a Chinese, I felt it was my duty to introduce our culture," showing slides of Beijing in addition to lecturing on Confucius and Mencius.[44]

Chen Lifu's intersecting experiences in the United States of racism, ambiguous class identity, technological expertise, and ascribed authority regarding China's Confucian heritage all left their mark on his burgeoning nationalism. The racism that he experienced left him with the sense that "one must not reveal weakness to foreigners."[45] Having arrived in the United States in 1924, when the National Origins Act renewed exclusions on Chinese immigration, he was acutely attuned to American racism's institutional underpinnings.[46] He nevertheless remained entranced by American industrial prowess, particularly by its managerial practices and the potential benefits of translating these practices beyond factory walls. Chen later recalled how "emphasis on practicality and efficiency required every phase of work be meticulously studied"; the system of incentives moreover fostered "loyalty among employees toward the company."[47] Chen's 1924 master's thesis lauded ideals of efficiency, in particular a system of work discipline typically called Taylorism after the champion of "scientific management" F. W. Taylor. Taylor had advocated labor-management cooperation, standardization of the labor process, and scientific studies of time and motion to render worker movements as seamless and productive as possible.[48] "Drillers only need to know how to drill at a rapid rate," Chen observed in his thesis; "Men who take charge of the cutter are only required to be expert on cutting, but each needs more skill to carry on his work efficiently."[49] Although Chen's thesis displayed a deep sympathy for the abysmal conditions under which such relentlessly specialized workers labored, its overriding emphasis was on the national-collective benefits of mechanizing the Chinese mine industry and overcoming inefficient practices writ large.

Chen Lifu's interest in the broad social applications of scientific management developed amid his immersion in various forms of class conflict. When his elder brother Guofu recalled him to China to join the United Front, Chen Lifu was on strike with the United Mine Workers, and he arrived in Canton during the Hong Kong–Canton strike boycott.[50] In Canton, Chen swiftly dissociated himself from such class conflictual activism while honing his new technological expertise and sense of Confucianism as "our culture." His family connections facilitated his rapid rise within GMD ranks: by 1926 he was serving as Chiang Kai-shek's confidential secretary and was working with Chen Guofu, Dai Jitao, and others to formulate plans for their own and China's political future, the most immediate of which was to sever relations between the GMD and the Communist Party. Chen family connections played an important role in this process, as their uncle Chen Qimei had introduced Chiang Kai-shek to Shanghai's gang leaders a decade earlier.[51] When Chiang Kai-shek's forces reached Shanghai in spring 1927, they worked with Shanghai gangsters to attack the Communist-organized Shanghai General Labor Union. Affiliating with gangsters was an expedient means of eliminating Communists before formal state organs could be established to do the same; gangsters also helped to broker deals with French Concession and (British) International Settlement authorities who were themselves "anxious to purge their factories of radical influence."[52] While such alliances have been interpreted as a sign of Nationalist betrayal of their stated revolutionary ideals, they could be readily justified as temporary compromises to advance greater goals. Elizabeth J. Perry has underscored that the objective of these operations, "in classic corporatist fashion, was to create a network of tamed labor unions under government direction."[53] In 1927 corporatism was a globally nascent form of state-society relations primarily associated with Fascist Italy that aimed to control class conflict and the instabilities of laissez-faire capitalism.[54] The architects of the GMD party purge could, in this way, reasonably understand themselves as clearing the slate for the construction of a new type of society.

In his memoirs, Chen Lifu expressed "lifelong regret" that he never became a practicing engineer.[55] Yet after the Nationalists took power, Chen's engineering expertise became amply manifest in his cultural and philosophical writings, where he communicated his visions for an efficiently managed society in which everyone performed their allocated tasks. His CC Clique may have fought turf wars with another group of Chiang Kai-shek supporters known as the Blue Shirts, but both groups articulated similar ideas about the hierarchically rationalized direction in which they desired China to change. The Blue Shirts' social model was derived primarily from the military rather than the modern capitalist firm, but they likewise valorized efficient and coordinated operations performed under strict chains of command.

Broadly speaking, the terrains of the modern factory and military have been so entwined that critics of modern industry have inevitably employed military metaphors to grasp the hierarchical and disciplined structure of factory production. Others have traced the deep historical connections between these terrains. As early as 1848, for instance, Karl Marx and Friedrich Engels wrote of how "masses of laborers, crowded into the factory, are organized like soldiers. As privates of the industrial army they are placed under the command of a perfect hierarchy of officers and sergeants."[56] Max Weber subsequently observed that "no special proof is necessary to show that military discipline is the ideal model for the modern capitalist factory" and saw this discipline most fully elaborated in principles of "scientific management" that had set new norms for productive output.[57] Michel Foucault's later discussions of the "temporal elaboration of the act," furthermore, saw the rigid regulation of workers' behavior on and off the clock presaged in the precise choreographing of early seventeenth-century French troop movements. Insofar as a "disciplined body is a prerequisite of an efficient gesture" and such disciplining appears "most clearly in military organization," links between army and workplace discipline were not just rhetorical but deeply social and historical.[58] In this sense, the CC Clique and the Blue Shirts may have been on different sides of the Nationalist Party's thin civil-bureaucratic and military divide, but the highly militarized nature of Chiang Kai-shek's regime and their shared anti-Communist developmentalism spelled a distinct convergence between their hierarchically rationalized visions of a reborn China.

THE BLUE SHIRTS

In late March 1945, FBI director J. Edgar Hoover sent a memo to the U.S. State Department's director of foreign activity correlation, Frederick E. Lyon, introducing several hundred translated pages of Japanese Foreign Ministry reports from 1937 and 1938 on the Chinese Lan-i-she Society. Hoover's memo noted that the society "apparently played an extremely important and secret role in China's internal affairs prior to 1937 and supported General Chiang Kai-shek in his rise to power. It apparently dominated directly and indirectly the Chinese Central Army and operated with the greatest secrecy, much of its activities allegedly being known only by its leaders."[59] While the existence of the Blue Shirts—the popular name for a series of overlapping, clandestine groups led by Whampoa graduates—allegedly came as a surprise to the FBI director, it was an open secret in 1930s China. Despite Chiang Kai-shek's official denials, their existence could be surmised from their violence toward Japanese settlers and collaborators in northern China, toward Communists in the rural southwest, and toward urban intellectuals critical of the Nanjing regime.[60] This violence was fueled by aspirations to refashion Chinese state and society in a hierarchical manner modeled on the modern rationalized military. Like the CC Clique, the Blue Shirts also publicized their aspirations via a range of media outlets, compelling us to understand them not just as henchmen but as men driven by a specific ideology and evangelistic purpose.

The Blue Shirts formed in response to the September 18, 1931, Mukden Incident, drawing its core members from the first six classes of the Whampoa Military Academy. During the Mukden Incident, officers of Japan's Kwantung (Kanto) Army framed Chinese nationalists for a bomb that they had planted near their own barracks in the Manchurian city of Mukden, using the attack as a pretext to assume control over Manchuria. While Nanjing responded with a fraught policy of appeasement and appealed to the League of Nations to mediate, radicalized Chinese officers—some sixty of whom were then studying in Japan—mobilized to take direct action.[61] In the fall of 1931, a young officer named Teng Jie organized fellow Whampoa alumni into an organization called the Sanminzhuyi lixingshe, or the Three Principles of the People Forceful Action Society. At the same time, another young officer named Liu Jianqun penned a tract, "The Path to Reviving the Chinese Revolution," that called for reinvigorating the GMD with a renewed revolutionary spirit to confront the myriad problems that China was then facing.[62] As the Manchurian crisis unfolded, Chiang Kai-shek faced severe challenges to his leadership. He resigned from his civilian (though not military) positions and reportedly placed considerable blame on the CC Clique for his troubles.[63] When organizers of the Three Principles of the People Forceful Action Society informed Chiang of the group that they had founded, he opted to become their patron, anointing them in a 1932 ceremony modeled on the dramatic oath-swearing rituals of Chinese secret societies.[64]

Although the men involved with this secret organization never officially called themselves Blue Shirts, this is how they became known to Chinese and foreign publics during the 1930s, and how they and their myriad front organizations have been known to subsequent scholars.[65] From the twenty-odd men present at Chiang's 1932 inaugural ceremony, Blue Shirt front groups mushroomed to include as many as 500,000 members by the time Chiang officially disbanded them in 1938.[66] The structure of the Blue Shirts has been varyingly described as "pyramidal" or as "concentric circles," with the top of the pyramid, or innermost circle, retaining the name Forceful Action Society (Lixingshe). Led by Chiang Kai-shek, it eventually had five hundred members.[67] The second tier, or ring, of the organization had two branches, one called the League of Young Chinese Revolutionary Soldiers and the other called the Chinese Young Comrades Association. The former group dissolved shortly after founding, while the latter went on to become the main front group for the Forceful Action Society and is estimated to have had nearly forty thousand members by 1938. The Lixingshe in turn organized a third ring or tier known as the Renaissance Society (Fuxingshe), which included up to 500,000 members by 1938. Operating with the same democratic centralist principles that theoretically governed the GMD as a whole, the core members of the Lixingshe controlled all of the lower and outer organizations in one way or another.[68] Given the concern of Blue Shirt leaders for hierarchy and discipline, it is reasonable to assume that the actions and ideas of their myriad front groups were in relative sync with those of the men at the top of the pyramid, such as He Zhonghan, Dai Li, and Chiang Kai-shek himself. In this regard, when I examine the ideas and illustrations produced by pseudonymous contributors to Blue Shirt periodicals, or those whose biographical information has been lost to history, we can consider these to have been generally approved by the organization's better-known leaders, and hence important voices in the collective chorus of Chinese fascism.

Despite their small numbers relative to the total Chinese population, Blue Shirts exerted an outsized influence within the Nationalist military, which itself expanded its power within the government as a whole over the course of the 1930s. The expansion of Blue Shirt power was facilitated by the Nanjing government reorganization that took place in the wake of the Mukden Incident and Japan's January 1932 aerial attack on Shanghai. Wang Jingwei became head of the Executive Branch, while Chiang Kai-shek became chairman of the newly reorganized Military Affairs Council (MAC), responsible for conducting counterinsurgency campaigns against rural Communist soviets and prepping for war against Japan.[69] It was through the MAC that Blue Shirts were funded and found room to expand—they soon controlled nearly every bureau under the MAC's jurisdiction.[70] The structure of the MAC enabled Blue Shirts to operate beyond the reproach of the Chinese public or even other factions of the GMD. By design, their secretive nature was also a thorn in the side of Communists and Japanese imperialists. In the latter case, Blue Shirts were accused of circumventing Nanjing's appeasement policies—reportedly even placing a bounty on the head of Manchukuo's Japanese-appointed puppet emperor Puyi—which so irritated Japanese officials that they pressured Nanjing to make them cease and desist.[71]

The military contexts in which Blue Shirts operated indelibly shaped their visions for a transformed China. Their economic development aspirations focused on defense industries and their cultural sights trained on fostering order and discipline within the population at large. Dooeum Chung has summarized Blue Shirt views as encompassing "ultra-nationalism, dictatorship, opposition to individualism and democracy, state domination of the economy, totalitarian control of culture, the militarization of society, and the use of secret police against political enemies."[72] Their ideology was therefore far more totalizing than a specific concern with military affairs, even as it was forged in military milieus and had national defense at its core. Demographically, Blue Shirts came from all regions of China and had varying class backgrounds, though the majority were born around the turn of the twentieth century in Yangzi delta provinces, converging first at the Whampoa Military Academy after its founding in 1924.[73] After graduating from Whampoa, many continued their educations together at military schools in Japan, the USSR, and Europe. According to historian Deng Yuanzhong, of the dozen-odd Whampoa graduates who went on to study in the USSR, all became members of the Blue Shirts' core organization.[74] Many Whampoa graduates who subsequently studied in Japan also became Blue Shirts, while only a few of the men who studied in Germany eventually joined. In this respect, Blue Shirt worldviews were forged in closer dialogue with Soviet Communism and Japanese imperialism than with European fascism, and were deeply tied to the military-institutional contexts in which they came of age. These institutional contexts conditioned but did not determine their subject positions: they absorbed Soviet and Japanese military discipline while explicitly rejecting Bolshevism and Japanese imperialism, just as many of them had studied Marxism and worked closely with Chinese Communists until turning violently against them in 1927. In other words, military institutions helped to shape Blue Shirt approaches to revolution but did not determine them any more than did their class backgrounds.

One of the Blue Shirts' most prolific proponents of revolutionary nationalism in an anti-Communist mode was Blue Shirt leader He Zhonghan. Scholar-turned-ROC-official Hung-Mao Tien observed that even though He's role in Nanjing Decade politics is often overlooked, "available evidence suggests that he was one of the pivotal figures in Chiang's political and military enterprises of the 1930's."[75] Born in Hunan in 1898 to a relatively prosperous peasant family, He Zhonghan received a classical education before attending modern schools in Wuchang in 1915, where he became a student leader. After studying Russian at a Shanghai school founded by Communist Party founder Li Dazhao, He Zhonghan went as a delegate to the 1922 Congress of the Toilers of the East in Moscow. He apparently left the USSR impressed by Soviet governance but convinced that its revolutionary direction was unsuited for China.[76] He entered the first class of Whampoa in 1924—where he helped found its Sun Yat-senism Study Society along with other anti-Communist cadets—and went back to the USSR for further military training at Moscow's Frunze Military Academy in 1925, not returning to China until 1928.[77]

In Canton and Moscow alike during the 1920s, disciplining the body to render its actions as purposive and precise as possible was an integral aspect of military education. This schooling also reinforced notions of China's relative developmental backwardness and hence the imperative to refashion bodily habits as swiftly as possible. According to a circa 1925 Soviet-authored document, training at the Whampoa Academy was "conducted approximately according to the same standards as the training of the European armies before the great war, adding to it the political instruction."[78] The stated reason for this lag was that although in Europe, "the introduction of powerful technical equipment radically changed the tactics and conformably the training of the troops, in South China the extensive use of technical means will be hindered, on the one hand, by the lack of railways and the poverty of the government, and on the other hand by the special conditions of the theater of war, by the absence of roads, and by the fact that the regions are infested with bandits who make it impossible to supply the army regularly from the rear."[79] As a result of such constraints, Nationalist officers were frequently dispatched to military schools abroad for training in the kinds of warfare conducted in and by metropolitan countries—that is, of the sort waged against Chinese and other colonized and semicolonized populations. Such lived experiences of developmental difference, as much as the Whampoa training program itself, contributed to Blue Shirt obsessions with bodily discipline and collective cohesion as keys to national regeneration and assertion of strength on the world stage.[80]

Military schools abroad likewise cultivated Blue Shirt appreciation of hierarchical order. The rationalized military instruction to which Blue Shirts were exposed in the USSR and Japan, moreover, converged in fundamental ways with the scientific management practices celebrated by the CC Clique.

Moscow's Frunze Academy, where He Zhonghan studied, was named after a man closely associated with the rationalization of the Red Army. Mikhail Frunze's reforms emphasized "iron military discipline and high political consciousness," uniformity of training, efficient division of tasks, and the importance of personal hygiene.[81] So important was bodily tempering at the school that one Soviet conscript recalled, "Our military training began with a steam bath, the disinfection of all our clothes, a haircut that left our scalps as smooth as our faces, and a political lecture."[82] Blue Shirts who studied at military schools in Japan (which included He Zhonghan between 1928 and 1931) learned similar lessons. Chiang Kai-shek, who had himself attended Tokyo's Shinbu Military Training School in the early 1900s, was impressed by the "rigid discipline, political indoctrination, and technical education" of the Japanese armed forces.[83] When the Blue Shirt Teng Jie, studying in Japan in the fall of 1931, called for "a strong organization with a united will, with iron discipline, with a clear division of responsibility, and with the ability to act with alacrity" that would abide by democratic centralist principles, the stamps of Teng's training were evident.[84] So, too, was his consciousness of the differences between China's sociohistorical circumstances and those of countries whose military lessons Blue Shirts imbibed.

While the CC Clique elaborated its own ideas for an efficiently managed society, Blue Shirts moved into positions of state power from which they amplified their militaristic social visions and also expanded their capacities to wield coercive force. In 1931, He Zhonghan became propaganda director for the Armed Forces General Headquarters Antibandit Propaganda Bureau (Hailukongjun zongsilingbu jiaofei xuanchuanchu); he retained directorship when this bureau was reorganized under the newly established MAC in 1932 as a political training unit for counterinsurgency soldiers. In 1933 He took charge of the MAC's entire Political Training Bureau and in 1934 headed up the Organization Department's military affairs section.[85] Meanwhile, another former Whampoa student named Dai Li—later dubbed China's Himmler, apparently to liken his bloodthirst to that of the notorious Nazi architect of the Holocaust—was authorized by Chiang Kai-shek to establish a Special Services Department whose tasks intersected with those of the CC Clique's Bureau of Investigation.[86] Although technically independent of the Blue Shirts' core organization (i.e., the Forceful Action Society), Dai Li was very much one of them, as his bureau "could not do without the Renaissance Society and the so-called Blue Shirts that constituted its membership," and the department itself got off the ground with rechanneled Blue Shirt funds.[87] They trained their sights on conationals whose thinking and action appeared to deviate from the proper course of nationalist revolution.

Blue Shirt understanding of this course centered on fostering China's capacities for military self-defense and expanded to encompass total national rebirth. Following Sun Yat-sen, Blue Shirts pressed for state-directed heavy industrial development—varyingly called a "controlled economy" or "national capitalism"—to rectify the private and unequal accumulation profits as well as worker exploitation.[88] One Blue Shirt observed that because "modern wars are totally reliant on science," it was necessary to foster Chinese industrial, technological, and natural scientific knowledge in tandem.[89] Modern military power relied not just on weapons but on laboratories; wartime victory hinged "on basic research in the natural sciences."[90] It also required developing domestic coal, iron, and steel production capacities, while military transport required petroleum—all of which remained under foreign control or were not yet established within Chinese territory.[91] Whatever the Nanjing regime's actual track record in rural areas, Blue Shirts positioned themselves as revolutionary in part by denouncing "feudal remnants" and landlord exploitation in the hinterland. Though they apparently disagreed among themselves as to whether landholdings should be equalized (privatized into relatively equal small plots after Sun Yat-sen's suggestion) or collectivized for the sake of introducing mechanization and nationalistic organization to the peasantry, both courses entailed sweeping transformation to extant rural social relations.[92] No stone was to be left unturned; everyone and everything would serve a newly prescribed purpose.

In this way, logics of hierarchical rationalization pervaded both Blue Shirt and CC Clique worldviews. Whether their revolutionary model was derived from the military or the scientifically managed factory, both involved elite leadership and top-down chains of command. Both were proindustrial and required mass participation but were deeply hostile to popular input. Aspects of Blue Shirt and CC Clique elitism certainly bore the imprint of Confucian paternalism. There is, however, no reason to view this elitism or their hostility to popular input as signs of modernity's absence. As Geoff Eley has observed, "early twentieth century resistances against democracy, right-wing defense of privilege, coercive systems of authoritarian rule, and attacks on civil liberties" were all abundantly manifest in the Western liberal democracies that scholars typically laud as models of normal modernization.[93]

Blue Shirt and CC Clique militants were interested in controlling the direction and character of China's modernization, not in precluding it. Their recourse to violence revealed impatience with the protracted duration of "making the people new," as the reformist scholar Liang Qichao had put it decades earlier, as well as fury that other political forces continued to compete for the masses' hearts and minds. Hierarchical command structures, in their view, were efficient and effective ways of eliminating such competition and capturing the masses for themselves.

While I discuss in chapter 2 how this rationalized, efficient social order was to remain animated by an enduring Confucian national spirit—what fascists disenchanted with one hand they reenchanted with the other—in the remainder of this chapter I examine Blue Shirt and CC Clique media engagements. Their simultaneous efforts to hide from public scrutiny and to put their ideas into wide circulation bespoke a desire to be appreciated in addition to being feared. They wanted others to know what they believed and they wanted to persuade others to share these beliefs. Via the stakes that they held in technologies of mechanical reproduction, it is clear that their organizational elitism and insularity were twinned with populist and popularizing impulses. They recognized the importance of newspapers, radio, and film for capturing the popular imagination and took pains to position themselves within these spheres as more progressive than any actual or potential rival. They opined about events occurring the world over and displayed their conversancy in the latest artistic, literary, and scientific trends. By deploying modernist graphics akin to those favored by China's interwar commercial publishers and political left wing, they communicated their commitment to the revolutionary-new. If fascist media efforts ultimately spoke primarily to the already converted, they nevertheless aimed far wider. Believing themselves to be locked in mortal struggle with Communist, liberal, and imperialist forces for sway with the supposedly dimwitted masses, communications media and ultimately culture writ large became integral to their political project.

Fascist Media and Machine-Age Aesthetics

From the start, both the CC Clique and the Blue Shirts were engaged not just in internal party-state affairs but in circulating their unfurling understanding of revolution within society at large, soon exerting considerable influence in educational as well as media circles.[94] It was through their media forays and their efforts to construct and control what they called Chinese culture that their behind-the-scenes work of party recruitment and military training assumed a public face. The fact that these men propagated their views widely in the first place bespeaks Arno Mayer's observation that the "bayonets of revolution and counterrevolution need ideology as much as ideology needs them," while the forms that their propagandizing assumed revealed key dilemmas faced by the Nanjing regime.[95] Although Nanjing had criminalized, with threat of imprisonment, people who "propagate[d] ideas discordant with the Three Principles of the People and detrimental to the People's Revolution," when the Nanjing regime was first established its jurisdiction barely extended beyond several Yangzi delta provinces and it had no control over the kinds of works disseminated through the colonial concessions.[96] It was not until the 1935 Fifth Party Congress, when the Blue Shirts and cc Clique had considerably expanded their power and Chiang Kai-shek was more firmly in charge, that they registered a shift in state policy from a negative cultural agenda based on suppression to a positive one with solidified power to delineate the contours of a new order.[97] It was, moreover, not until 1936 that the state even generated a detailed picture of what was actually published within the areas that it controlled.[98] When fascists got into the media business in the late 1920s and wrote about the pressing need to ferret out Communist and imperialist influence there, this impression was derived largely from their own rootedness in treaty port–based circles rather than a comprehensive awareness of what was actually produced and disseminated within China's borders. Despite or perhaps because of this fact, fascist media endeavors were fueled by the desire to achieve such total knowledge as well as by a conviction that channels of mass communication were dominated by enemies of the revolution who were preventing the kind of collective unity that national regeneration required. In and through their mass communications initiatives, and particularly in their embrace of modernist visuals, we can see how both the cc Clique and the Blue Shirts positioned themselves on the Chinese political spectrum as anticonservative revolutionaries. Like Italian Futurists, they celebrated representational forms that conveyed speed, dynamism, and not infrequently, the renewing properties of violence.[99] At the same time, the national-particular rarely fell out of view, celebrating bodies, structures, and motifs that communicated continuity with an illustrious past.

Blue Shirt and CC Clique media endeavors included magazine, book, and newspaper publishing, radio broadcasts, and film production. They also opened bookstores in major cities across China. These endeavors followed a two-pronged course of attacking what they regarded as degenerate and divisive influences—as I discuss in chapter 5, compensating for the state's limited censorship capacities by terrorizing individuals deemed responsible for such influence—and by attempting to saturate the market with their own political writings, cultural theory, and fiction. In 1933 and 1934, both the Blue Shirts and the CC Clique founded cultural organizations to better coordinate their hitherto fragmented forays into publishing, radio, and film, and to provide these efforts with more substantial theoretical foundations. The Blue Shirts established a Chinese Culture Study Society (Zhongguo wenhua xuehui) in the city of Nanchang in late 1933, while the CC Clique quickly followed suit with a Chinese Cultural Construction Association (Zhongguo wenhua jianshe xiehui) in early 1934.[100] The latter association in particular marked a step toward the 1936 establishment of an official state committee, headed by Chen Guofu, dedicated to planning and coordinating the activities of what were called "cultural enterprises."[101] This committee proceeded from the assumption that culture was a resource that could be mapped and managed by the state in the manner of coal or forests in the service of national regeneration, tentatively surmounting what, earlier in the decade, had constituted deliberate yet relatively disjointed approaches.

The CC Clique made their first organized forays into print media in the late 1920s and early 1930s with daily papers such as the Nanjing-based *Chenbao* (*Morning Post*) and *Jingbao* (*Nanking Times*), the weekly *Shidai gonglun* (*Era Public Opinion*), the monthly *Xinshengming* (*New Life*), and by establishing bookstores in Nanjing and Shanghai.[102] While newspapers like the *Jingbao* focused on local and global current events, magazines like *New Life* (1928–31) and *Shidai gonglun* (1932–35) pondered broader problems like national-spiritual decadence. *New Life* described its mission as propagating the theory and spirit of Sun Yat-sen's Three Principles of the People, as well as "researching construction and planning, and introducing and critiquing doctrines and policies from around the world."[103] The desire of the *New Life* group to present themselves as champions of modern life is manifest in a 1928 photograph in which Chen Guofu, Chen Bulei (secretary to Chiang Kai-shek), and others involved with the magazine pose in front of two recent-model automobiles (fig. 1.1).[104] The urban street setting, prominent positioning of the cars, and the sartorial choices of the people photographed—which include a Western summer suit, fatigues, and a long gown—together convey a sense of embracing and creating something historically novel, both nationally particular and fully modern. This is further suggested by a 1931 photograph of Chen Lifu in Shanghai speaking through a broadcast microphone to an art and literary gathering (fig. 1.2).[105] Shot from below and staged in front of a large poster of a traditional Chinese opera character, the image suggests Chen's authority vis-à-vis both modern communications technologies and indigenous art forms.

The cc Clique launched *Wenhua jianshe* (*Cultural Construction*), the flagship monthly journal of its Chinese Cultural Construction Association, in Shanghai on October 10, 1934. Visually and linguistically, *Cultural Construction* negotiated tensions between nurturing China's "native culture" and launching the nation into a new world of science, technology, and industrial productivity. The magazine's title conveyed the engineering expertise that its contributors brought to the project of nation building (as well as the unacknowledged but likely influence of the multilanguage Soviet publication *USSR in Construction*), while its pages delineated the totalizing nature of their undertaking. Prefatory pages of the two-hundred-plus-page first issue, which included essays by Dai Jitao, Chen Lifu, and Shanghai mayor Wu Tiecheng, explained the magazine's purpose "to promote China's native culture and to propagate the construction of modern China," requesting that readers send in their own photographs of China's past architectural, painting, and sculptural accomplishments, as well as of its new construction projects.[106] A photo spread in the first issue spotlighted "Crystallizations of Chinese Culture," slotting engineering marvels like the Great Wall and the Temple of Heaven, as well as art objects like Ming vases and Tang pottery horses, into a visual narrative of national development (fig. 1.3).[107] In the context of a magazine devoted to the forward-looking project of construction—and anticipating the photographs of cutting-edge technology from around the world featured in subsequent issues—*Cultural Construction*'s visual assemblage of dynastic triumphs with contemporary building efforts suggested a national phoenix rising from the ashes of postdynastic ruin. The Nationalists were presented as simultaneously effecting a historical break and suturing a historical rupture, bringing the greatest possible expertise to bear on decades-germinating problems that no other organization could solve in a way that accorded with the nation's rich heritage.[108]

FIGURE 1.1 » Founders of the magazine *Xinshengming (New Life)* in Shanghai, January 1928. Chen Guofu is fourth from the right. From Wan et al., *Jiang Jieshi yu guomin zhengfu*, 75.

Magazines like *Cultural Construction* further stressed how only the GMD was capable of regenerating China in a manner that delivered modernity's promises without leading the nation to debauchery and chaos. This was visually conveyed by pictorial spreads showcasing scientific and technological marvels, including renderings of planets, rocket ships, and exploratory missions to the Antarctic (fig. 1.4). Depictions of outer space heralded wondrous future discoveries, while the aerodynamic form (streamlined style or *liuxianxing*) of the U.S. Union Pacific Streamline Express train emblematized the kind of rationalized efficiency that Chen Lifu wanted to foster among the nation at large (fig. 1.5).[109] This train's art deco aesthetic was in keeping with designs then popular in Shanghai's hotels, department stores, cabarets, and movie sets. By circulating these kinds of images, the CC Clique reinforced the modernizing, futuristic orientation of their political agenda. They laid claim to popular industrial aesthetics in a way that attempted to remove them from the clutches of imperialists, leftists, and commercial advertisers. This would render emergent, socially recognized

FIGURE 1.2 » Chen Lifu speaking to an arts assembly in Shanghai, 1931. From Wan et al., *Jiang Jieshi yu guomin zhengfu*, 94.

中國文化的結晶（一）

㊀ 萬里長城（參看第一百十頁）
㊁ 天壇（參看第一百十頁）
㊂ 明陵牌樓（參看第一百十一頁）

★ ★ ★ ★

FIGURE 1.3 » "Crystallizations of Chinese Culture": photographs of dynastic engineering triumphs in *Wenhua jianshe* (*Cultural Construction*) 1, no. 1 (1934).

signs and symbols of modernity their own and interpretable in a delimited number of ways, avoiding the "kaleidoscopic" multiplicity of meanings perceptible in images that circulated in popular nonpartisan magazines like *Liangyou* (*The Young Companion*).[110]

With an eye toward eliminating interpretive and political ambiguities, the cc Clique also ventured into radio and film. In 1932 Chen Guofu established a Central Broadcasting Station that cc Clique members used for science-related programming.[111] That same year Chen Lifu established a Chinese Educational Film Association, whose productions aimed to foster a national revolutionary spirit, encourage productive labor, impart scientific knowledge, and cultivate Confucian moral standards.[112] The younger Chen elaborated on his film association's work in the self-authored booklet *The Chinese Film Industry*, which was published in 1933 by the cc Clique's Shanghai-based Chenbao Press.[113] As I discuss in greater detail in chapter 5, in this booklet Chen stressed the importance of film in wresting China's national self-understanding away from foreign control. This archetypically modern medium was not to be shunned but turned into a useful tool as it was considered uniquely suited for fostering a collective, national sense of purpose. It was thought to have the capacity to convince the masses to experience their own labor not as an individual hardship but as an enjoyable contribution to national well-being. Filmmakers, Chen argued, should join forces with conventional soldiers to launch "psychological attacks" against the "latent, expanding influence of despicable mentalities."[114] Seizing control of communications technologies was thus a critical component of their broader struggles for national regeneration. These were key to fostering the right kind of nationalism and producing a hierarchically ordered, disciplined society capable of obeying strict chains of command.

After the Blue Shirts were founded in 1932, they quickly entered the media business and circulated their visions of militarizing society via bookstores, newspapers, and magazines in cities including Nanchang, Hankou, Shanghai, Nanjing, and Beiping.[115] By stepping from military affairs into publishing, the Blue Shirts apparently ignored Chiang Kai-shek's request that they leave media work to the cc Clique.[116] Yet it would be surprising if they had heeded it, as they were motivated by a virulent nationalism that they believed all others should share. Within the first three years of the Blue Shirts' existence, they published some two hundred different periodicals and works related to fascist propaganda.[117] Like the cc Clique, they were

FIGURE 1.4 » "The Latest in the World of Science": renderings of outer space in *Wenhua jianshe* (*Cultural Construction*) 1, no. 4 (1935).

FIGURE 1.5 » "Streamlined Forms": late art deco trains and planes in *Wenhua jianshe* (*Cultural Construction*) 1, no. 5 (1935).

also interested in the powers of cinema: He Zhonghan founded a China Film Studio and named as its first director a man who had penned a tract called "Seizing the Weapon of Film."[118] Still, their most important media interventions took the form of print, which was cheaper to produce and circulated more readily. Even more so than periodicals issued by the CC Clique, those of the Blue Shirts embraced modernist aesthetics in a way that deliberately positioned the group as militantly forward looking.

On the surface, some Blue Shirt publications appeared indistinguishable from China's many other papers, carrying innocuous titles like the Nanjing-based *Zhongguo ribao* (*China Daily*), which was published by Blue Shirt leader Kang Ze from 1932 to 1936.[119] Others had titles and cover art that readily announced the militancy of their contents, such as *Tiexue yuekan* (*Iron and Blood Monthly*), *Hanxue zhoukan* (*Sweat and Blood Weekly*), and *Saodang xunkan* (*Mopping Up Thrice Monthly*).[120] The Shanghai-based monthly *Qiantu* (the *Future*), one of their most successful publications, heralded the Blue Shirts' transformative aspirations.[121] Its title, which can also be translated as the *Path Forward*, signaled anticipation of the world yet to come, while its genre-diverse contents suggested the broad scope of Blue Shirt interventions. As with titles like *Sweat and Blood Weekly*, the *Future*'s graphic design underscored its contributors' vanguardist self-understanding, frequently deploying geometric fonts and industrial imagery. Such magazines thereby contributed to Shanghai's burgeoning trend of synchronizing magazine design and content while also staking claim to a visual repertoire that signaled an embrace of the new.[122] This was particularly the case with the 1933 cover discussed and pictured in this book's introduction, which featured a charioteer whose arrow is aimed at the masthead characters for "the future," fusing in a single image China's ancient military traditions and the modern industrial age. The cover's blue and white blocks referenced GMD party colors, while red suggested bloodshed, good fortune, and a communistic ethos concentrated in the national body. Readers would be unlikely to interpret this image as signaling a desire to unwind history's clock or decelerate the pace of change, or to thus expect such ideas to be expressed in the pages of the magazine.

The Nanchang- and then Shanghai-based Blue Shirt magazine *Sweat and Blood Weekly*, edited by Liu Daxing, also championed modernist designs throughout its five years of publication between 1933 and 1937.[123] With the slogan "expend one's own sweat to sustain one's own life; pool our blood to save our nation," the magazine covered domestic and international events with a decidedly militaristic slant. Elaborate pictorial spreads, often employing collage techniques that suggested the organized reassembly of disjointed modern experiences, appeared with *Sweat and Blood Weekly*'s third volume. The magazine's cover images also grew increasingly technically sophisticated over time, evolving from simple inked characters to sharp-resolution photographs bordered with bright colors. The second issue of volume 1, for instance, highlighted the character "blood" with dripping red ink and the character "sweat" with a coal-like black (fig. 1.6), while numerous issues from volume 5 featured photographs of male and female Chinese athletes.[124] Like the female javelin thrower depicted in fig. 1.7, many of these athletes were captured in vigorous poses that suggested a strengthened national body striving toward a regenerated future. Others were more casual and salacious. In other words, interspersed with pictorial spreads that unambiguously registered successful eugenics and national exertion were those that might be found in contemporaneous mainstream magazines like *The Young Companion*.

How should we make sense of the fact that magazines produced by fascists during the Nanjing Decade often employed graphics, fonts, color schemes, and pictorial techniques that scholars have come to associate with Shanghai's progressive and nonpartisan commercial publishing houses? *Sweat and Blood Weekly*'s 1934 special issue on the New Life Movement (fig. 1.8), for instance, strongly resembled a 1933 red and yellow cover design by Qian Juntao for *Shidai funü* (*Modern Woman*).[125] *Sweat and Blood Weekly* also utilized repeating industrial motifs—such as the orange and black cog designs framing a photograph of the 1935 funeral of a Polish leader—markedly similar to those favored by left-wing publications, including Lu Xun's *Wenxue* (*Literature*) (figs. 1.9 and 1.10).[126] We also see illustrations evocative of woodcuts—such as those of an airplane and of Adolf Hitler that appeared alongside a *Cultural Construction* news brief (fig. 1.11)—that were contemporaneously in favor with the left.[127]

Such similarities suggest that GMD fascists were attuned to, enmeshed in, and actively contributed to media and aesthetic developments for which leftists and politically ambivalent commercial firms have long been credited. Both the Blue Shirts and the CC Clique took pains to differentiate their visuals from those that would have appeared to readers as conservative or backward looking. These similarities further indicate that visual claims upon the modern and revolutionary-new remained contested in 1930s China: no single party or organization successfully monopolized a particular aesthetic

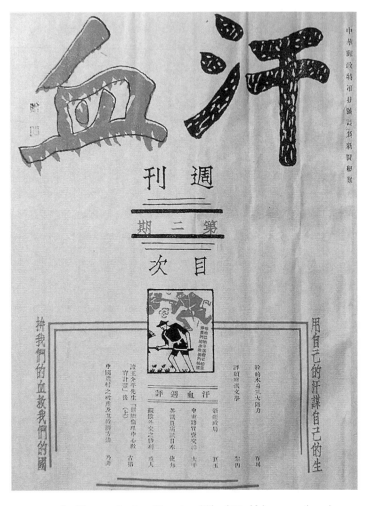

FIGURE 1.6 » *Hanxue zhoukan (Sweat and Blood Weekly)* 1, no. 2 (1933).

汗血週刊

第五卷

第三期

FIGURE 1.7 » *Hanxue zhoukan (Sweat and Blood Weekly)* 5, no. 3 (1935).

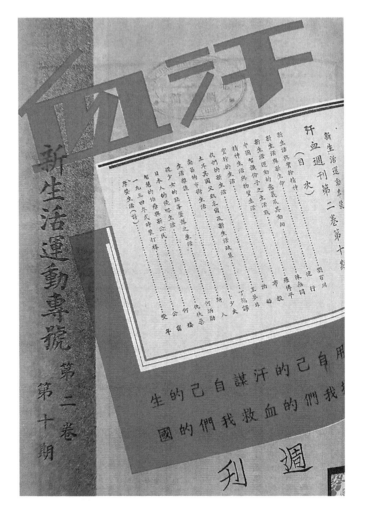

FIGURE 1.8 » *Hanxue zhoukan* (*Sweat and Blood Weekly*), New Life Movement Special Issue, 2, no. 10 (1934).

FIGURE 1.9 » *Hanxue zhoukan* (*Sweat and Blood Weekly*) 5, no. 1 (1935).

FIGURE 1.10 » Cover of the left-wing periodical *Wenxue* (*Literature*) 1, no. 4 (1933).

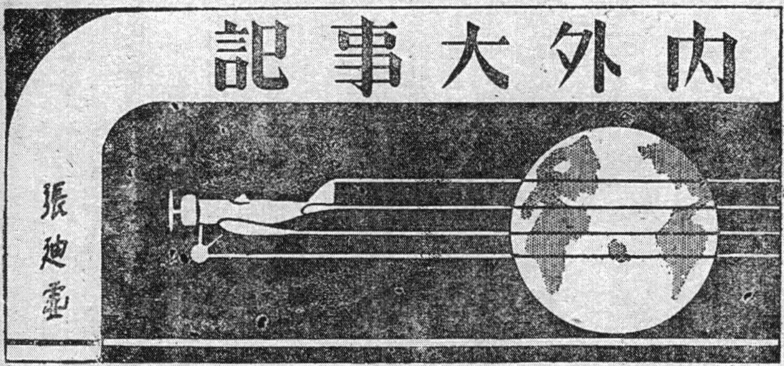

內外大事記

張蜒靈

一　希德拉聲勢今年不如去年

七八月的中歐，誠所謂是多事之秋也。先有七月廿五日「小拿破崙」奧總理陶爾斐斯的遇害驚動全世界，陶案發生後未滿兩星期德意志全國景仰的英雄與登堡總統又以病故聞了。

奧國的事變希德拉在歐洲列強尤其是意大利，怒目相視之下，態度軟化平日聲威大受影響同時與登堡逝世後的德國國內情形也表示希氏的黃金時代似乎已經過了。

與登堡逝世在八月二日清晨九時同日十時希德拉暫行攝代總統職務兼陸軍大元帥翌日由政府預布攝代法律命令將總統及總理職權合而為一任命希德拉為德國國家人民最高領袖。九日政府決議擇定十九日舉行公民投票以表決希德拉兼任總統及總理職權之法律。

總投票以前國社黨照例作盛大的宣傳，國社黨宣傳部長戈培爾斯照例大顯身手其對羣眾的演辭中有云：「德意志全國人民俱信常今除希德拉外實無人能擔當前總統與登堡氏所遺下之重任此次舉行人民複決之用意，不在使人民明瞭希德拉為當今必需之人物，而在使外國了解德國人民一致擁護希德拉而已凡屬人民為有投票之神聖義務因此次投票人數如較去年十一月十二日所投之票數有一人之缺少者外國勢將謂希德拉已至日暮途窮之日矣……」

大選的前兩夕希德拉親臨漢堡用無綫電

希德拉

FIGURE 1.11 » Hitler and airplane graphics evocative of woodcuts in *Wenhua jianshe* (*Cultural Construction*) 1, no. 1 (1934): 1.

or effectively fused it to their own political program. Fascists of the GMD nevertheless attempted to claim popular modern repertoires and to politically circumscribe their meanings—dissociating art deco in particular from luxurious private consumption and linking it instead to a national project of technological development. Blue Shirt and CC Clique magazines also evidence concern to represent dynamism via recognizably Chinese-national signifiers. Occasionally, these efforts masterfully succeeded, as with the *Future's* archer-charioteer. More typically, they involved unsubtle juxtapositions, as with pictorial spreads in *Cultural Construction* that varyingly showcased Ming vases, rocket ships, and newly constructed factories.

Such CC Clique representations of historical regeneration were matched in Blue Shirt magazines by positive depictions of violent struggle for national survival. A 1933 cover of *Jingcheng yuekan* (*Absolute Sincerity Monthly*), for instance, echoed the *Future's* abstracted charioteer (fig. 1.12). Though drawn with rounded lines and organic referents, this rendering of a mounted soldier leaping past a blazing sun similarly conveyed a militant striving. The skulls and bones over which the soldier leaps indicate that their struggles required a willingness to kill or to sacrifice one's own life, while the sun's red rays suggest harnessed life forces.[128] Photo spreads in *Sweat and Blood Weekly*, meanwhile, showcased military armament and national-racial competition in a Darwinist world.[129] This is, for instance, illustrated in a 1936 issue that opens with a collage, "The Revival of the Aryan Race," in Nazi Germany. Here, we see orderly formations of fighter planes, submarines, and tanks that Germans had amassed under Hitler's emboldened leadership.[130] This same issue of *Sweat and Blood Weekly* also highlighted Ethiopian resistance to Italian fascist aggression—a situation that many in 1930s China, including the Blue Shirts, likened to China's resistance against Japan.[131] The issue's back cover carried photographs of Ethiopians mobilizing to defend themselves against Italian aggression. The caption reads, "For the survival of the nation, Ethiopians use armed force to defend themselves."[132] Like Germany, Ethiopia is depicted as having a strong male head of state—Haile Selassie is pictured in the upper left-hand corner. But rather than enjoying national resurgence in the manner of the Nazis, Ethiopians are shown struggling for national survival. And rather than mobilizing tanks, submarines, and aircraft, Ethiopians are presented resourcefully using available modes of military transport (camels) and their familiarity with local terrain to defend themselves against invasion by the more powerful Italy. In Blue Shirt eyes, all nationalities required unity, discipline, and

FIGURE 1.12 » *Jingcheng yuekan* (*Absolute Sincerity Monthly*) 1, no. 3 (1933).

the resolve to fight if they were to survive and ultimately thrive in a competitive world. But some, like the Ethiopians and the Chinese, had greater obstacles to overcome and farther distances to travel than did others, like the Germans, Italians, and Japanese, whose renaissances already seemed well under way. With an acute sense of the relative military and industrial backwardness spelled by their nation's semicolonized circumstances, China's fascist media marshaled modernist imagery to push for ever greater degrees of militant cohesion.

Conclusion

In the semicolonized context of interwar China, where coastal treaty port cities often had more in common socioeconomically with metropolitan cities than with the vast rural interior, fascism's revolutionary aspirations must be taken as seriously as its counterrevolutionary violence. Many young Nationalist recruits did not abandon their revolutionary fervor in the wake of Chiang Kai-shek's spring 1927 coup d'état. Instead they reassessed their situation and continued to fight, particularly by positioning themselves as more radical than other members of the Nationalist Party who, they believed, settled too comfortably into positions of state power and too meekly confronted domestic and international threats. Two different groups of Chiang Kai-shek supporters emerged in the second half of the 1920s—the CC Clique and the Whampoa Clique (eventually Blue Shirts)—who understood it as their mission to advance Sun Yat-sen's revolutionary vision and eliminate all forms of dissent. Although tensions between these two groups certainly negatively affected the overall functioning of the Nanjing regime, the clear convergences between their technocratic and military worldviews—seeking to remodel Chinese society along the lines of a scientifically managed factory and a rationalized military—suggest a shared developmental logic at work. The ruthlessness with which they worked to crush political opposition, particularly Communist, cannot be separated from their developmental ambitions.

These men orchestrated the White Terror behind a veil of secrecy and hence beyond public reproach. But they also pointedly put their visions for China's revolutionary transformation on display for all to see via bookstores, publications, radio broadcasts, and so on. This desire to communicate broadly is among the reasons why we should understand them as fascists and not merely as authoritarians. They had visions of national renaissance that they wanted to render collectively held. That GMD fascists embraced a modernist repertoire that scholars have hitherto associated with China's progressive left and commercial advertisers indicates their immersion in treaty port culture, an awareness of what was popular, and a keen desire to harness the visual language of the revolutionary-new. They self-consciously positioned themselves as anticonservative and as more capable of delivering on the promises of modernity than any other organization. Still, the CC Clique in particular gained a reputation for hidebound conservatism because they championed Confucian values as the bedrock of what they termed China's native culture. This championing was, however, not conservative in any meaningful sense. It was a reaction against the anti-Confucianism of the New Culture and May Fourth movements and also against the longer-term degradations of imperialism. In chapter 2, I sketch an intellectual genealogy of GMD fascist promotion of Confucianism as the glue binding the national subject together, revealing how they worked to remove Confucianism from the hold of "feudalism" and fuse it to a revolutionary corporatism.

2 » SPIRIT IS ETERNAL

Cultural Revolution from the Right

Nationalism, many have observed, is Janus-faced.[1] Turning simultaneously toward the past and future, nationalists reassemble the inherited past to remap the present and the world to come, continually drawing upon its resources to foster a sense of shared destiny among disparate populations.[2] Many twentieth-century Marxist internationalists, including members of the Chinese Communist Party (CCP), countered this nationalist tendency by furthering Marx's admonition in the "Eighteenth Brumaire" that a workers' revolution needed to "create its poetry . . . from the future."[3] During the interwar and wartime years, nationalist movements on the far right claimed that they, too, desired to begin history anew. Yet, contra Marxism, fascists promised not only to reset history's clock but also to honor ostensibly timeless national traditions in the process. The paradoxical nature of this promise marked an intensification of temporal contradictions already inherent in nationalism, and staked a claim that everything about the world could be changed while everything would remain as it always had been. That the traditions fascists conjured typically bore little resemblance to past or present realities—images of conflict-free and ethnically pure national communities engaging in industrial production and enjoying the fruits of modern technology looked more like feudalism in capitalist garb than life as it ever had been or ever could be lived—mattered little. What mattered was that the fantasy made sense to its proponents and appeared to offer modernity's bounty without its attendant social dislocations.

The cultural revolution outlined and fitfully implemented by Chinese fascists during the 1930s intensified nationalism's historical posture. It harbored a promise to simultaneously change everything and nothing about China. Scholars continue to interpret the interwar GMD's rhetorical respect for indigenous traditions, in particular their promotion of Confucianism, as evidencing their conservatism.[4] Yet when we compare the cultural discourse of GMD fascists to that of noted Republican-era conservative intellectuals like Liang Shuming, differences quickly become apparent. To be sure, historian Edmund S. K. Fung's rethinking of conservatism in Republican China as a modern response to modern problems helps illuminate how GMD fascists and conservative intellectuals shared points in common. They both reacted against the anti-Confucianism of the New Culture and May Fourth movements, and their shared reactions opened possibilities for their intermittent cooperation. Moreover, like their conservative counterparts, GMD fascists harbored what Fung has called, following Paul Gilroy's elaboration on a core idea of W. E. B. Du Bois, "a modernizing outlook and reflective double consciousness" in their articulation of Chineseness in the shadow of a white-coded West.[5] Perhaps most importantly, fascists and conservatives shared a strong desire to see the restoration of gender and class hierarchies—though the forms of hierarchy that they supported were historically novel and had to supplant remnants of China's dynastic order.[6] However, fascists explicitly rejected the gradualism that conservatives rhetorically favored. Fascists clamored for immediate sociopolitical transformation, threw their weight behind a state rhetorically committed to modernizing all aspects of Chinese life, and even frequently denounced fellow GMD members that they perceived as too cautious. Fascists moreover skirted conservatism's avowed elitism by speaking in the name of the masses, and they flouted conservatism's concern for order by insisting that destruction was necessary to clear the way for the new. We must therefore take the Blue Shirts' and CC Clique's self-professed concern for revolutionizing culture seriously, for only then will the tensions of this concern become intelligible signs of a distinct political position.

The project of creative cultural destruction in which Chinese fascists engaged necessarily emerged from context-specific struggles and intellectual genealogies.[7] Its modernizing, vanguardist rhetoric drew heavily from the New Culture and May Fourth movements, from United Front Leninism, and from military and technical schooling received in China and abroad. Blue Shirt discussions of culture, for instance, bore an unmistakably militaristic tone. We hear them speaking of cultural fronts, struggle, and total mobilization. "Culture is the advance brigade of social thought," wrote the editors of the Blue Shirt periodical *Shehuizhuyi yuekan* (*Socialism Monthly*) in 1933; "It is the source of revolutionary power."[8] Like the military that they populated, culture to Blue Shirts was inherently nondemocratic and hierarchical. Its essential spirit needed to be drilled and disciplined; its different elements were, like a national army, supposed to work together as a coherent whole to deflect China's myriad internal and external enemies. Meanwhile, in CC Clique writings on "cultural construction" and "cultural enterprise planning," we hear unmistakable echoes of early twentieth-century managerial and engineering techniques.[9] Culture was to be managed by the state like a Taylorized factory—in which channels of communication were open in a strictly top-down fashion—to foster cohesion between the leaders and the led for the good of the nation writ large. Chen Lifu's 1934 best-selling tract *Weishenglun* (*Vitalism*) sketched a picture of Chinese society as an animate machine manned by a sagacious state, whose individual parts had to perform their designated functions for the "efficiency" (a word that Chen liked to render in English) of the larger whole.[10] Just as modern armies follow strict chains of command and require maximal coordination, conceptions of the nation as efficient firm were underpinned by elitist notions of who had the authority to plan and who would be the objects and executors of said planning. Whether militaristic or technocratic in emphasis, fascist cultural discourse emphasized hierarchical unity. Both emphases privileged disciplined divisions of labor, while the latter's recourse to scientific metaphors implied the naturalness of the culture invoked and suggested an underlying immutability that even the most radical of historical-material transformations could not alter.

While Joseph Levenson argued that the "nationalist-traditionalist impulse" of men such as Chiang Kai-shek and Chen Lifu "was for Chinese to be Confucian because Confucius was Chinese, not because he told the simple truth," this "impulse" was not a direct engagement with dynastic tradition as such (whatever that might be) but an intervention in ongoing politico-intellectual debates about the status of Confucianism in a postdynastic world.[11] Their primary point of reference was the 1910s New Culture and May Fourth movements. Men who became fascists in the 1920s and 1930s participated in these movements, imbibing their modernizing, socially engaged ethos but reversing their dominant conclusions regarding Confucianism.[12] In United Front Canton and after, GMD rightists found inspiration in the words of Sun Yat-sen, who maintained not only that Confucianism and industrial modernity were compatible but that Confucianism constituted a necessary ground of national cohesion upon which China's development depended. Whatever Sun Yat-sen had argued before his death, fascists struggled throughout the late 1920s and 1930s to distance Confucianism, as well as their own political position, from the tarring feudal designation that Confucianism had acquired during May Fourth. Chen Lifu, among others, insisted that "renaissance does not equal resuscitating the past" (*fuxing fei fugu*), as *fugu* was a "conservative" and "not progressive" stance involving the blind worship of old ideas and the stubborn rejection of foreign things, whereas *fuxing* entailed rescuing China from its present state of decline by resuscitating its national spirit (*minzu jingshen*) while remaining open to the new.[13] "National spirit" thus emerged as an unstable resolution to the problem of revolutionary restoration, allowing fascists to argue that their revolutionary program would change China materially beyond recognition while the nation's enduring Confucian ethos would remain as it had always been.

Imperialism and the "Nightmare" of Tradition: Nationalists Respond to the New Culture and May Fourth Movements

That Sun Yat-sen and his founding generation of Nationalist Party revolutionaries were geographically and preoccupationally distant from the northern loci of the New Culture Movement, typically dated to the 1915 appearance of the journal *Xin qingnian* (*New Youth*), did not mean that they were unaffected by its paradigm-shifting powers. Beginning in 1915, a group of Beijing-based intellectuals including *New Youth* editor and soon CCP-cofounder Chen Duxiu began attacking ethics and institutions associated with China's recently collapsed dynastic system. The New Culture Movement was multilayered, involving first and foremost the promotion of science and democracy as the basis for a new national culture. These demands led to an "unprecedented affirmation of Euro-American culture and to a total repudiation of the native hegemonic tradition, Confucianism, which now represented all that was backward and superstitious against the 'enlightenment' of modernity."[14] The movement targeted key textual and social sites through which "tradition" was reproduced, prompting demands for a new colloquial written language and the dismantling of institutions with which Confucianism was indelibly associated. The family was primary among the targeted institutions; its undoing appeared necessary to create a new generation of people unencumbered by patriarchal authority. Confucian precepts like filial piety were regarded as particularly enfettering. Wang Zheng has written of how New Culturists focused their attacks on the ostensible barbarism of Confucian social bonds: "the three cardinal principles in Confucianism—ruler guides subject, father guides son, husband guides wife—were held responsible for turning the Chinese into slaves. Or even worse, the Confucian ethics that maintained a hierarchical social order were nothing but 'eating human beings,'" as the writer Lu Xun suggested in his 1918 short story "Diary of a Madman."[15] Although the New Culture and May Fourth movements had differing social bases (the latter involved mass nationalist demonstrations against the 1919 Versailles Treaty), the first helped give way to the second. Arif Dirlik has underscored how the New Culture Movement "blended in 1919 with the May Fourth Movement, which spread the message of 'new culture' broadly beyond the small group of intellectuals (mainly in Beijing) to which it had been restricted initially."[16] By the early 1920s, New Culture Movement ideas—the promotion of science and democracy and the critique of Confucian traditions—were increasingly woven into the fabric of mass nationalism and inevitably appeared on the GMD radar. The New Culture and May Fourth movements involved a wide range of epistemological and political standpoints, and not everyone who championed science and language reform, or even the idea that China needed a new national culture, believed that attacking Confucianism was a necessary part of the equation.[17] This became an increasingly clearly articulated position of veteran GMD revolutionaries like Sun Yat-sen and Dai Jitao, as well as a younger generation of men who were inspired by the social-transformational momentum of the New Culture and May Fourth movements to join the formalized agitational structures already established in China's southern city of Canton. There, GMD activists began to collectively craft a picture of China's Confucian tradition that was in many respects as unnuanced as that of their Communist counterparts and which soon became a ground for action.

In Canton, the GMD capitalized in various ways on the anti-imperialist mobilizations that erupted on May 4, 1919, while many New Culture-turned-May Fourth-Movement participants soon made their way south to the GMD's Canton power base.[18] This group included a new generation of revolutionary activists who joined the GMD after the 1924 Soviet reorganization provided the party with firmer ideological and military foundations—men like Chen Lifu and He Zhonghan, who had themselves been students in northerly cities during the 1910s and early 1920s and experienced the New Culture and May Fourth movements firsthand. He Zhonghan, as noted above, was a student leader in Wuchang in the late 1910s, following which he moved to Shanghai and studied Russian at a school established by New Culture leader and soon CCP cofounder Chen Duxiu. After attending Moscow's 1922 Congress of the Toilers of the East, He Zhonghan returned to Wuchang and founded the People's News Agency as well as another news agency in Changsha, where he was also involved in that city's Youth Service Society. He's activism soon took him to Canton, where he joined the first class of Canton's Whampoa Military Academy in 1924 and helped to organize the academy's anti-Communist Sun Yat-senism Study Society.[19] Chen Lifu, meanwhile, entered Tianjin's Beiyang University to study mine engineering in 1917.[20] When the May Fourth Movement erupted in 1919, Chen was in charge of publishing the school's daily paper, a position that granted him "access to a great variety of publications, including magazines such as *New Youth* or *La Jeunesse* [*Hsin ch'ing-nien*], *New Tide* or *The Renaissance* [*Hsin Ch'ao*], and books related to the Russian revolution and communism." Though Chen "devoured these with great interest" and regarded himself as a leftist at the time, he recalled being uncomfortable with the May Fourth slogan "Down with Confucius." Chen wrote, "I thought [it] was too radical and antitraditional. I had thoroughly studied *The Four Books* and *The Five Classics* and could not agree that Confucius' teaching was that bad. My way of thinking was that any rotten tradition certainly ought to be discarded or rejuvenated but that to condemn old traditions as bad and demand they be destroyed was overemotional and irrational."[21] Though Chen expressed this sentiment in his memoirs many years after the fact, his decision to lecture to American audiences on the Confucian classics while studying in the United States, as well as his subsequent intellectual labors, lend weight to this retrospective narration of his own engagement with the May Fourth Movement's antitraditionalism. He Zhonghan, Chen Lifu, and others who went on to form the core of the GMD right wing had firsthand experience of the intellectual

debates, associational forms (student clubs and reading groups), and communications media (newspaper and journals) that were cornerstones of these
movements.[22] Under Comintern influence during the United Front (1923–
27), May Fourth debates were translated into the idioms of Communist internationalism, but their stamp remained clear. The emerging pro-Confucian
traditionalism of the GMD right wing concertedly engaged with them.

By Chen Lifu's own recollection, his primary concern at the time of May
Fourth was with imperialism, and he had come to believe that "extremism
[condemning China's Confucian heritage] to correct a wrong would only
produce a greater loss."[23] Chen was equally convinced that his advanced
training in mine engineering—which, as discussed in chapter 1, he undertook at the University of Pittsburgh in 1923–24—would help strengthen
China's position on the world stage.[24] Chen's dual desire to acquire developmental expertise and to protect China's Confucian heritage from further
desecration should not be regarded as contradictory or confused. Chen's
interests resonated strongly with those of nationalist elites across the colonized world at the time, who grappled in varying ways with the forms of
violence that colonial authorities had wrought against precolonial ways of
life while they also fought to achieve national independence. From such a
perspective, to argue that received traditions encouraged people to canni-
balize others, as Lu Xun had written, or that they weighed "like a nightmare
on the brain of the living" (as the modernist Marx put it in the "Eighteenth
Brumaire") added insult to imperialist injury, contributing to what Chen
Lifu called a "greater loss." Precolonial traditions, in this latter view, were
not a nightmare from which one had to awaken but rather a realm of forced
dispossession to be reclaimed as a condition of emancipation from imperialist domination.[25] Still, just as the cultural discourses of elite anticolonial
nationalists from South Asia to North Africa have been criticized for repress-
ing or ignoring forms of difference within the nation as well as subaltern
demands for social justice, the repressions and blind spots of the GMD must
also be examined.[26] Whose loss did Chen Lifu have in mind, and who stood
to gain from this act of retrieval? What did defending Confucianism signify in the context of revolutionary Canton, where everyone affiliated with
the United Front endorsed some form or another of radical sociopolitical
transformation? How did this defensive posture, moreover, affect the ways
in which the subject and object of revolution were conceptualized?

In Canton during the early 1920s, ideological positions were far from
fixed; social forces of many kinds converged and clashed; and momentum

for radical social transformation was not only building but was gaining a newly disciplined, militant structure with the aid of the Communist International. "Going to the people" and figuring out how to mobilize them was a constitutive, but not at all straightforward, part of the United Front's work.[27] Who were the people and what did they believe in the first place? Historian Tong Lam has written of how the first decades of the twentieth century witnessed the rise of the social survey in China.[28] Organizers and investigators of all kinds, armed with new epistemologies, traveled across the country and discovered it anew, researching the kinds of social imaginaries and work rhythms that animated everyday life. Surveys of villages and factories produced new conceptualizations of China's diversity of languages, practices, professions, and religious beliefs. In the context of the 1920s, during which organizers and researchers were confronting and tabulating China's extraordinary internal diversity, the emerging cultural discourse of the GMD right wing appears all the more striking for its lack of interest in investigating what actual people thought and did all day. Instead, we see an increasing GMD confidence that China had a unitary culture that encompassed the entirety of its claimed territory and stretched back five thousand years. China's problems stemmed from the fact that Confucian values had waned, and these problems could be resolved only if people remembered the social obligations that China's native culture was supposed to cultivate in them. If the GMD exponents of this position sounded like they themselves had not yet been "enlightened" from the despotism of an elite, text-based Confucian tradition, the technocratic-developmentalist and anti-Communist terms in which they articulated their views suggests that they were as attuned to the ways of the modern world as their "enlightened" political opponents. Building on ideas that were explicit and implicit in the thought of Sun Yat-sen, GMD right-wing cultural discourse began to function like a language of capture, defining the national-revolutionary subject, refusing the category of class, and forcing the diversity that was then being "discovered" about China into an orderly national box.

SUN YAT-SEN AND THE COMPATIBILITY OF
CONFUCIANISM WITH INDUSTRIAL MODERNITY

According to Sun Yat-sen biographer Marie-Claire Bergère, Sun "did not pronounce officially on Confucianism until 1924, at which date he praised it, paying homage to its role in the formation of the national culture."[29]

The fact that Sun, a man whose own thinking was as indebted to Confucian categories as it was to Euro-American post-Enlightenment thought, felt compelled to officially praise Confucianism at all bespeaks the ways in which the New Culture and May Fourth movements had shifted the national conversation about its role in social transformation.[30] In his 1924 "Three Principles of the People" (*Sanminzhuyi*) lectures, which aimed to strengthen the GMD's ideological foundations in the wake of the party's Soviet reorganization, Sun vocally rebutted the anti-Confucianism of the New Culture and May Fourth movements. These lectures conveyed Sun's enthusiasm for the machine age and presented Confucianism as compatible with its wonders if not in fact capable of animating a form of modernity superior to anything the metropolitan world had yet generated. As many scholars have noted, Sun's oeuvre was riddled with ambiguities, and his 1924 Canton lectures walked a fine line between upholding the United Front and criticizing Marxism. Moreover, Sun's criticisms of Marxism, in particular its theory and practice of class struggle, readily blended into his criticisms of the New Culture Movement. This was partially due to the fact that many Communists in Canton had emerged from the New Culture and May Fourth movements and were themselves fierce critics of Confucianism. But it was also because Sun's criticisms of Marxism shuttled between historical and cultural lines of argument. That is, Sun's criticisms of Marxism stemmed, in part, from his productivist belief that class struggle hindered the development of a given nation's productive capacities, and that class struggle had been rendered historically obsolete—evidenced, Sun argued in his first lecture on the principle of popular livelihood (*minshengzhuyi*) by America's Ford automobile factories. But productivity for Sun also required interclass cooperation on a national basis, and Sun's nation was held together by blood and culture. Historian Guannan Li has underscored that for Sun, "the Chinese nation had maintained its racial cohesion since earliest antiquity." This cohesion was bolstered by "other cultural factors such as style of life, language, religion, and customs," which had rendered the Han Chinese into a "single pure race. . . . Sun's concept of race thus went beyond biological conditions and included a number of sociological, religious, and cultural qualities that created the foundation for the Chinese nation."[31] In this regard, Sun's criticisms of Marxism were both historical and cultural. To attack Confucian values, as the New Culturists and Communists were then doing, was to attack the basis of national cohesion and to threaten its capacity for productivity and thereby the possibility of China regaining its sovereignty on the world stage. Listeners so inclined, like Sun's longtime comrade Dai Jitao, as well as young nationalists like Chen Lifu and He Zhonghan, did not have to strain to hear in Sun's words validation for the idea that critics of Confucius and advocates of class struggle posed intertwined dangers to the nation and to the revolution that the GMD was waging. This opened a door for emerging GMD right-wing arguments that China's native Confucian culture naturally supported interclass cooperation and that class struggle was alien to enduring Chinese ways of being. By the 1930s, all of these ideas—Communism's threat to a primordial national culture, to productivity, and to the GMD's capacity to fight for China's sovereignty against imperialism on the world stage—would be woven together in fascist discourse.

Sun Yat-sen's most direct statement on the New Culture and May Fourth movements appeared in his sixth lecture on the principle of nationalism (*minzuzhuyi*), delivered in Canton on March 2, 1924, in which he argued that recovering China's "native old morality" was necessary for the Nationalist revolution to succeed:

> If we want to recover our national standing, not only must everyone unite into an organized nation-state, we must first recover our native old morality. Once we have recovered our native morality we can plan to recover our nation's former standing. Chinese people to this day will recall that, according to China's native morality, first comes loyalty and filial piety [*zhongxiao*], then benevolence [*ren'ai*], then sincerity and righteousness [*xinyi*], followed by peace [*heping*]. Chinese people still frequently speak of these old morals. However, oppression by foreign nations has also entailed the invasion of a new culture and this new cultural influence is ravaging China. People infatuated with this new culture reject the old morality with the assumption that a new culture means that the old morality is no longer desirable. They don't realize that if a native thing is good then it is of course worth preserving, and if it is not, then it can be discarded.[32]

Here, Sun maintained that recovering China's "native morality" was a precondition for liberating China from imperialism and reestablishing its preeminence on the world stage. Native morals were presented by Sun as synonymous with Confucian precepts like filial piety—then under attack by New Culturists for their role in reproducing patriarchal norms and socially submissive mentalities. Far from seeking to overturn such precepts,

Sun insisted that they were to be revived and transmuted into a basis for national unity. This included transferring obligations one might have previously held toward the emperor to the modern state, and likewise by shoring up family and clan organizations as key mediators between the state and the individual.[33] From such a perspective, challenging the family structure threatened an organizational platform of Sun's nationalism. In the passage above, Sun further cast New Culturists as abetting imperialists by threatening values that Chinese people held dear. He thereby figured this people as holding a unitary set of values and the GMD as defending them against imperialism and its New Culture handmaidens.

Sun's criticisms of the New Culture and May Fourth movements extended to their cosmopolitanism (*shijiezhuyi*), against which he defended his own doctrine of nationalism (*minzuzhuyi*). In lectures delivered in Canton in February 1924, he rebutted "new youth advocates of a new culture," noting that he often heard "new youths saying that the 'Guomindang's Three Principles of the People are not in accord with new world trends.'" But, Sun challenged, the reason why China had become a "lost country" was because China had an indigenous tradition of universalism (*tianxiazhuyi*) akin to cosmopolitanism that stretched back two thousand years. It was precisely because of this worldly openness, Sun argued, that China had been lost to the Manchus, who themselves had championed such a view. Cosmopolitanism, according to Sun, entailed a "failure to distinguish between foreign tribes and the Chinese."[34] In the modern era, cosmopolitanism was at best a luxury that colonized populations could enjoy after national sovereignty had been achieved, and at worst it was a fig leaf for imperialist global domination.[35] Here, Sun's position may have been consistent with United Front and Third Communist International principles of a two-stage revolution—that is, that colonized populations needed to first achieve national independence and experience a bourgeois revolution before advancing toward socialism—but it was hardly a stretch to see in Sun's criticisms of cosmopolitanism an objection to Marxist internationalism, or, relatedly, to see the resurgence of a long-standing ethnocentrism in his criticism of Manchu universalism. The nation and its unity were paramount in Sun's program.

Sun's distaste for class struggle was entwined with his belief that China would only regain its sovereignty if it developed its own productive capacities. This in turn required interclass cooperation on a national scale. History had proven class struggle unnecessary, and China's circumstances made it particularly inappropriate. Sun's first Canton lecture on the principle of popular livelihood, delivered on August 3, 1924, pointed to America's Ford factories to evidence the former point. Ford, according to Sun, demonstrated that remunerating workers well, limiting their work hours, and monitoring their off-duty welfare resulted in greater productivity than did the class conflict that Communists advocated:

> Everyone is aware of America's Ford factories, that they are enormous in size and produce a tremendous number of cars that sell well in countries all around the world, and that their annual profits are also enormous. What are the production and management conditions of these factories? Whether the factories themselves, the management offices, or the machinery, everything is perfect and exquisite and accords with worker sanitation. Workers' time in the factories—even those doing the most manual of tasks—does not exceed eight hours per day. As for wages, even the most unimportant work is given five dollars per day. . . . [Factories] also provide playgrounds for workers' recreation, there are hospitals and clinics to treat worker illnesses, and schools have been established to educate newly arrived workers and their children. . . . Marx said that capitalists try to reduce workers' wages, but the Ford factories are increasing workers' wages; Marx said that capitalists wish to increase the cost of commodities, but Ford is reducing their costs. . . . Marx may have diligently researched social problems over the course of several decades, but the facts that he grasped now belong to the past. He did not foresee these subsequent developments.[36]

Ford's experiments proved that advocating class struggle, as Marx's followers did, was historically passé. To Sun the welfarist, disciplinary role assumed by these factories properly belonged to the state. In certain respects, Sun's vision for the Chinese Republican state resembled a Ford factory writ large. His recourse to automotive metaphors to describe state functions further underscores the hierarchical yet cooperative class relations upon which his political program rested—relations that Sun's fascist followers would soon amplify as intrinsically Confucian and therefore intrinsically Chinese.

In Sun's view, Nationalist revolutionaries had the opportunity to create a form of state and society superior to anything the world had yet seen; to do so they had to learn from the West's mistakes as well as its innovations. Class struggle was clearly detrimental to social progress. Instead it was best to "eliminate business monopolies, increase income and estate taxes on capitalists, increase the wealth of the state and then reinvest this wealth in public transport and communications, improving worker education, improving sanitation and workplace facilities, and thereby increasing society's overall productive capacities."[37] Governing itself, or managing the state, was best left to experts. Government by experts was like the novelty of a chauffeured car. "Government is like a large automobile; government officials are like drivers," Sun explained. "When democracy first emerged in Europe and America, there were no experts. It's like when cars first appeared on the road twenty-odd years ago and people who owned them had to maintain and drive them themselves." History had since given rise to repairmen and to chauffeurs, so there was no need for car owners to deal with annoyances like maintenance and driving. The same was true of governing.[38] Europe and America had proven class struggle unnecessary, and they also demonstrated that government functioned better in the hands of experts. If Chinese people came to recognize this fact, they were poised to industrialize and reap the benefits of modern technology without producing the kinds of social strife that had emerged in the West.

Like an efficiently run Ford factory, Sun's notion of government by experts rested on the assumption that certain men were destined to manage and others to be managed, and that people would embrace whatever their allotted role happened to be. Here Sun's historical argument regarding a stage in the global development of capitalism merged into a cultural one about China's difference, which also rejected the idea of natural human equality.[39] To Sun, China's primary divisions were not between classes, but between three different tiers of people: the *xianzhixianjue* (a term that can be rendered as "those who know and become conscious first," "foreknowers," or "vanguards" depending on context), the *houzhihoujue* ("those who know and become conscious after the fact" or "after-knowers"), and the *buzhibujue* ("those who do not know and are unconscious," or more simply, "the ignorant and unconscious"). These three groups were inclined toward cooperation rather than conflict. It was possible and indeed morally obligatory for the state to provide each group with opportunities according to their abilities, but absolute equality was neither a proper starting point nor a proper goal.[40] Regarding the foreknowers, Sun argued that only because of their insight and initiative "does the world progress and mankind have civilization."[41] The middling strata of after-knowers were more numerous and less capable than the first, and their role was to follow and imitate what the first had the foresight to invent. Unlike the lowest and largest tier of ignorant and unconscious people, after-knowers could at least understand the first tier's inventions. One might try to educate people in the lowest tier, but they ultimately "cannot understand; they can only implement."[42] Sun took care to stress that all of the world's industry and progress required implementation and hence rested on the labor of the third group. Despite fundamental differences between these groups, it was selfish for any one of them to work for their own benefit. Rather, they had an obligation to work together for the public good.

While it is possible to interpret Sun's social vision as residually feudalistic with respect to social stratification, it was quite modern in its assumptions about planning and the division of labor. This was particularly clear in an example Sun furnished about the construction of a foreign-style building. To construct such a building, Sun explained, it had first to be envisioned by an engineer, here representing the elite group of foreknowers. Once the engineer had sketched his designs, these could be turned over to a foreman (here standing in for the after-knowers), who would in turn hire workers (i.e., the ignorant and unconscious) to gather materials and build according to the engineer's designs. Sun maintained that "the workers constructing this foreign building cannot read the plans themselves. They can only listen to what the foreman tells them and would otherwise be laying bricks and tiles wherever, making the simplest of things. The foreman, similarly, would not be able to come up with the comprehensive plan sketched by the engineer; he could only direct the workers in how to lay the bricks and tiles."[43] Sun's point was not only to illustrate differences of ability between his three tiers of people, but to underscore that each could not and should not work on his own: the only way for the building to be built properly was if they all cooperated. By extension, in constructing a new polity it could take "several thousand years" for the ignorant masses to recognize of their own accord the importance of the present political struggle.[44] Left to their own devices, their progress would be glacially slow. Men of foresight within the GMD therefore had to show the ignorant how to advance. For their own welfare, the latter were obliged to listen to instructions relayed by the middling tier that originated with visionaries at the top. Otherwise, China's masses would just be laying bricks and tiles wherever, milling about with no purpose or goal.

In Sun's schema, workers, much less peasants, were not the vanguards of revolution but rather its drones. The ignorant would be cared for—nurtured and protected and provided with basic human needs like clothing, food, shelter, and transportation (*yi, shi, zhu, xing*)—but they would not have a voice. Their role was to provide the necessary labor in the fields and factories, to implement what vanguards had invented. To be sure, Sun's explication of expertise involved contradictions, and he elsewhere tempered his elitism by insisting that all men should be respected for their respective areas of knowledge. Indicating its modern orientation, this idea was also illustrated with reference to automobiles. In his fifth lecture on the principle of popular sovereignty (*minquanzhuyi*), Sun told a story about hiring a taxicab in Shanghai's French concession after suddenly remembering that he had an appointment across town fifteen minutes later.[45] Given traffic, he expected that his destination would be impossible to reach in such a short span of time. Sun recalled growing impatient as he rode along since the driver seemed to be taking him on a roundabout route, only to find that the driver delivered him to his destination on time. Sun's point was that he should not have questioned the driver's expertise, that all men have special varieties of insight, and that there was no reason for anyone to look down upon workers, whether drivers, cooks, carpenters, or patrolmen.[46] But Sun's plea for respect did not translate into power or voice, at least not for the foreseeable future. A governing official should respect the expertise of the cook, but the cook had no business being something other than a cook or acting like he knew how to participate in governing. Lenin, for his part, had also maintained that "an unskilled [laborer] or a cook cannot immediately get on with the job of state administration," but Lenin believed not only that they were capable of learning how but also "that a *beginning* [should] be made at once in training all the working people, all the poor, for this work."[47] Sun wanted the cook to stay put. His impulse to set society in motion—evident not just from his frequent references to locomotion but also in his identification of transportation as a staple of livelihood—was distinctly shadowed by a desire for social fixity.

This discussion of Sun's elitism is not intended to suggest that it represented the entirety of his thought, or that many of his ideas did not also point in a more egalitarian direction. Rather, it is to highlight tendencies that GMD rightists soon represented as the true Sun that in turn informed their project of cultural revolution. In Sun's 1924 Canton lectures, themes of efficiency and productivity abutted allusions to canonical Confucian texts and stories drawn from popular historical tales like the *Romance of the Three Kingdoms*.[48] Sun likened state organs to machine parts as readily as he praised the moral governments of the ancient mythical emperors Yao and Shun, and he explicitly presented a plan for modernizing China that did not entail abandoning traditions then being criticized by New Culturists and Chinese Communists.[49] Sun's insistence that the success of the Nationalist revolution required the revival of Confucian values, as well as his racialized-culturalist remarks about China's ancient unity, provided fodder for activists within the GMD who were already dismayed by the party's alliance with the Communists to recast the latter as an explicit threat to the nation and its revolution. When Sun died in 1925, leaving the future of the party and the revolution in question, they began to reread Sun's doctrine as defending not only native Confucian values against the onslaughts of liberalism and Communism, but Sun himself as an industrial-era Confucian sage. Sun's interests in Fordism and in redistributive socialism were recast as a cultural predisposition expressive of Sun's Confucian sagacity, while the interclass cooperation upon which Fordist production depended was reread as naturally fostered by China's Confucian culture. Guomindang right wingers thereby placed Sun and Confucianism on the side of the Chinese nation, and aligned political positions that seemed to challenge either or both with imperialism. The power struggles that erupted within the GMD after Sun's death entailed a sharp nativization of Sun's thought.

NATIVIZING REVOLUTION: DAI JITAO READS SUN YAT-SEN

As Brian Tsui has elaborated, the transformation of Sun into an industrial-era Confucian sage who fused ancient wisdom with revolutionary developmentalism was greatly indebted to the politico-intellectual labors of Sun's longtime personal secretary Dai Jitao.[50] Born in 1891, Dai was quickly swept up in anti-Qing activism, and he participated in publishing and in Nationalist politics until his death by suicide in 1949. In the early 1910s, he worked as secretary for the Railway Development Bureau; railways represented to Dai "more than conveying goods and thus curing poverty; they were the emotional symbol of strength and physiological sinew of national unity."[51] Dai soon became editor of the Chinese Revolutionary Party's (a GMD predecessor) main propaganda organ, *Minguo zazhi* (*The Republic*), and at the time of the May Fourth Movement he was involved with several other publications. In the early 1920s, like many younger radicals, Dai had a strong interest in Marxism, participating in study groups in Shanghai.

Dai's pioneering Chinese-language introduction to Marx's *Capital*, based on a Japanese translation, was serialized between November 1919 and April 1920.[52] Whether despite or because of his Marxist expertise, Dai remained deeply skeptical of class conflict. Dai never advocated a leadership role for workers and instead, according to Arif Dirlik, "wished to educate laborers to raise their class consciousness, but with the professed objective of preventing, not fomenting, class struggle."[53] Throughout this period Dai remained close with Sun Yat-sen and grew increasingly anti-Communist. Dai initially declined to participate in the United Front at all but acquiesced to serving a number of roles in Canton, including becoming, in January 1924, a member of the Nationalist Party's Central Executive Committee as well as its propaganda director. In May 1924, Dai became the political director of the Whampoa Military Academy, working alongside future Communist leaders.[54] The introduction of political work into the military was a pivotal development of the United Front, and Dai Jitao's reinterpretation of Sun's thought soon exerted a powerful sway over young nationalistic cadets.

After Sun's 1925 death Dai began to underscore how morality set Nationalists apart from Communists and how Confucian interpersonal obligations bound the larger national revolutionary subject together.[55] That year Dai published two serialized articles, later reissued as pamphlets, addressing the party's future. These two tracts—"Philosophical Foundations of Sun Yat-senism" (soon retitled "Philosophical Foundations of the Three Principles of the People") and the "People's Revolution and the Chinese Nationalist Party"—provided theoretical grounds for the GMD to sever its United Front ties with the CCP. They made the case that the true subject of a truly Chinese revolution was not the proletariat, much less the peasantry as heterodox Marxists like Mao Zedong would soon suggest, but rather an awakened nation bound together by Confucian culture.

Narrowing revolution or the theories that aid it to an exclusively national enterprise necessarily involves multiple erasures. This is as true of the French Revolution as of the Chinese, where colonial and regional entanglements invariably shaped conceptualizations of revolution's agents and aims. As Tani Barlow has observed, "Scholarship in the semicolonial frame can never be uncomplicatedly national, since the borders of the semicolonial nation are, by definition, compromised."[56] The same pertains to the sociohistorical processes of revolution and counterrevolution, particularly in the technologically and imperialistically interconnected world of the twentieth century. Yet in Dai Jitao's hands, "revolution was reduced from an international struggle to an indigenous Chinese enterprise." It was removed, as Herman Mast and William Saywell argued, from the "grip of enormous historical forces" and "returned to human moral striving" on a specifically national basis.[57] Dai's writings subsumed Sun's eclectically inspired corporatism under a discourse of Confucian moralism that presented Chinese culture as naturally producing social harmony. Class struggle–fomenting ideologies like Communism were, in this view, irrevocably alien.

Dai's 1925 "Philosophical Foundations of the Three Principles of the People" positioned Sun's political philosophy as a transmission of ancient Confucian wisdom directly to the twentieth-century GMD elite. In Dai's presentation, Sun's openly acknowledged debts to Euro-American thinkers from Henry George to Henry Ford disappeared behind a mystical shroud of native morality stretching back to the ancient sage emperors Yao and Shun. Dai honed in on elitist, anti-Communist tendencies in Sun's thought and recast them as an expression of an ancient national culture, thereby fusing Sun's developmentalism with an enduring set of nationally particular values. Sun's thought not only protected indigenous Confucian values but was a modern-day expression of them, while Communism constituted an attack on a revolutionary course that China's native culture naturally directed the nation to follow. Ever since European culture had arrived in China, wrote Dai, Chinese intellectuals had undergone radical transformation and had come to oppose the ways of Confucius. Within revolutionary circles, "extreme opponents of Confucian influence are always in the majority."[58] Sun Yat-sen was not among them. His thinking directly inherited Confucian orthodoxy and carried it forward. To Dai, Sun possessed the cultural self-confidence necessary for the revolution to mature. He not only supported reviving Chinese culture but "believed that China's ancient ethical philosophy and political sages were crystallizations of the greatest human spiritual civilization in the history of world civilizations."[59] The "genuine liberation of all mankind" rested, in Sun's view, on the foundations of China's native culture.[60]

In his modern sagacity, Sun offered a blueprint for industrializing without generating social conflict. Unlike Communism, Sun's program did not declare war on capitalism but was instead akin to "aborting the fetus of a recently impregnated capitalism"; it eliminated capitalism's unwanted offspring, like the social pathology of class struggle, without compromising its overall productive capacities.[61] Forces of revolution and counterrevolution in China were divided between conscious and unconscious actors; society itself was stratified less by class than by the divisions based on knowledge and ability that Sun had identified.[62] As far as the revolution was concerned, Dai regarded it as not only selfish but counterrevolutionary for any one group to work for its own benefit. Confucian ethics provided the basis for revolutionary cohesion.[63] Organizing efforts were therefore to focus on fostering recognition of the chain of responsibility from the self to the family to the state, creating a new mass of people possessed of cultural self-confidence and conscious of their social obligations, as well as of the unnaturalness of class-conflictual activism.

Communist organizers in Canton quickly denounced Dai's invocation of Confucian culture as a ground for revolutionary solidarity, sensing in it not only an explicit threat to United Front unity but also a new form of elitism dressed in a familiar garb. Chinese Communist Party leaders Qu Qiubai and Chen Duxiu sharply denounced what they called "Dai Jitaoism" for threatening to turn the work of mass mobilization into a "philanthropic enterprise" undertaken by benevolent Confucian gentlemen.[64] Chen and Qu's rebuttal underscores the historically novel aspects of Dai's Confucian paternalism. Dai may have invoked long-standing Confucian categories and ascribed to them an ancient power, but he spoke in the name of the masses and a revolutionary nation. He was concerned with industrial production and how it affected China's relations to imperialist powers and other oppressed nationalities. Moreover, Dai's theorization of nationalist revolution directly reacted to the challenge of an organized Communist movement, steering the Chinese revolution in a specifically national direction and attempting to render a Communist (or any other) revolutionary path impossible on cultural grounds.

Whereas Communist organizers were quick to see threats in Dai's writings, other activists in United Front Canton found inspiration in them. These included Whampoa cadets as well as the academy's leader, Chiang Kai-shek. They also included Chen Guofu, who was then working as a Whampoa recruiter, and his brother Chen Lifu, who was then a personal secretary to Chiang. In late 1925, under the spell of Dai Jitao's writings, Whampoa cadets including future Blue Shirt leader He Zhonghan formed Sun Yat-senism study groups in opposition to the Communist cadet group, the League of Chinese Military Youth.[65] These study groups marked the incipient translation into practice of a nativist interpretation of Sun Yat-sen by Soviet-trained soldiers who gained new experience propagating their ideas via publications and street demonstrations.[66] Sun Yat-senism Study

Society branches were soon founded across the country.[67] The ideological and organizational foundations of Chinese fascism thereby appeared in nascent form in revolutionary Canton.

To GMD rightists in the wake of the May Fourth Movement, Confucianism was not a nightmare from which China had to awaken but rather a heritage of which the nation was still being forcibly dispossessed. May Fourth had made clear that struggles over this heritage were as much about the distribution of social power in the present as the details of the past itself. Many of the men who defended Confucianism in United Front Canton were as invested in China's broad-based social transformation as those who opposed it. Still, May Fourth had put proponents of Confucianism—at least those who explicitly styled themselves as revolutionaries—on the defensive. They increasingly found it necessary to clarify how defending Confucianism constituted something other than defending feudal ways of life. After GMD rightists violently ended the United Front in 1927, they strove to clarify the differences between their own revolutionary program and that of the Communists, and relatedly how native morality could underpin a future-oriented, proindustrial revolution. Invoking Confucianism as a kind of national spirit—rather than as a historically grounded and evolving system of thought and practice—emerged as a means of skirting the contradictions of revolutionary restorationism. Echoing Dai Jitao, Chiang Kai-shek soon encouraged his loyalists to marshal "the spirit of traditional Confucianism in their being and actions to carry out the premier [Sun Yat-sen's] deathbed behests, to overcome present difficulties, and establish a country based on the Three Principles of the People."[68] The future depended on a particular understanding of the ways in which the past animated the present.

Spiritual Resolutions: Revolutionary Nativism during the Nanjing Decade

Although most strains of interwar and wartime fascist discourse were comfortable with logical inconsistency—Jews in much Nazi propaganda, for instance, were simultaneously affiliated with global financial capitalism and revolutionary Bolshevism—some evinced concern that such inconsistencies might grate too harshly against received common sense. This is evidenced by what Claudia Koonz has called "the Nazi conscience," whereby National Socialists "removed entire categories of people from most Germans' moral map" by generating a new discourse concerning who was human and who was not.[69] Nazis thereby found ways to make murder "moral," persuading and coercing their constituencies into seeing the world differently. As I examine in chapter 3, GMD militants did not simply kill Communists but attempted to justify it to themselves and others in specific ways. These justifications typically hinged on Communist violation of Confucian norms, which were in turn understood as the basis of the revolutionary nation's unity and coherency. Yet for activists shaped by the New Culture and May Fourth movements, vouchsafing the nation's Confucian heritage and advancing a revolutionary agenda did not readily appear compatible. In the pages of their post-1927 publications, Blue Shirt and CC Clique thinkers openly wrestled with the tensions of creating a new social order while defending national traditions against Communism and imperialism. They ultimately resolved these tensions not by working through the challenges of bringing Confucian tenets into accord with modern social dynamics, as New Confucian philosophers were then doing. Instead, the Blue Shirts and CC Clique insisted that Confucian values were the animating impetus of an enduring national spirit. In their understanding, this spirit was not particular to any historical era or mode of production. By invoking a Confucian-based national spirit, these GMD militants distanced their agenda from the taint of feudalism and found a highly malleable rallying cry.

Nearly as soon as the new Nationalist state was established in Nanjing, Chiang Kai-shek's CC Clique and Whampoa alumni supporters put their visions for a new China into circulation via a range of periodicals. Waging a nationalist revolution while suppressing a Communist one required explanation to themselves and others; the very world-historical newness of their situation meant that it had to be continually theorized. Their work necessitated differentiating the new that would be constructed from the old to be destroyed, and they also had to reconcile their work of destroying the past with that of protecting and reviving native values. In the process, nationalism's Janus-faced posture assumed increasingly mythic dimensions. An ancient spirit, whose power only the Blue Shirts and the CC Clique presently recognized and which they empowered themselves to awaken in the masses, became key to creating a radiant new future. In fusing this spirit to Sun's Three Principles, fascists made clear that pursuing any other developmental course was aberrant and unnatural.

Fascist efforts to differentiate the new that the Nationalist revolution desired to construct from the old slated for destruction began as soon as the
Nanjing regime was established.[70] Because they were concurrently tarring
Communists for abetting imperialism and despoiling native traditions, however, distinguishing the new that they would create from the old that they
would destroy was far from straightforward. The January 1, 1928, cover
of the CC Clique monthly *New Life* carried a drawing of a radiant twelve-
pointed GMD star flanked by cherubs heralding the new life that the regime
was bequeathing. Introductory remarks by Chiang Kai-shek's secretary Chen
Bulei announced that the magazine's purpose involved preparing readers
not only for a new life, but also for the kinds of pain and destruction that
realizing it necessitated.[71] Over the course of its three-year run, *New Life*
contributors including Dai Jitao, Chiang Kai-shek, and Chen Guofu underscored their commitments to building a new society. The second volume
of *New Life*, for instance, ran an essay by Chiang, "Revolution and Not-
Revolution," in which he rebutted accusations then being spread by Communists among the masses that the GMD was "not revolutionary." Other
contributors worked out what they understood to be the proper relationship between Sun's principle of livelihood and capitalists as a class, how to
destroy remnants of feudalism, and the "progress of Confucian doctrine."[72]
Contributors to this early CC Clique monthly thereby attempted to affirm
the GMD's revolutionary credentials in opposition to remnants of China's
dynastic regime that lingered in the present while also conceptually separating Confucianism from the old slated for destruction.

New Life discussions made it clear that the CC Clique would be the ar-
biters of what was valuably new and what was harmfully new and what was
valuably versus harmfully old. Similar sentiments appeared in early Nanjing decade publications of Whampoa graduates. The first 1930 issue of a
short-lived magazine called *Zhongguo wenhua* (*Chinese Culture*) included an
essay by soon-to-be Blue Shirt leader Deng Wenyi, "China's Problems in
1930." Here, Deng addressed the ways in which a new culture of Sun's Three
Principles was fitfully overtaking remnants of conservative decrepitude in
the fields of culture and education, and how much more work needed to be
done to destroy these remnants.[73] Far from casting Confucianism as one of
them, however, this issue of *Chinese Culture* opened with an essay by Chiang

Kai-shek emphasizing how the Confucian bonds of *li*, *yi*, *lian*, and *chi* (propriety, righteousness, integrity, and humility) had to ground the party and the state in its revolutionary struggle against the chaos fomented by Communism and imperialism.[74] Confucianism was being extracted from the feudal designation attached to it since the 1910s and placed in the camp of the revolutionary-new.

The work of distinguishing the revolutionary-new from the feudal-old continued in Blue Shirt and cc Clique publications throughout the 1930s. The conceptual and historical grounds of these distinctions grew increasingly arbitrary, and fascists displayed increasing confidence that it was their prerogative to simply declare what was what. In this vein, Blue Shirts at times expressed a deep hostility to all remnants of the past in a manner that suggested not only that they worried about their revolutionary credibility but also that they wanted to leave the past behind in its entirety. In a recorded speech distributed by the Blue Shirt–run Tiba bookstore, for instance, He Zhonghan complained of how remnants of China's "native culture of the past" were still "etched deeply into the mentality of our average countryman."[75] He identified this culture as an obstacle to national unity, arguing that when people referred to China as the "sick man of Asia," they meant that "China had an exceedingly glorious history, that it was a country with a culture of great duration, and if others intended to conquer us, our country could never be extinguished. . . . But this five thousand years of culture is a culture of the past. Although this culture of the past is a native culture and certainly has important value, its value is historical and in this new era it is backward, and under present conditions, much of it is unsuitable."[76] He Zhonghan's point here was that merely reviving past practices would not suffice to resolve current crises; doing so might actually deepen Chinese subjection to imperialist forces. Turning this native culture "into something that can serve as an amulet to secure the country's foundations or build the country up would be akin to the sons of a large family, because their ancestors were eminent scholars, taking that standing to be their own, thus deceiving themselves and others."[77] One only had to look at countries that had been influenced by China's native culture such as Burma, Vietnam, Korea, and Taiwan to appreciate that it was little match for the forces of imperialism.[78] "We know," moreover, "that culture doesn't perpetually advance. Sometimes it must also retreat and even be destroyed."[79] National survival, He reasoned, required overcoming nostalgic attachments to past ways of being and destroying whatever needed to be destroyed.

At the same time, He Zhonghan and other Blue Shirts strove to differentiate their work of destruction from the attacks on the past then being waged by liberal and left-wing heirs of the New Culture and May Fourth movements. In this vein He celebrated the Blue Shirts' own work of protecting and reviving Confucian values, extolling the nation's superior moral culture, and emphasizing that its people needed to recognize its centrality to revolutionary progress.[80] Similar lines of argument appeared in the thrice-weekly Blue Shirt newspaper *Shehui xinwen* (*Society Mercury*) and the magazine *Socialism Monthly*. Numerous articles in these virulently nationalistic publications, whose contributors frequently used pseudonyms, condemned China's dynastic culture for its weakness in the face of capitalist-imperialist onslaughts and lobbied for eradicating its remnants in the present.[81] Yet they also attempted to distill from China's past a kind of nonfeudal essence that could help overcome these remnants in a manner different from May Fourth–descended liberalism or Communism.

While Sun Yat-sen had condemned the dangers that May Fourth cosmopolitanism spelled for national cohesiveness, Blue Shirts took this further by arguing that the bourgeois nationalism that emerged during May Fourth was inextricably tied to a decaying global capitalism. Its decrepitude meant that it could not successfully challenge the remnants of feudalism that persisted in China's countryside. A series of 1933 editorials in *Society Mercury* examined how capitalism had taken root in China in a belated and malformed way, generating uneven development between coastal cities and the rural interior.[82] Cities were swamped by modern forms while the latter remained beholden to "provincial" and "clannish" ways. Imperialist disruptions to China's "feudal culture" had undermined its long-standing capacity to resist all barbarian invasions. While the country had been reduced to a "subcolony by the capitalism of the great powers," remnants of the old regime still persisted and "feudal thought still ha[d] considerable power among general society and culture—especially in the countryside."[83] These remnants constituted a major stumbling block to the creation of a unified nationalist consciousness: "Feudal thought cannot move beyond the confines of petty provincialism and clannishness. What is a nationality? What place does the Chinese nation occupy in the world? This is not something that feudal thinking understands."[84] The problem was therefore that feudal worldviews remained entrenched in rural areas and blocked the progression toward national unity. Moreover, the bourgeois nationalism of May Fourth, irreparably tainted by the foreign, was too weak to remove these obstacles.

In Blue Shirt eyes, May Fourth attacks on China's native culture had exacerbated the nation's crises. Political liberals that emerged from the movement blindly worshipped foreign things that were inherently rotten because they were imported from Europe at a time when capitalism was on the verge of global collapse: "The bourgeois culture that was relayed to China was an imperfect, disease-harboring culture."[85] Thinkers like Hu Shih called for liberal democracy despite the fact that it had proven itself "rotten refuse" in Europe and America. Since "bourgeois liberal democracy" was something comparatively new in China, it could easily deceive a portion of the masses. This would only serve to "exterminate the nation's spirit and cause China to be even more deeply subjected to imperialism."[86] As far as the development of a national culture was concerned, Communism was far worse. May Fourth–turned-CCP leaders like Li Dazhao and Chen Duxiu were revealing themselves to be tools of the USSR who championed a "fatherland-less proletariat."[87] That is, they were instruments of yet another foreign invader who sought to finally destroy everything that was particular about the nation and fundamental to its survival. Instead, *Society Mercury* argued, it was necessary to destroy remnants of feudalism via the construction of a new yet indigenously grounded national culture.[88]

Feudalism, in this line of argument, remained an obstacle that could only be overcome with a purer and more forceful kind of nationalism than had emerged during May Fourth—one that eschewed the cultural insecurity of liberals and the total cultural sellout of Communists. Looking elsewhere in the world, both the Blue Shirts and the CC Clique found examples of the kind of cultural regeneration they desired. The CC Clique came to admire the Nazis' "*volkisch* and Germanic ideology" as it suggested how "regeneration was rooted in a people's cultural heritage."[89] Blue Shirts meanwhile favorably observed, "Hitler's party has . . . spared no effort in establishing [a] fascist culture, and has not hesitated to burn books and lay plans to destroy and [purge the remnants] of the old culture." And in Italy, Mussolini was eradicating "all culture blocking the development of extreme nationalism."[90] In the eyes of GMD militants, this work of destruction helped to clear the way for the resurgence of a purer national essence. The GMD was tasked with removing the rubble of China's now-conquered old regime. Their appeals to Confucianism did not entail resuscitating a dying feudalism but rather identifying an uncorrupted foundation of national unity. By invoking something that they called the national spirit, they positioned themselves as revolutionary vanguards committed to destroying the old and constructing the new in a manner that eschewed degenerate foreign ideas.

In March 1933, Chiang Kai-shek exclaimed that the Three Principles of the People "have inherited the morality and essential spirit of ancient China— that of Emperors Yao and Shun, of Kings Wen and Wu, of the Duke of Zhou and Confucius—they employ the native spirit of the Chinese race to lead the revolution and revive the nation."[91] Here Chiang reiterated nearly verbatim a passage from Dai Jitao's "Philosophical Foundations of the Three Principles of the People" and communicated that a particular spirit was guiding GMD efforts to realize Sun's developmental vision. In Chiang's presentation, the Nationalist Revolution was oriented toward the future while also remaining true to an ancient national essence. Over the course of the Nanjing Decade, spirit (*jingshen*) in fascist discourse came to denote Confucian traits particular to China. These traits were unmoored from specific historical contexts while linking the ancient past with the twentieth century and beyond. They regulated the nation's material development and rendered it different from everywhere else. This spirit, Blue Shirt and CC Clique activists argued, had been beaten down by imperialism, and it was presently endangered by myriad forces, especially the crass materialism of the Communists. But it still bound the nation's people together across time and space, subsuming all differences of class, region, ethnicity, and gender. It was neither feudal nor retrograde; it was a necessary compliment to material development that prevented the emergence of social diseases and ensured that China would retain its unique qualities. Ultimately, the arbitrariness of the category "spirit" allowed fascists great latitude to define the parameters of national belonging and fueled their confidence as reenchanters of a rationalizing, industrializing world.

A 1937 *Sweat and Blood Weekly* cover of a phallic pagoda, whose base is inscribed with the phrase "Spirit Is Eternal," illustrates the aggressiveness with which fascists asserted spirit as a salient analytical and mobilizational category (fig. 2.1).[92] As early as 1933, Blue Shirts were demanding that Nationalists clarify for themselves and the nation as a whole that material and spiritual development were equally essential. They were also insisting that navel gazing over philosophical questions concerning the precise relationship between the material and the spiritual would never produce the kind of unity that China's crisis conditions required. Among other things, this

FIGURE 2.1 » "Spirit Is Eternal," *Hanxue zhoukan* (*Sweat and Blood Weekly*) 8, no. 23 (1937).

suggested that they did not want to be pressed to clarify what exactly *spirit* was supposed to mean. Frequent *Future* contributor Ru Chunpu, for instance, quipped, "There is no such thing as material culture without the spiritual, and at the same time there is no spiritual culture without the material."[93] In a similar vein, *Society Mercury* argued that China's "new culture cannot be established on purely spiritual foundations nor can it be established on purely material foundations." The GMD, they insisted, should not lean too heavily toward either the spiritual or the material, or fret excessively about the philosophical grounds of these distinctions. It should just focus on the problem of "mankind's evolutionary struggle for survival" in a hostile world.[94]

Whether due to the principles of democratic centralism by which Blue Shirts operated or to a general ideological convergence, the idea that culture comprised material and spiritual components had widespread purchase among them. They thereby explained how they would transform China materially beyond recognition without altering its enduring national particularities. In a 1934 piece for *Sweat and Blood Weekly*, "On Cultural Revolution," a contributor named Ye Fawu wrote of culture as an unfolding process and a social product governed by a spiritual impetus. Struggles between nations were perpetuated by differing spirits. Ye explained that "culture is a product of social life, a creation of the talent of a nationality, the historically accumulated and formed foundation of human life, and it is that which distinguishes humans from animals."[95] The average scholar, Ye wrote, tended to define culture very broadly, furnishing explanations that encompassed "religion, art, technology, even all aspects of ways of life, knowledge, beliefs, and behaviors." However, these sweeping definitions were still not broad enough: "Each kind of culture must have its own kind of spirit, and it is this spirit that serves as the foundation of culture."[96] The global dissemination of natural science and communication technologies meant that once-distinct national cultures had tended "toward convergence." Although technological development was important, in the present world in which, Ye wrote, "national struggles become more extreme every day, if a given nationality wants to subsist, it must on the one hand absorb the influence of other cultures, while on the other it must foster its own [so it will not be] exterminated by another's culture."[97] Spirit in Ye's understanding was key to the maintenance of national difference. It regulated material development and allowed for the absorption of technological advances generated elsewhere without the loss of national particularity.

The "cultural revolution" in which they were to engage to defeat both Communism and imperialism had Sun Yat-sen's Three Principles at its core.[98]

Other Blue Shirts emphasized how China's particularly Confucian national spirit animated and regulated Sun's development plans and set China on a unique historical course. Writing for the *Future* in 1934, a contributor named Sun Xiyu explained that the "native morality of the Chinese nation is the spirit of the Chinese nation. Because the nation has lost its spirit, its culture has degenerated."[99] This native morality stressed "propriety, righteousness, integrity, humility, filial loyalty, benevolence, good faith, and peace."[100] As Sun Yat-sen had told them, for China to materially progress it was necessary to revive this native morality. The nation's present-day scientific and technological achievements, particularly with respect to machinery, clearly could not match those of the West. Yet for several thousand years, when China's native moral spirit had been honored, China's scientific and technological culture had flourished, giving rise to inventions of world-historical significance including the compass, gunpowder, the printing press, and suspension bridges, as well as silk and tea.[101] Whereas scholars like Lewis Henry Morgan had argued that culture advanced in successive evolutionary stages, Sun Yat-sen had said otherwise.[102] If the Chinese and other weak nationalities struggled "to awaken themselves, to rise up against the imperialism which is destroying the culture of humankind, and with a fearless spirit promote the revolutionary Three Principles of the People, they would be able to overtake the scientific culture of Europe and America, and build a new world culture."[103] That is, in order for China to overcome its present material backwardness, its people had to tap into and regenerate the national spirit that had flourished in previous historical eras, enabling history to accelerate. The emphasis laid by Sun Yat-sen and Chiang Kai-shek on reviving native morality was precisely to this end.[104] In Sun Xiyu's presentation, there was nothing feudal or backward about China's native morality. It did not belong to any historical era; its revival would actually hasten China's leap into the industrial age.

Theorists of the cc Clique arrived at a similar conclusion regarding the equal salience of spiritual and material forces in historical development. They were likewise convinced that the Chinese nation's spirit was essentially Confucian and had grossly degenerated. The cc Clique magazine *Cultural Construction*, as well as the Chinese Cultural Construction Association's in-house *Wenhua jianshe xiehui huikan* (*Periodical of the Chinese Cultural Construction Association*) underscored how China's feudal past had to be overcome through the development of science and technology and how the nation's enduring spiritual attributes vouchsafed its unique character. Articles in *Cultural Construction* explicitly referenced *ti-yong* [substance-function] debates that had commenced among Chinese literati during the 1860s, which had newly posited the possibility of delineating discrete bodies of indigenous versus Western knowledges and thereby signaled the impossibility of henceforth conceptualizing one without the other. But unlike their late Qing antecedents, CC Clique activists understood material-technological progress to already be an intrinsic part of China's native culture, albeit a dimension that had been inadequately cultivated at the expense of moral-spiritual concerns while the West had surged ahead during the Industrial Revolution. Like deciding what was valuably versus harmfully new in the modern world, CC Clique activists arrogated to themselves the authority to decide what fell within and outside the purview of the nation's spirit. Just as Dai Jitao had domesticated Sun Yat-sen's globally sourced ideas and pushed unwanted sociopolitical tendencies into the category of the foreign, *Cultural Construction* contributors including Chen Lifu, Tao Baichuan, and Dai himself worked to distinguish positive elements of the West that could facilitate China's national rebirth from poisonous things like Marxism, dance halls, and licentious Hollywood films.

Introductory remarks to the first issue of *Cultural Construction* explained how China urgently needed a new culture, stressing the importance of neither blindly worshipping the West nor seeking to return to the past.[105] Its new culture had to embrace science and technology and supplant remnants of dynastic clannishness as well as abstruse doctrines like Buddhism. It also entailed regenerating the spirit of the past in a forward-looking manner. Chen Lifu pursued this line of argument in a contribution to the issue. Here, Chen maintained that the nation's present state of decline could be attributed to the fact that its people did not appreciate the greatness of their own past.[106] Chinese and Western cultures respectively had a spiritual and material "center of gravity," and these differing centers underpinned their differing strengths. China, Chen argued, had excelled in moral-spiritual endeavors and had emphasized them excessively since the Song Dynasty, while the West's material emphasis had led to its scientific and industrial revolutions and hence its global ascendancy. Referencing the classic Confucian text *Zhongyong* (*Doctrine of the Mean*), Chen argued that it was not healthy for any society to lean too heavily toward either the material or the spiritual, as both had to balance and complement one another.[107] The task before

Nationalist revolutionaries was to rectify China's own internal balance, reviving its spirit while also strengthening a weakened disposition toward material advancement. As historian Terry Bodenhorn has noted with respect to Chen's observations about relations between man and nature in Chen's 1934 *Vitalism*, the idea of balance here did not idealize acting in harmony with nature.[108] Instead, Chen stressed the complementarity of material and spiritual development within the Chinese national sphere to counteract the oppressive weight of the West. In other words, Chen's position was deeply modernist in its assumptions about mankind's rightful domination of nature and the imperative to exploit it for the sake of national strength.

Spirit in this discourse fostered hierarchical national unity. It absorbed differences into a stratified sameness. In *Cultural Construction* as in *Vitalism*, Chen Lifu underscored how the universe was ordered into natural hierarchies, and how, in the modern world, the nation constituted the most important community to which an individual belonged. Chen's recourse to natural scientific metaphors to explain this belonging—noting, for instance, that culture was cyclical and cumulative—was not merely reflective of his training as a mine engineer. Such claims also indicated that national belonging was an immutable aspect of earthly life that modern methods of inquiry had revealed and verified. In the same way that gravity acted on everyone whether they knew it or not, a given individual was bound to the larger national community regardless of whether he or she was yet cognizant of this fact. In Chen's schema, individuals were supposed to become aware of their duties to the national collective and carry out their proper functions for the efficiency of the whole.[109] According to Bodenhorn, Chen believed that "the chief concern of national leaders . . . was in determining how best to structure an efficient society, and how best to get people to perform their appropriate roles in that society."[110] Carrying Sun Yat-sen's interest in government by experts several steps further, Chen wrote of "society as productivity" and, in Bodenhorn's words, he "envisioned a utopia of machine-like happy toilers directed by the state in such a manner that needs and goods coincided."[111] The national spirit was one of mutual obligation and respect for authority. As Dai Jitao had stressed in United Front Canton, the organizing work for Nationalist leaders entailed awakening the populace to their national-social obligations.

Even when spirit was not directly invoked, CC Clique and Blue Shirt thinkers emphasized the ways in which a given nation's culture bound it together through time and across space, forging a collective body that super-seded the individual as well as any kind of social stratification. It organized the national revolutionary subject in a particular direction, subsuming differ-ences internal to the nation into a world of sameness and knowability. This was the overriding message of a 1934 special issue of the *Future* on cultural control. Ru Chunpu's contribution argued that culture was all encompass-ing yet nationally particular; it was the product of the actions of national collectivities, not the privately possessed results of individual striving. Con-servative thinkers, Ru chided, still thought of culture in dynastic Confucian terms of "historical incidents of value, things that the average person can-not understand, things they cannot do." Others viewed it as merely meaning "loyalty, filial piety, chastity, and righteousness," while still others "regard[ed] locales that have produced many successful civil service exam candidates as places with a flourishing culture." Moreover, some "see only historical relics as culture. . . . Others see writers of essays as culture; others see essays them-selves as culture."[112] To Ru, none of the dynastic signs of human cultivation—success with imperial examinations, strict observation of behavioral norms, literary-artistic facility, and so on—were broad enough to encompass culture's modern significance as the totality of a nation's collective life. He explained,

> In the past, one intervened in one's own life—[as demonstrated by] methods of self-restraint and ritual observance, of strict uprightness in one's private life and the disciplining of one's own temperament—now we want to make these kinds of practices writ large, to regard collective life as an individual was once viewed. Collective life dis-tinctly resembles an individual life, with the responsibilities of a pub-lic life added to the present responsibilities of an individual life. In the past, there was no adequate term for the collectivity's power to intervene. There is no other term but "culture" to adequately represent the totality of the meanings of social life, so cultural control exceeds in scope the control of life and involves methods requiring a more painstaking attention to detail.[113]

At bottom, culture clarified differences between nations and erased differ-ences within them, becoming a means of gauging who belonged to the col-lective and what kinds of behavior this collective ought to mandate. Ru's framing of the problem, moreover, revealed how 1930s fascists worked to distance their own social ideals from those of conservatives past and present.

Conclusion

The idea of the nation as a cultural unity whose self-confidence had waned gained considerable public attention in 1935 via a manifesto issued by a group known as the Ten Professors. Their "Manifesto for the Construction of Culture on a Chinese Basis" first appeared in the CC Clique magazine *Cultural Construction*, was reissued in their *Periodical of the Chinese Cultural Construction Association*, and was republished later that year as a book by the Longwen Press along with dozens of positive and negative public responses.[114] Guannan Li has observed that the manifesto invoked culture as "simultaneously 'scientific' and spiritual for the purposes of overcoming the limitations of both Western materialism and Eastern spiritualism." It carefully distinguished things that were Chinese from things that were traditional and insisted that China remain open to the West.[115] The manifesto's authors explained that on the one hand, China's spatial and temporal characteristics were so unique that any attempt to emulate the historical course of another country was bound to fail. On the other, China's particularity had become barely perceptible in the modern world: "It is, at present, impossible to discern China in the realm of culture. It is like standing in a fog and being unable to see the figure in front of one's eyes. . . . Chinese people are frustrated, struggling, and groping about in the dark."[116] In the wake of imperialism their countrymen barely "count[ed] as Chinese." The professors insisted that efforts to rectify this situation should neither unilaterally glorify nor outright condemn China's ancient systems of thought, nor those of the modern West.[117] While more research is needed to discern the political allegiances of the manifesto's authors and to what extent they knew about the CC Clique's clandestine activities, the fact that the CC Clique circulated their manifesto at the very least indicates the clique's efforts to forge connections with patriotic intellectuals likewise concerned with the "greater loss" of China's dynastic heritage. Whatever the limitations of their power during the Nanjing Decade, the CC Clique as well as the Blue Shirts certainly tried to tap into and fan popular concerns about the eclipse of a dynastic cultural inheritance. Given nationalism's affective and irrational powers, fascist insistence that the degeneration of the national-cultural spirit explained present crises might readily have gained wider purchase.

In the hands of GMD fascists after 1927, Sun Yat-sen's development program shifted course. They transformed the late leader's interest in defending Confucianism and in promoting this culture as the ground of national unity into a violent mythology. Sun's suggestion that national unity and hence economic development required recuperating native Confucian values lent fodder to emerging claims that these values naturally gave rise to a cooperative form of state-society organization. The homage that men including Chen Lifu and He Zhonghan paid to Confucianism during the Nanjing Decade constituted rebuttals of predominant May Fourth characterizations of this dynastic heritage. On the one hand, they inverted May Fourth (as well as Orientalist) arguments that Confucianism and economic and political modernity were incompatible. On the other, they deflected left-wing charges that this tradition reproduced social inequalities within the nation, and they mined it for ideas that specifically buttressed a class-harmonious project of industrial development. Fascist recourse to the category of national spirit enabled them to distance themselves from feudal or conservative positions while also arrogating to themselves the right to define what was properly national and what was not.

Confucianism invested the Blue Shirt and CC Clique's work of creative destruction with continuity of historical meaning, lending a veneer of stasis to the ruptures they otherwise fomented. Confucianism, as they understood it, also helped to avert the generation of what Dai Jitao called "social abnormalities," particularly the social anomie and class conflict that attend processes of industrialization. Violence and repression were necessary to achieve the kind of social harmony that Dai and others envisioned. While fascists infused urban print media with militant, revolutionary-nationalist rhetoric, they also waged war against Communists and leftists on rural battlefields and urban streets. This warfare's ideological arsenal included the revolutionary nativist rhetoric traced in this chapter. That is, it had immediate social consequences. In granting themselves the authority to define what the national spirit encompassed, fascists authorized themselves to kill people who did not conform to it. Communism, as I examine in chapter 3, was cast as posing intertwined threats to Sun Yat-sen's vision of industrial development and to Confucian values of family, social order, and sexual morality. It is in the Nationalists' counterinsurgency campaigns, and in the propaganda efforts that bolstered them, that interwar fascism's counterrevolutionary dimensions were most pronounced. These campaigns prompt us to reckon with the violence that underpinned Blue Shirt and CC Clique appeals to native culture and the nature of the alternative modernity that they desired.

3 » SPIRITUAL OFFENSES

The Nativist Prose of Counterinsurgency

Speaking in 1936 to an assembled crowd of Nationalist administrators in the recaptured Jiangxi Soviet capital of Ruijin, philosopher Zhang Junmai declared that the city marked "the spiritual front line of anti-Communism."[1] From the text of his speech, reprinted in the 1937 volume *Visitors' Accounts of Jiangxi* published by the Blue Shirts' Sweat and Blood Press, we can see that Zhang's views of Communism dovetailed with those of his Nationalist hosts. Zhang explained to his listeners that he had long ago concluded that Marxism was incompatible with Chinese life. Though the Chinese Communist Party (CCP) held lofty ideals, "their methods involve[d] murder and arson, and southern Jiangxi had become an inhuman place."[2] After reminding his audience of Communists' evidenced disrespect for property and time-honored gender norms, Zhang chided that their professed historical materialism claimed the world to be composed only of matter and denied the role of *xinling*, or mind-spirit. Their singular concern with class struggle, moreover, obviated the kinship sentiments that rendered humans human. The absence of such sentiments portended a society in which "fathers and sons cannot act as fathers and sons, brothers cannot act as brothers, husbands and wives cannot act as husbands and wives, nor could there be a nation-state to speak of."[3] With the specter of a world so alien to Confucian social norms still haunting their present, Zhang cautioned that when the Red Army had fled from Ruijin just two years before, its commanders, Mao Zedong and Zhu De, had declared that they would return within five. Given the urgency of the situation, Zhang pleaded with the "gentlemen bearing administrative and educational responsibilities" then gathered in Ruijin to address the roots of the Communist scourge. Doing so was key to preventing Communism's return and was "naturally a responsibility for the nation as a whole," even if the former red capital remained a critical front.[4]

Zhang Junmai's willingness to appear at a Nationalist assembly lent an air of highbrow respectability to the party's counterrevolutionary violence and signaled that nativist sentiments, when it came to Communism at least, radiated beyond Blue Shirt and CC Clique circles.[5] Yet where the conservative philosopher fell silent on how to actually confront the Communist threat—suggesting only that the "spiritlessness of China's old culture" needed to be rectified—Nationalist soldiers and officials had already experimented with tactics ranging from military campaigns to community policing to repentance camps (*fanxingyuan*), where incarcerated Communists and sympathizers were being rehabilitated as productive and properly Confucian members of society. Although Communists had been targets of organized violence since the spring of 1927 and their activities rendered illegal with the formal inauguration of the new Nanjing regime in 1928, the process of defining what a Communist was, why they posed a threat to the state and nation, and why they should be eliminated (rather than, for instance, politically defanged through reintegration into a coalition government) was still unfolding. Blue Shirt and CC Clique activists came to see the Communist threat lurking everywhere. If immoral people gravitated toward Communism and Communists by nature engaged in debased activities, their reasoning went, how could one tell if a cohabitating Shanghai couple, cabaret patrons, or idle male peasants were Communists or not? Even apparently apolitical manifestations of rural banditry and urban vice likely masked something politically sinister.

During the Nanjing Decade, CC Clique and Blue Shirt activists produced reams of written material—from handbooks on bandit suppression to magazine special issues to collections of military speeches—parsing how and why to eradicate Communism. These materials seldom engaged in high theoretical debate, but instead conjured a Communist specter animated by nativist tropes and stressed the need for resolute action. Communists violated Confucian social norms, were sexually licentious and irrationally destructive, and abetted processes of imperialism that had already laid waste to familiar ways of life. Communists perpetuated and capitalized on the worst aspects of May Fourth, particularly what CC Clique spy chief Xu Enceng called the era's "glass-of-water-ism" (yibeishuizhuyi).[6] Xu's oblique reference to Soviet Marxist feminist Alexandra Kollontai's oft-misquoted plea to liberate sexuality from morality—to regard it instead as being as natural as quenching a thirst—harbored the dual charges of foreignness and debauchery.[7] The threat that Communism posed was thus not to democracy or private property, as anti-Communist refrains went in the contemporaneous United States, or to the free world as they would go in Cold War Taiwan and elsewhere. It was instead to a national community bound together by a Confucian spirit, and to the possibility of this community developing the productive capacities needed to successfully confront multiple imperialist challenges. This in turn hinged on the reconstitution of a stable familial and social order, vouchsafed by patriarchal authority, in which both men and women could be counted on to make "correct erotic choices" and engage in productive activity.[8]

This chapter examines the ways in which Nanjing Decade fascists apprehended their Communist enemies, both in the figurative sense of how they construed them and in the literal sense of how they hunted them down. The Communist specter that they conjured was invisible and omnipresent, apolitical and hyperpolitical, and simultaneously alien and cancerous to the national body. In his seminal essay on the "prose of counter-insurgency," Ranajit Guha considered how peasants resisting British Raj structures of oppression were rendered into "insurgents" and "fanatics" by multiple layers of colonialist discourse, which stripped peasants of reflective agency and meaningful political intent. Such framings, according to Guha, constituted a "code of pacification which . . . was a complex of coercive intervention by the state and its protégés, the native elite, with arms and words."[9] Nanjing was not a colonial state, nor can the majority of Communist leaders be understood as subalterns. Yet Chinese fascists addressed Communist insurrection with similar forms of military and epistemological violence, attempting to turn both Chinese and foreign-imperialist common sense against the possibility of a Communist revolution in China. Like a colonial archive, the code of pacification articulated by interwar fascists must be read against the grain for compelling information about the Communist movement itself.[10] It speaks relatively straightforwardly, however, about fascists' own fears and aspirations for the nation. Most importantly, it tells us what kind of people they thought did and did not belong to it, and about the kinds of force that could legitimately be brought to bear on people on either side of their desired divide.

In the pages of their publications, fascists continually charged Communists with violating Confucian social norms, to the point of behaving like beasts rather than civilized human beings. Communists allegedly killed, burned, raped, and looted wherever they went; they preyed upon ignorant masses too dimwitted to know what was best for them. Such phrasing may have shared a name-calling tendency common to much modern Chinese political rhetoric (cf. the denunciation of "snake-demons" and "ox-monsters" during the Great Proletarian Cultural Revolution), but its content and intent must be taken seriously.[11] Its key refrains reveal Blue Shirt and CC Clique anxieties about the gender, sexual, and mass-participatory transformations of the post–May Fourth era. More broadly, they disclose the kind of militantly policed, hyperproductive society that they were fighting to create. Fascist characterizations of the Communist scourge were, of course, also literally matters of life and death for thousands. If counterinsurgency warfare, by definition asymmetrical and fought on behalf of a presumed victimized population, relies on historically accreted ways of "telling" allies from enemies, Nanjing Decade fascists deployed long-standing tropes to virulently nationalistic new ends.[12] It is in their ways of telling that we can discern fascists' distrust of the national masses in whose name they waged revolution, their discomfort with new gender roles and relations, and logics behind their ever-widening anti-Communist dragnets. These dragnets ultimately meant that the period of Nationalist political tutelage could never end, and persistently undermined the above-board juridical procedures that figures like Zhang Junmai, and other increasingly silenced members of the Nationalist Party, were then advocating.

Apprehending the Enemy

Lecturing in September 1931 to personnel with the Armed Forces General Headquarters Bandit Suppression Propaganda Office, Whampoa graduate and soon-to-be Blue Shirt leader He Zhonghan explained that "military force can only eradicate banditry that has an objective form, and only politics can cleanse banditry that does not. Objective banditry hatches from formless banditry. . . . Because the banditry that has an objective form is relatively scarce, eradicating it is relatively easy, while formless banditry is more prevalent, and extinguishing it comparatively difficult, for it breeds the most quickly."[13] In this speech, He Zhonghan pointed to the fact that actual flesh-and-blood Communists had, by 1930, been largely expelled from China's cities and geographically contained within soviet base areas in the mountainous southwest. At the time, he was helping the Nationalist military prepare for the first of five "encirclement and suppression" campaigns against these base areas, which were launched in December 1930 and did not succeed until late 1934.[14] In certain respects, He Zhonghan's 1930 remarks anticipated the Three Parts Military Seven Parts Politics approach adopted by the Nationalists in June 1932 after the third encirclement campaign—the first of the campaigns personally led by Chiang Kai-shek—had failed to oust them.[15] But here Mr. He was pointing not just to the importance of winning local hearts and minds, or of successfully implementing a rigorous development agenda to resolve problems of male unemployment and to link Jiangxi economically, via dense transport and communications networks, to areas under Nationalist control. Rather, He was speaking about the ways in which Communism posed an existential threat to the nation and its enduring ways of being. Potential Communists, moreover, were everywhere. Men in charge of the bandit suppression campaigns thus presented themselves with the challenge of recognizing and eliminating Communism's actual as well as possible manifestations. In either case, how would they know it if they saw it? How could one successfully combat, as former U.S. defense secretary Donald Rumsfeld notoriously put it, such "unknown unknowns"?

In the following two subsections, I trace how the anti-Communist discourse of Blue Shirts like He Zhonghan merged with that of the CC Clique to construct two interlocked figures: the national-revolutionary combatant and the Communist he was supposed to eliminate. I use the broad term *combatant* to designate the range of soldiers, intelligence personnel, and civilian officials that the Blue Shirts and CC Clique attempted to train because their speeches and writings invested these varying types of state actors with a common mission. I also use the gendered pronoun *he*, because until the New Life Movement began to invoke women (*funü*) as a category that also needed to attain a battlefield consciousness, fascists understood Nationalist combatants to be men, albeit men whose masculinity required fortification. They did not necessarily assume that their Communist enemies were male (and often impugned their masculinity), but tended to make clear when they were speaking about female Communists, whose sexual depravity they invariably noted. In this discourse, Communists appeared as foils to the Nationalist cause. Whereas Nationalist combatants were productive, spiritually fortified, and morally upright, Communists were destructive and debauched. Nationalists had inherited the modernizing, patriotic ethos of May Fourth; Communists its anarchic and anti-Confucian aspects. One could therefore potentially discern political allegiances from a given person's outward adherence to Confucian behavioral norms and engagement in productive activity. The result was to regard everyone as a likely criminal; as conationals bearing obligations to prove themselves innocent rather than as fellow citizens bearing rights, whether natural or legal.

Although aspects of this code of pacification had been articulated within military ranks and in CC Clique–run, urban-focused police and secret service apparatuses since 1927, multiple intersecting sociopolitical developments prompted its consolidation in the early 1930s. These included the continued expansion of rural Communist soviets, a process partially facilitated by the Nationalists' own internal disarray.[16] They also included the escalation of Japanese continental imperialism, which compounded the animosity that many Nationalists felt toward a Communist internationalism that undermined national cohesion. Japan's seizure of Manchuria in September 1931 and its January 1932 aerial bombing of Shanghai prompted a redivision of responsibilities within the Nationalist government to address these crises. As noted in chapter 1, a new coalition government was forged between Wang Jingwei's left wing and Chiang Kai-shek's right wing, lasting from 1932 until 1935. At the start of 1932, Wang assumed control of the Executive Branch in Nanjing, while Chiang assumed leadership of a revamped Military Affairs Council (MAC/Junshiweiyuanhui). Chiang quickly took advantage of the MAC's relative independence from Nanjing, as well as the provincial and well-armed remove of the field headquarters under MAC jurisdiction, to consolidate his own as well as his loyalists' power.[17] The Blue Shirts found room and resources to expand their operations, establishing new security apparatuses, training programs, and publishing initiatives that paralleled those already run by the CC Clique. During this time, Japanese imperialism certainly remained a key focus of their collective ire. Yet they were blocked by Nanjing's official appeasement policies from tapping into and fanning widespread anti-Japanese nationalism.[18] They channeled their nationalist fervor instead onto the figure of the Communist, who bore the full brunt of their anger for undermining the unity that they believed necessary for deflecting attacks such as Japan's.

The early 1930s uptick in the intensity of anti-Communist rhetoric can also be linked to the rise to power of the Nazis in Germany. Even more so than the Italian example and less awkwardly than that of Japan, the establishment of Nazi Germany in 1933 helped to consolidate and affirm Blue Shirt and CC Clique beliefs, in particular the exigency of dealing ruthlessly with internal dissent. In a fall 1933 speech to Nationalist personnel, Chen Guofu lauded Germany's recent exit from the League of Nations, which had followed closely on the heels of Japan's departure from the league over the Manchuria crisis. Chen praised how the German people had faced their World War I losses with "one heart and one mind. With a resolute spirit they prepared for renaissance, and by living lives of utmost fortitude they were able to reap the results of bolstering national power." Lambasting the inertia of China's own public servants, Chen exhorted his trainees to overcome their discouragement in the face of China's weakness and rally the nation to unite behind them.[19] The politico-moral panic that Chinese fascists strove to foment over the domestic spread of Communism consistently indexed these larger crises.

CULTIVATING COMBATANTS

Under the cover of the MAC, Blue Shirts seized opportunities to shape the consciousness of counterinsurgency combatants. They played key roles at the July 1933 midlevel officers' training sessions at Lushan in Jiangxi, where they worked with German military advisers.[20] By the winter of that year, He Zhonghan's Bandit Suppression Propaganda Office was responsible for politically indoctrinating all soldiers involved in the Communist suppression campaigns, including local militia and a notoriously vicious Special Operations Brigade (Biedongdui) (fig. 3.1).[21] Blue Shirts also attempted to broaden the audience of their training sessions and to cement the knowledge imparted there by putting their ideas about proper soldiering into print. He Zhonghan's addresses, for example, circulated in the 1933 volume *Selected Speeches of Mr. He Zhonghan*, issued by the Blue Shirts' Tiba Bookstore. Military speeches by Mr. He, Chiang Kai-shek, and other commanders also circulated in myriad new combatant-focused periodicals. While

FIGURE 3.1 » Militia members flying Nationalist-affiliated flags. From Tang, *Chinas Kampf gegen den Kommunismus.*

mainstream newspapers like Tianjin's *Dagongbao* and Shanghai's *Shenbao* reported on the Nationalists' encirclement campaigns according to globally developing norms of journalistic objectivity, Blue Shirt outlets such as *Saodang xunkan* (*Mopping Up Thrice Monthly*), *Jingcheng yuekan* (*Absolute Sincerity Monthly*), and *Donglu yuekan* (*East Route Monthly*) were self-consciously partisan in their representations thereof. These titles, as well as magazines like *Tiexue yuekan* (*Iron and Blood Monthly*), proudly announced themselves as political interventions intended to bolster combatant morale and to enable them to grasp their historical missions clearly.

These publications sharply delineated what Nationalists were fighting for and what they were fighting against; drilling into readers the contrast between wanton Communist destructiveness and the revolutionary purposiveness of Nationalist undertakings. Harrowing stories of life in bandit areas appeared alongside inspirational work reports on Nationalist redevelopment initiatives. Art and literature sections carried poetry, plays, and short stories pertaining to the work of bandit suppression. Boldly colored cover images of battlefield violence, and high-quality inserts featuring the calligraphy of military and civilian officials, conveyed the Nationalists' successful fusion of military and civilizational refinement.[22] Meanwhile, titles such as the *Saodang huabao* (*Mopping Up Pictorial*) targeted minimally literate soldiers with serialized drawings and simple text.[23] This flurry of publications worked to render combatants' struggle against Communism into an all-encompassing way of life. Calligraphy, cartoons, work reports, photographs, and personal reflections by men of varying ranks bombarded readers with the sense that their entire being pertained to the fight. Soldiers' Sections and Reader's Sections, in which rank-and-file soldiers could share their battlefield experiences and their own motivations for joining the struggle, helped to complete the loop of combatant indoctrination. Testimonials published there signaled to readers that they belonged to an elite group of clairvoyant men, and that if they similarly worked to attain a correct consciousness they too might be given a platform from which to speak. Conversely, their failure to do so spelled national ruination and the end of everything that respectable people considered meaningful.

"Our revolutionary movement, as directed by the premier [Sun Yat-sen], is an uprising of righteousness, while Communist revolutionary methods are those of violence. . . . Sun Yat-sen informed us that the mission of revolution is to enact righteousness. . . . If we do not find a way to resolve our counterinsurgency difficulties and exterminate the bandits, it would suggest that 'righteousness' cannot conquer 'violence,'" explained He Zhonghan in an October 1933 speech at the Central Military Academy, soon reprinted in *Mopping Up Thrice Monthly*.[24] The topic of He's lecture—"The Effort and Consciousness Required for Bandit Suppression"—reiterated what had quickly become key Blue Shirt talking points. Nationalists followed Sun Yat-sen and were on the correct side of history. Those who challenged this course were purveyors of violence and thus rendered themselves into legitimate targets of violence. Nationalist combatants therefore first and foremost had to understand Sun's program, its exclusive suitability to China's social conditions, and to mold their thinking and behavior accordingly. Combatant training, He emphasized elsewhere, aimed to "consolidate revolutionary power," to "eradicate reactionary forces," and to "organize sympathetic powers."[25] Soldiers had to overcome their own inner dispiritedness and lack of discipline, paying renewed attention to their own "spiritual education" because they bore responsibility for the spiritual education of others.[26] They also had to learn how to marshal this spirit—resurrecting it from the dead and regarding it as a pill of immortality, as Chiang Kai-shek put it—to effectively and fearlessly kill their enemies.[27]

Modern soldiers the world over are trained to willingly sacrifice them-selves for a cause—typically though not exclusively for the nation and the ideals for which it is supposed to stand. They demonstrate courage and valor in their readiness to die, and often to kill, for these ideals. They are expected to be disciplined, obedient, efficient, and orderly. Blue Shirt expectations of Nationalist soldiers, in these respects, were not particularly remarkable. Comparable expectations of self-sacrifice and self-subjection, usually ar-ticulated in hypermasculine terms, could be found in modernized armies everywhere. The political specificity of Blue Shirt training endeavors is ap-parent instead in the ideals for which they wanted combatants to kill and die, and, as I discuss in chapter 4, in their desire to restructure civilian life along military lines. Blue Shirts fleshed out the nation for which combat-ants were fighting via persistently reiterated catchphrases referencing Sun Yat-sen and canonical Confucian texts like the *Record of Rites* and the *Great Learning*. Noticeably, they avoided reference to popular martial traditions such as those associated with stories like *Outlaws of the Marsh* and *Journey to the West*. This is striking in part because these stories had, as Meir Sha-har has noted, contributed much to the "shaping of masculinity at large." Yet these well-known stories also had a rich history of providing "symbolic resources for insubordination" and inspiration to those "who strayed from or challenged the existing order."[28] The nation for which Nationalist com-batants were supposed to fight was structured by an elite Confucian heritage that championed stability and respect for authority. Violence that shored up state power and advanced Sun's Three Principles was righteous. Appar-ent subversions constituted banditry.[29] Locutions like "red bandits," "bandit party," and "bandit suppression" thus became cornerstones of Nationalist counterinsurgency prose, as they positioned Nationalists on the side of law and order and their Communist opponents on that of mayhem.

Under Blue Shirt instruction, Nationalist combatants learned that they were responsible for defending and reviving an ancient yet lapsed Confu-cian spirit that supplied the nation's worldly uniqueness. Infantry drill regu-lations, for instance, emphasized, "Our soldiers' spirit is exclusively composed of propriety, righteousness, integrity, and humility." Soldiers had to cultivate within themselves "moral qualities of fraternity and absolute sincerity." This was because "propriety and righteousness beget confidence, integrity and humility beget valor, fraternity begets benevolence, and absolute sincerity begets wisdom."[30] In all of their actions they had to render themselves wor-thy of already-deceased officers, of Sun Yat-sen's memory, of the parents who brought them into the world, and of the suffering masses.[31] The message that the CC Clique was concurrently imparting to civilian party personnel did not significantly differ from what the Blue Shirts were conveying to soldiers. Chen Guofu, leader of the CC Clique, similarly emphasized in his speeches that "party members must first be properly trained, then they can go and train the people." Comrades, Chen emphasized, had to foster within themselves a "spirit of fraternity and absolute sincerity."[32] They had to not only cultivate themselves but also manage their households well. Lauding the "dutiful wife and good mother," Chen cautioned his trainees to choose their wives prudently, as modern higher education had put fanciful ideas into women's heads and extravagant women rendered their husbands corrupt.[33] Successfully exercising this kind of self-discipline, as well as control over one's interpersonal relations, formed the backbone of social order. Demonstrating that one was spiritually rectified in this way clarified outward distinctions between Nationalists and Communists; between those who could successfully wage what He Zhonghan called an "uprising of justice" and those who merely spread debauchery and chaos.

Such commonplace Confucian moral exhortations—which were certainly patriarchal but not intrinsically fascistic—were invoked by the Blue Shirts and CC Clique alike to sanction violence against people who did not conform. Revolutionary nativism thus authorized anti-Communist violence. Although the high Confucian canon from which GMD militants drew is often cast as averse to violent force, this received understanding is unwarranted.[34] What matters here regardless is not what the Confucian canon actually authorized Chinese fascists to do or not do, but what they believed it authorized them to do. Men involved in combatant training invoked certain time-honored Confucian ideals—particularly *li, yi, lian,* and *chi* (propriety, righteousness, integrity, and humility) and the social importance of keeping one's household in order—and wove them into exhortations to kill. Confucian norms of benevolence and restraint simply did not apply to Communists. Because Communists did not abide by these norms and overtly threatened them, they could not be considered conationals at all. It was therefore not immoral to kill them. Doing so could be construed as a righteous defense of the nation and its proper revolutionary course.

Whereas the CC Clique trained personnel who had relative bureaucratic distance from acts of killing, Blue Shirts trained men to fight physically. Rationales for killing Communists thus saturated Blue Shirt magazines, and were articulated with particular ferocity at the 1933 Lushan Officers'

Training Conference. In conference speeches attributed to Chiang Kai-shek (compiled in a 1947 volume by Blue Shirt Deng Wenyi, and perhaps penned by Deng as well), Chiang repeatedly stressed the importance of self-examination, self-restraint, and spiritual fortitude.[35] Good soldiers had to be wise, benevolent, and brave. They should observe propriety, righteousness, integrity, and humility. Chiang exhorted his officers to put their households in order for the sake of stabilizing the country and pacifying the world.[36] This was not to obviate the need to wield coercive force but to do so more formidably. The entire point of their efforts, Chiang stressed, was to "annihilate the red bandits and build a new country."[37] Demonstrating filial respect for one's parents and honoring Sun Yat-sen meant committing every fiber of one's being to the task. It meant garnering the furious yet controlled rage that Chiang exuded in his speeches and steeling one's own body to kill others. Eliminating Communists, Chiang explained, did not hinge on the numbers of guns, cannons, and bombs that their forces possessed. More rudimentary weapons like bayonets and rifle barrels could also be used. If bayonets and rifles were not available, each man had "two hands and two feet with which to punch and trample the enemy—precisely what heaven and earth and our mothers and fathers bequeathed to us for fighting enemies."[38] In the absence of hands and feet, each man had teeth with which to bite and tongues with which to verbally lash. "Not until our teeth are extracted and our tongues cut off," Chiang admonished, "will it be permissible to die or to achieve the status of a true soldier and disciple of Sun Yat-sen!"[39] Filial devotion was thus linked to national-revolutionary devotion and the willingness to ruthlessly kill enemies of the nation.

Dehumanizing the enemy has constituted an enduring cornerstone of modern warfare. In the 1930s, Nationalist combatants learned that the difference between someone worthy of life and someone worthy of death centered on adherence to Confucian norms. As those who did not adhere to them were essentially uncivilized animals, "exterminating and cleansing" such people would vouchsafe the nation and humanity writ large.[40] Chiang Kai-shek stressed how Communists were amoral and therefore uncivilized beasts:

> Everyone must understand that the red bandits seek to destroy ethical relations. They want neither ancestors nor parents, and we do not want this scum of the nation! They want to turn the entirety of humanity into a nationless, amoral mass, without hierarchy or order

and without any integrity. They want to turn the world of humanity into a world of beasts! The behavior of the red bandits is therefore that of beasts; the true nature of the red bandit is that of a beast. Our bandit suppression is therefore akin to a struggle against beasts, the same as exterminating beasts. It is to save the citizens of the Chinese Republic, to allow them to live as humans and not be turned into beasts! Safeguarding the entirety of humanity and preventing it from being turned into a world of beasts is precisely the responsibility facing our revolutionary soldiers! . . . This will allow us to be worthy of our ancestors and parents. . . . The singular mission before us is to exterminate the red bandits . . . and to be willing to die to exterminate them![41]

The problem was not, as Chiang framed it here, that Communists were untutored in civilized ways. Rather, they self-consciously rejected the kinds of ethical practices that made humans human. They therefore invited their own extermination. Nationalist combatants were taught that it was necessary to isolate or kill them in order to protect the humanity of valued members of the national community.

Such dehumanizing refrains were incanted by lesser-known contributors to combatant periodicals as well, who likewise stressed that Communists evinced no sign of the Confucian national spirit and should hence be shown no mercy. A man named Ding Wenyan, writing from Nanchang for a 1933 issue of *Mopping Up Thrice Monthly*, in an article titled "Reviving the Chinese Nation and Promoting the National Spirit," underscored that Communists fundamentally lacked it. Nationalist combatants should take pride in eliminating them. "Narrowly speaking," Ding elaborated, "the spirit of a nation points to the goodness and purity of a nation's prevailing customs, and broadly speaking, it points to a nationality's native morality."[42] He himself believed that, stretching back to the Yellow Emperor, the Chinese spirit had historically been "creative and boldly progressive" and that it was important to always bear in mind that "China is the world's oldest civilized country."[43] In previous historical eras, the "Chinese people's spirit could weather any blow." While striving for their own spiritual regeneration and that of their countrymen, Nationalist soldiers were not to assume that Communists harbored this spirit. Ding reasoned, "If we speak of 'benevolence' or 'good faith' in regard to bandits it will cause these terms to lose their meaning, and moreover we will lose sight of the purpose of bandit extermination. Because what we are doing by exterminating the bandits is saving the people from harm, plotting an escape route for the country, and honestly, doing our faithful duty on the nation's behalf and campaigning tirelessly for the country."[44] Even referring to Communists with Confucian terms that properly belonged to the national people would cheapen their purchase. Officers tasked with bandit extermination therefore had to appreciate that Communists were entirely excluded by the spirit that the Nationalists were trying to revive, and that this spirit was synonymous with filial piety, loyalty, propriety, righteousness, integrity, and humility.

It is, of course, difficult to know how seriously ordinary combatants involved with the Communist suppression campaigns took such commands. Nevertheless, Blue Shirts went to some length to present their training efforts as successful. This is evidenced by the publication of soldiers' letters in Blue Shirt magazines that were in sync with ideas expressed by men higher up the command chain. A particularly telling example is an "open letter to the bandits" that appeared in a 1933 issue of *Mopping Up Thrice Monthly*, attributed to a soldier with the National Revolutionary Army's Eighth Division named Huang Lisen. Here, Huang fumed that the Communists were "social vermin" that behaved like animals, casually shared wives, killed their own parents, and reallocated land. Shared racial characteristics between Nationalists and Communists should have been grounds for their compatriotism—"We are both yellow-raced," Huang insisted. However, Communists could not actually be considered conationals at all because they were forcing the Chinese "to become a different race" by imposing upon them ideas that did not accord with Chinese national sentiments.[45] If permitted to expand their power, the CCP would effectively deracinate the entire Chinese population, transforming them into Soviet Russians. The country would moreover become so internally disorganized that it could not survive in a Darwinist world. For these reasons, Communists belonged neither to the nation nor to humanity as such.

To Huang Lisen, such charges justified the violence that the Nationalists were meting out. They also grounded the apparent pleasure he derived from participating in it: "If we want to pacify society, we cannot but eradicate you. If we want to save the country, we cannot but put you to death! . . . Is not a dense cloud of an army crowding in around you? . . . Do you not see the planes setting their targets on you, raining bombs upon your heads?"[46]

Huang had prefaced his letter by recounting his recent experience of killing Communists. Huang recollected that he had nearly failed in his pursuit of several Communists that he had spotted on a nearby hill ("just like a cat spotting a rat"), even though they were "hobbling along elegantly" like "bound-footed girls." When he finally succeeded in killing one, he felt "so carefree and happy, all humiliations vanished."[47] Still, Huang reassured readers that his delight in killing did not compromise his own moral rectitude: "Gentlemen! My heart is at bottom harmonious, benevolent, and compassionate. Under normal circumstances I cannot bear to even see lice eggs meet their deaths, so why is it that I have just now killed a man?—bandits—have brought what kinds of joys and gratifications? You gentlemen understand the function of this kind of sentiment—there's no need for me to describe it further here."[48] Communists were, in Huang's rendering, less worthy of life than larvae. Still, his comment that readers intuitively grasped his sense of satisfaction in killing suggests that it was a shared sentiment that still required reinforcement. Magazines like *Mopping Up Thrice Monthly* thereby helped to create a community in which such ideas—and a willingness to act on them—were normalized and encouraged, bolstering more formal training sessions.

Whether Huang Lisen existed or not, the published letter attributed to him indicates Blue Shirt concern to showcase the purchase of their combatant training efforts. The successful Nationalist combatant embodied revolutionary nativist ideals. He had a rectified spirit and he understood the Confucian qualities of the nation for which he was fighting. He respected authority, understood the teachings of Sun Yat-sen, honored his parents, and vowed to regulate his own actions as well as those of his family. Killing Communists did not compromise Confucian ideals of benevolence, and so on, but instead constituted a righteous defense of them. Blue Shirts, as well as the CC Clique, thereby figured the Nationalist combatant as a foil to the Communist, who became recognizable for his depraved undermining of the family structure, his compromised masculinity (he was in reality no more formidable than "bound-footed girls," as Huang put it), and his deceptive, bestial nature. One could therefore tell if someone was a Communist, or likely to become one, from participation in debased, antiproductive, and unpatriotic activities. They did not need to have a copy of *The Communist Manifesto* tucked under the arm; promoting free love and criticizing Confucius could constitute sufficiently damning evidence.

Historian Yan Lu has recounted how Nationalist theorist Dai Jitao, sometime after his first suicide attempt in 1919, ruefully reflected on his own youthful romantic dalliances. These dalliances, as already noted, had resulted in a son born to a Japanese mistress, whom Chiang Kai-shek adopted and raised as Chiang Wei-kuo. Dai came to blame such transgressions on "'Shanghai, this cesspit that degraded humanity" and more broadly on what Lu identified as "the influence of new thoughts and ideals popular during the May Fourth era." In this vein, Dai excoriated "the Communists who follow blindly the few slogans of Communism imported from the West and use such slogans to cover up their own pursuit of sexual desire and appetite."[49] Although the tenor of Dai's accusations suggests a man in the midst of a midlife crisis disavowing responsibility for his own past choices, his characterization of Communists as depraved followers of poisonous foreign ideas was in fact general consensus among the CC Clique and Blue Shirts during the Nanjing Decade. Communists, they insisted, perpetuated the worst aspects of May Fourth. They found cover and encouragement in Shanghai's colonial concessions for libertine, anti-Confucian, and irredeemably foreign ideas. Communists who had managed to flee to Jiangxi and surrounding rural areas spread their toxic notions to an already benighted countryside. They aimed to turn China into one giant cesspit and drag everyone else down with them.

There are of course no necessary connections between libertine, Communist, and feminist politics. Yet, from the menacingly unbridled sexuality of the red woman in the 1920s German Freikorps imagination to the lavender scare in the McCarthy-era United States, nonnormative sexual activity and gender identities were read across the twentieth-century world as signs of Communist subversion. In this vein, the café-haunting modern boy in interwar Japan, as well as his self-fashioning modern girl counterpart, were coded as Communist conspirators in Japan's right-wing press.[50] During the Nanjing Decade, many Nationalists similarly believed that "political radicalism and cultural permissiveness were cut from the same cloth."[51] Although the specific fears informing such links were particular to given national contexts, it is not difficult to see how Communism could be universally construed as a total assault on existing (or desired) structures of power and property. Because such structures are inevitably maintained by hierarchies of gender, sexuality, race, and ethnicity, the Communist specter in any given context could readily assume the hodgepodge guise of local power holders' deepest fears—however incoherent the traits attributed to the specter may have been, and whatever the actual gender and sexual politics of the Communists in question. The further to the right the accuser stood on the political spectrum, the more contradictory the specter conjured. This is not to say that all accusations leveled against Communists were totally groundless—even paranoids have real enemies, as Golda Meir is said to have once retorted to Henry Kissinger.[52] Rather, it is to suggest that even though the traits ascribed to the specter did not add up coherently, its agglomerated malevolence served to justify sweeping and draconian eradication measures.

As we have already seen, links drawn during the Nanjing Decade between Communism and cultural permissiveness had roots in the Nationalists' repudiation of certain New Culture ideas and their often misplaced or exaggerated attribution to the CCP of these ideas, in particular free love and anarchic iconoclasm. New Culture Movement leaders had indeed stressed during the 1910s that gender hierarchies and family arrangements were indivisibly also those of power, property, and social order. The practices and aspirations that the CC Clique and Blue Shirts attributed to Communists in the 1930s referenced these earlier critiques and portended total social ruin, paranoiacally fixating on the CCP's wanton destructiveness, patricidal fanaticism, and sexual rapaciousness. At the same time, the stress that they placed on Communist threats to all that was holy helps to throw the radicalism of GMD militants themselves into relief. What, ultimately, is more culturally permissive than authorizing oneself to kill an alleged moral deviant? Or more threatening to social order and family integrity than covert assassinations, rapid industrialization, and a massive military mobilization to expunge insurgents from the ranks of a civilian population?

In certain respects, Xu Enceng, a CC Clique affiliate and cousin of the Chen brothers, could be said to have known Communists well. Although Xu had received an engineering degree from Shanghai's Jiaotong University, studied at Pittsburgh's Carnegie Institute of Technology, and worked briefly for the U.S. electrical company Westinghouse during the early 1920s, his contributions to the Nanjing regime involved intelligence rather than development work. While heading up Nanjing's Special Services Group after 1930, Xu credited himself with netting thousands of Communists, including the cultural theorist Qu Qiubai, the New Culture Movement luminary Chen Duxiu, and the peasant organizer Peng Pai, as well as the famed Comintern agent known as Hilaire Noulens.[53] He also took credit for decimating the ranks of the Young Vanguards and the All-China General Labor Union, eliminating "thirteen of the twenty-eight Bolsheviks," and imprisoning the feminist writer Ding Ling (see chapter 5).[54] The pride that Xu took in such accomplishments is evident in the boastful prose of the memoir that he penned from 1950s Taiwan. His pride is further evident in a graph included in this memoir depicting the rise and fall of CCP numbers over time, in which Communists killed, captured, or turned by his agency are represented as x/y plot points.[55] To the extent that Xu felt compelled to justify this work at all, he highlighted Communist immorality and deceitfulness.

Eight or nine out of ten Communist leaders were scions of wealthy families, Xu explained. They had no reason for joining the Communist Party other than its provision of an excuse to break from family-arranged marriages.[56] Capitalizing on what Xu called the May Fourth era's "flood of sex," the CCP trumpeted its opposition to arranged marriage and to "feudal sexual morality." It used such "immoral deceits" to drive wedges between young people and their families, and hence to attract people who would not otherwise have had anything to do with Communism.[57] In a similar fashion, after the Nationalists had forced the CCP underground and out of the cities in 1927, Communists attempted to elude capture by holing up in Shanghai's colonial concessions, thus taking advantage of, rather than challenging, China's imperialist exploitation. In the concessions, Communists donned outrageous disguises evidencing their debauchery. A single male renting an apartment in the French Concession might attract police notice, Xu explained, so undercover CCP cadres often paired up with a "female comrade" to present the appearance of an ordinary married couple. "Only Communists, who completely lack a sense of morality, could come up with such amusing rules," Xu reasoned.[58] In other words, only Communists would think it acceptable for an unmarried man and woman to cohabitate.

On the flip side, some Blue Shirts insisted that Communists were in fact indistinguishable from garden-variety hedonistic denizens of the colonial concessions, whether Chinese or foreign. Communists, in this telling, did not merely disguise themselves in a manner that revealed their immorality and craven acquiescence to colonial violations of Chinese sovereignty. Rather, a Communist was essentially the same as any other self-indulgent bourgeois. A 1934 article in *Sweat and Blood Weekly* came to this conclusion based on the readiness with which Communists took cover in Shanghai's colonial settlements. Communists might proclaim themselves to be anti-capitalist and anti-imperialist, but they in fact delighted in the decadent pastimes on offer there. "Like capitalists," the author explained, Communists reveled in "its Western-style buildings, cars, mistresses, roulette wheels, dancing, horse and dog races, and massages—all manner of earthly delights."[59] They might champion things like "proletarian literature" but they certainly did not live like proletarians. The charge that Communists were basically club-going playboys is visually registered in a cartoon on the cover of *Society Mercury*, in which a cadre (indicated by his worker's cap) welcomes a proposition from a cartoonishly curvaceous, *qipao*-clad waitress (fig. 3.2).[60] From this perspective, Communist hedonism and high living revealed a kind of deceitfulness different from that sketched by Xu Enceng: Communists lived the good life while inflicting ruin on everyone else. Indecision over whether Communists merely disguised themselves as bourgeois, were actually bourgeois at heart, or were just generally debased gave rise to various mash-up charges, including that they advocated "wife sharing" and the "nationalization of wives."[61] A propaganda team in Jiangxi reported on the casual sexual relations permitted in the Communist areas, connecting for readers the CCP's flippant disregard of sexual norms with its lust to murder and burn.[62] Communists reportedly exhorted soviet residents with slogans like "abolish husbands," "support adultery," and "support marriage between fathers and daughters!"[63] Whether these relations were cast as depravedly Marxist or bourgeois, the GMD point was that the CCP mocked established social norms to the extreme of flouting the incest taboo. And because Communists were innately deceitful—sometimes donning disguises and acting in unobvious ways—it was ultimately reasonable to regard with suspicion everyone who did not conform to GMD behavioral expectations.

Communist disregard for norms of social propriety threatened to unmoor people from institutions in which they should find comfort and familiarity; it also undermined the nation's productive potential. The question of Marxism's suitability to China's social conditions—with its demonstrably small industrial proletariat—was certainly an open one that was concurrently being debated by leftists as well. Nationalist counterinsurgency prose supplied a definitive answer: it was an alien imposition that necessarily deceived the masses and fostered among them unnatural familial and class hatreds. Chiang Kai-shek stressed how Communists "not only do not want parents, they often beat and even kill them; they sell out their ancestors

FIGURE 3.2 »
Shehui xinwen (*Society Mercury*) 8, no. 2 (1934): back cover.

and worship foreign elders. . . . They regard Marx and other foreigners as their ancestors. . . . They are exactly like animals. How can they count as people?"[64] They in turn pressured recruits into killing their own friends and families while also seducing them with false promises of land and factory management.[65] Yet China's population was large, its land scarce, and its factories too few to redistribute in a manner that could sustain anyone's livelihood. The CCP was thereby turning "people of society" into the "utterly destitute poor."[66] It was not just that Communists attempted to socialize insufficient wealth. They dissipated the productive potential of fields and factories by redistributing them prematurely and by burning, pillaging, and looting everything in sight.

As early as 1928, the CC Clique newspaper *Nanking Times* trumpeted how Communist revolution begat nothing but destruction. This exacerbated problems of idleness and vagrancy, tendencies that historians Janet Chen and Zwia Lipkin have shown had been varyingly condemned and criminalized in China since the early 1900s.[67] According to the *Nanking Times*, in the areas to which the CCP had fled they shuttered shops, blocked communications, prevented workers with jobs from performing them, and prevented peasants with access to land from tilling it. Worse still, they colluded with "hoodlums and local ruffians."[68] He Zhonghan reiterated this point in a speech to Nationalist soldiers in the early 1930s, underscoring how Communist land reform policies had blighted the Jiangxi countryside. This was due in part to the fact that land redistribution was a magnet for people disinclined to work. It attracted hoodlums and ruffians who assumed control over the redistribution process and claimed the best parcels for themselves.[69] Since it was in the nature of hoodlums to be idle and loaf about, and since they themselves did not know how to farm, they had to hire peasants to till the land for them, who were in turn reluctant to work for wastrels. Grain requisitions by the CCP further undermined peasant work incentives. Production in the soviet areas had therefore come to a halt, Mr. He explained, and the land had become desolate.[70] Instead of helping the nation to recover its strength on the world stage, Communists were destroying it from within.

Such analyses indicate a recognition on the part of Nationalist counterinsurgency leaders that Communism might have appealed not merely to the morally debased but also to the socially disenfranchised. The fortitude with which the Nationalists committed to the economic redevelopment of Jiangxi and surrounding areas after the Communists were finally expelled in late 1934 suggests how moralizing discourse intermingled with a social analysis that located roots of Communism in underdevelopment and unemployment. Redevelopment programs implemented in mid-1930s Jiangxi foreshadowed those guided by modernization theory in the postwar period in their expectation that infrastructural improvements, scientific farming, and stable employment opportunities would diminish the appeal of left-wing mobilization. Moral-educational reforms were inseparably entwined with broader structural transformations—in CC Clique and Blue Shirt eyes, development was a Confucian project. That it proceeded in Jiangxi and surrounding areas under military rule was also in keeping with their conviction that the military's actions were righteous and there was only one, uncontestable path to a better future.

In the areas from which Communists were expelled, the Nationalists did not attempt to reverse the transformative tide that their adversaries had set in motion but rather to change its direction. Some Nationalist officials openly acknowledged that their own plans would be facilitated by Communist disruptions because the local population was now predisposed toward change.[71] Reconstruction efforts, which proceeded cooperatively between Chiang's MAC and Wang Jingwei's Nanjing-based National Economic Council, focused on rationalizing agricultural production, reviving mining exports, constructing new highways and railways, and reorienting the popular educational initiatives introduced by the Communists. As the CCP retreated, the Nationalists secured their gains by setting displaced locals to work building airstrips, bridges, and roads. Called "bandit-cleansing transportation policies," these public works projects employed displaced agricultural workers, facilitated troop movements, and prospectively reoriented local trade in the direction of other Nationalist-controlled provinces.[72] While great effort was made to restore CCP-redistributed land to prior owners, Nationalist officials were at least nominally concerned with enforcing Nanjing's 1930 Land Law, which limited rents to one-third of the harvest as well as the size of landed estates through a surtax on excess holdings.[73] This was to proceed with an unprecedented degree of planning and precision, relying on aerial surveys to map landholdings that had in many cases not been assessed since the Ming Dynasty.[74] The Jiangxi provincial capital of Nanchang, meanwhile, was supplied with electricity, paved boulevards, and running water—modernizing transformations of which the Communists could concurrently only dream.[75] In this way, Nanjing implemented, or at the very least aspired to implement, sweeping changes to local work patterns and daily routines. Conditions under which Communism had taken hold were addressed as concertedly as state resources allowed.

Nationalist counterinsurgency prose simultaneously presented the Nationalists as protectors of time-honored social bonds and as valiant creators of the new. Communists were figured as endangering these bonds and hence China's future development. Even as the Nationalists gained a decisive military upper hand, many remained fearful that "formless banditry" persisted. Such fear led the Blue Shirts and CC Clique to devise the New Life Movement (see chapter 4) in order to render all aspects of national life utterly known and predictable. It also led, as a kind of intermediary step between targeted anti-Communist military actions and the generalized New Life Movement, to the establishment of concentration camps. These prisons, which came to be called repentance camps (*fanxingyuan*), tapped into the moralistic and productivist concerns of postdynastic penal reform efforts, specifically in their stated intent to transform alleged political dissidents into diligently laboring and properly Confucian members of society. They shored up an image of the Nanjing regime as a benevolent patriarch extending forgiveness to his wayward children, as well as the idea that the nation beyond camp boundaries was uniformly Confucian and potentially productive.

Repentance and Revolutionary Truth

"True, there are gallows," wrote the Blue Shirt–hit listed writer Lu Xun in 1935, "but the gallows aren't so bad. Simply having a noose put around your neck can be considered preferential treatment." Execution, the writer intimated, might in fact be preferable to other forms of torture to which Nationalist prisoners were subjected. One could, alternatively, evade the gallows altogether by informing on a comrade—that is, by pulling "down with all of one's strength on the feet of friends whose necks are already caught in the hangman's noose." Such betrayals, Lu Xun quipped, served to supply "factual evidence of [a prisoner's] heartfelt repentance, and that those who are capable of repentance have the loftiest of spirits."[76] In other words, what Nationalist combatants regarded as demonstrations of spiritual rectitude were seen from the other side as coerced perfidy for the sake of self-protection. They were survival options that pitted citizens against one another, fostering mistrust among them as well as fear rather than respect for state authority. Whatever details Lu Xun may or may not have known about the Nationalists' incarceration tactics, he was correct that the cc Clique and Blue Shirts had devised elaborate methods for inducing Communists to turn on their comrades.[77] He was also correct that they prodded prisoners to repent (Lu Xun used the Buddhist term *chanhui*) for their political beliefs. Anticipating the "reform through labor" (*laogai*) camps instituted by the Communists in later decades, the Nationalists established political prisons to correct inmates' perceived twin deficits in Confucian rectitude and work discipline. These camps aimed to accomplish in a concentrated environment what the New Life Movement aimed at on a national scale: the elimination of unknown unknowns and the production of reliable subjectivities. The idea of repentance connected the Nationalists with a long history of Confucian self-reflection, now taking place behind barbed wire with the aim of mass conversion. It also fortified the authority of their nativist reading of Sun Yat-sen, insofar as the endpoint of the self-examination process was the moment at which a prisoner understood the truth of the Nationalists' revolutionary vision and accepted the criminal falsehood of all others.[78]

Over the course of the counterinsurgency campaigns it became clear that, if the Nationalists were fighting to save the people from Communist predations, those people had to be distinguished from their Communist predators in the first place. A person's willingness to accept Nationalist offers of amnesty, which at least demonstrated a capacity for correct thought, became one way of telling the difference between the redeemable and irredeemable. In a 1930 open letter to people "who have mistakenly joined the Communist bandit party," Chiang Kai-shek observed that most of the people living in the soviet areas could only have joined up with the CCP out of ignorance or fear.[79] His letter expressed hope that the deluded would "quickly come to [their] senses and decide to prevent indiscriminate destruction in the future, when it will be too late for regrets."[80] Chiang spelled out the terms on which soviet residents could seek amnesty, each of which stressed the importance of reflecting on one's political errors. To convince those who might not acknowledge their mistakes quickly enough, Chiang's letter called attention to the firepower that the Nationalists had already dispatched to annihilate them.[81] Violent force readily compensated for the limitations of moral suasion.

As the encirclement campaigns proceeded, the Nationalists formalized their amnesty policies and devised ways for defectors to demonstrate genuine changes of heart. Though Xu Enceng later maintained that he himself came up with the idea of "giving oneself up to the law and making a fresh start" (*zishou zixin*), these policies reflected the assumptions of the counterinsurgency discourse traced above, particularly regarding the subpar quality of the people who gravitated to the CCP. Military Affairs Council classifications of the various types of people who had cooperated with the Communists presumed widespread stupidity, self-interest, and immorality. Categories included the "ignorant" and the "weak willed"; people who were native to the bandit areas and cooperated with the CCP in order to protect themselves and their property; and "unemployed vagrants" and "ignorant workers and peasants" with few other options. Categories also included the relatively well-educated and talented who nevertheless found themselves "anesthetized" by the CCP, as well as those who had allowed themselves to be "seduced by female bandits." Whereas wealthier residents could reassert claims to CCP-requisitioned property and thereby prove their political loyalty to the GMD with relative ease, migrants and the landless necessarily had a more difficult time. Those without demonstrable property had to be vouched for by a trusted community elder and to demonstrate gainful employment. Those who could not prove their loyalty in such ways were recommended to reformatories.[82]

Rehabilitation programs implemented at dedicated political prisons followed logics of poor relief and criminal punishment that had been developing in China since the turn of the twentieth century. Janet Chen has examined how the boundaries of social belonging in China were redefined in the early 1900s in terms of an individual's capacity and willingness to work.[83] Intellectuals and activists of a wide variety of political persuasions began to conceive of idleness and inactivity as sapping the nation's strength and rendering it vulnerable to imperialist assaults. Workhouses sprang up to detain people classified as vagrants and paupers and to retrain them in trade skills that would ostensibly enable them to reenter society as productive individuals who need not rely on private charity or state aid.[84] The first decades of the twentieth century also witnessed the expansion of the modern social sciences of criminology and penology.[85] Criminal activity was reconceived as a personal moral failing generated by a combination of nature and nurture, including poor character, inadequate education, and adverse social circumstances.[86] Modern prisons (or, at least, the model prisons established across the country during the Republican period) aimed to simultaneously reform inmates' morals and to impart trade skills that would facilitate their reentry into society. Janet Chen therefore observes that modern prisons and noncriminal workhouses developed in China as closely entwined operations that "shared a common genealogy and a similar faith in the rehabilitative power of labor."[87] Political prisons established during the Nanjing Decade collapsed distinctions between such institutions: demonstrably lapsed individuals could regain social acceptability only via moral reform and learning how to labor.

The first fanxingyuan—which Frank Dikötter translates as a "place for self-examination," perhaps more aptly than the prevalent contemporary English translation "repentance camp"—was established in the city of Hangzhou in 1928, followed by fifteen more over the course of the Nanjing Decade.[88] In April 1933, Nanjing's Legislative Branch mandated that all political prisoners be moved from regular prisons into specially designated institutions. This decision was likely prompted by fears that political prisoners were organizing common criminals behind bars, and also to manage the flood of spiritually compromised people then being liberated from the soviets.[89] A repentance camp sentence was supposed to last from six months to five years, at the end of which a board would evaluate the extent of a given prisoner's rehabilitation.[90] Significantly, the existence of political prisons was not kept secret from the general public. The prison established in 1934 in the MAC headquarters city of Nanchang, Dikötter notes, served as a "showcase visited and promoted by political leaders and journalists."[91] Fanxingyuan were discussed in the Chinese-language gazette of the Judicial Branch, and favorable accounts of them also appeared in Nationalist-produced English- and German-language propaganda. Publicity surrounding these camps suggests that they served purposes beyond that of isolating and reforming accused political criminals. Among other things, the publicity bears out Émile Durkheim's observation that the identification of crimes and their proper punishment functions as much to constitute the community outside prison walls as to discipline those incarcerated within them.[92] They signaled to the former population that remaining a free citizen of the Republic of China required maintaining correct thought and behavior. Those on the inside had to acquire it. By not being kept secret, repentance camps helped to generate new norms for the public writ large as much as they divested actual inmates of unacceptable beliefs.

Repentance or self-examination here meant acknowledging one's political transgressions and coming to appreciate that productivity and Confucian morality were the bedrocks of national belonging. Inmates were subjected to military-like discipline, hygiene, vocational training, and political instruction.[93] Favorable accounts of a camp in Jiujiang, Jiangxi, penned by Nationalist partisans underscored the central role these ideals played in prisoner rehabilitation.[94] Prisoners who arrived mentally and physically filthy supposedly emerged sanitized inside and out. "In these camps," wrote an associate of Song Meiling under the pseudonym C. W. H. Young, prisoners "are taught the error of their former ways and emphasis is placed on the fact that the Communist doctrine is one which is not suitable for China and the Chinese people. They are taught ways of earning a livelihood. . . . Lectures are given on the New Life Movement and other worthy subjects, capable of transforming the erstwhile Red men and women into useful citizens of China."[95] An account penned by a German visitor to this camp observed that it primarily interred ignorant peasants who had "overwhelmingly stoic, almost mindless facial expressions, which leads one to believe that most belong to the fellow traveler train of the Reds." The author, identified as Dr. A. Kapelle, compared the enlivened demeanors of longer-term inmates with those of newer arrivals: "What a contrast!—a troupe of newcomers, watched by bayonets, passes by: figures draped in filthy scraps of cotton, many gray, sick faces, most with kerchiefs wrapped around their heads, barefoot or in straw sandals, with straw hats on their backs."[96] Conditions in what Kapelle identified as a "concentration camp" were, he believed, infinitely superior to living conditions the inmates experienced in the soviets. The camps were thus emblematic of Nationalist benevolence, who could not bear to inflict further suffering on their fellow *Volksgenossen* (a term favored by Nazis that merged *people* with *comrade*).[97]

Both Kapelle and Young emphasized the camps' successes in turning former Communists into productive citizens. The German visitor underscored that "important part[s] of the institution are the workshops, the textile, weaving, printing, canning, candle and soap-making workshops. Outside on the exercise yard you can even find small experimental stations for agricultural reform labor." While these initiatives were designed to bolster prison self-sufficiency, they also aimed to "prepare the prisoners for bourgeois occupations." C. W. H. Young similarly remarked on how the camps furnished inmates with skills that they could use upon regaining freedom: "Here we find carpenters, there are shoemakers, on the other side umbrella makers, and so on. Thus, former Reds are armed to go out into the world as independent men and women instead of forcing themselves on the communities as burdens. The better educated, instead of being given manual training, are given instruction in the big chemical factory" (fig. 3.3).[98] Whatever these inmates had done prior to their internment, it was assumed that they had been social burdens of one sort or another. Now, due to Nationalist benevolence, they were learning new trades—the less-educated steered toward manual labor and the better toward mental. Whereas the Communists destroyed productivity and moral rectitude, the Nationalists nurtured both.

In these laudatory accounts, China's political prisons fostered work discipline, Confucian morality, and respect for state authority. Not unlike the contemporaneous Nazi presentation of Germany's concentration camps as sanitary and comfortable spaces for rehabilitating political offenders

Sandal-making class in repentance camps

Pupils in a stock weaving class (repentance camps)

FIGURE 3.3 » Work training at a repentance camp. From Young, *New Life for Kiangsi*.

(Communists in particular, "who had to be incarcerated until they came to their senses," it was stressed at the time), China's camps were presented as gestures of mercy toward the wayward.[99] They cleansed inmates of mental and physical filth, showcasing the hygienic dimensions of modern life that only the Nationalists could provide. The fact that these institutions were made known to the general public meant that they also served to normalize the idea that political dissent was criminal. The condition of remaining a free citizen of the Republic of China, the camps implied, was to look and behave like a person who had already undergone a process of repentance and was not at risk of being sent inside. As one means of dealing with the problem that He Zhonghan called "formless banditry," the camps signaled that all good Chinese nationals should police their own thought and behavior accordingly.

Conclusion

To the GMD militants who tasked themselves with eradicating Communism, answers to the questions of who and what was a Communist were only clear in certain instances (e.g., self-identified CCP leaders). The 1927 party purge had required clarifying what their own party stood for and who its enemies were.[100] But after the GMD transitioned into administrators of a national state, identifying Communists among a large and largely unknown population presented new sets of challenges. How would one know a Communist if one spotted one in the course of police work? How could one tell the difference between an ordinary civilian and a Communist in disguise? Striking a tone of general paranoia, Blue Shirt and CC Clique activists soon saw Communists lurking everywhere. From their writings we learn that Communists were by nature deceptive, immoral, and cruel. They were "beasts with human faces," as Chiang Kai-shek explained using a popular adage, who assumed cunning disguises and flouted the Confucian morals that rendered a person truly human.[101] They engaged in wife sharing, incest, and patricide. They pillaged and set fires wherever they went and exacerbated problems of indolence and vagrancy.

The problem was not, in Nanjing Decade China, that Communists threatened ideals of democracy, private property, or religious freedom, as would be trumpeted in the first world during the Cold War. Rather, Communists threatened to corrode the nation from within and prevent its resurgence on the world stage. They fostered an unnatural class hatred and undermined

China's chances of developing the productive capacities needed to successfully fend off imperialist challenges. They were so monstrous that they deserved to be interred in concentration camps or exterminated outright. The punishments inflicted on people accused of such crimes indicate how the discourse of "spirit" traced in chapter 2 was far from happenstance or innocuous. It was deployed with a consistent logic and helped set the limits of national belonging, rendering Communism and ultimately dissent of any kind thinkable only to types of people who did not belong within the national fold.

On the one hand, the generalized paranoia of GMD militants had the effect of inflating the CCP's actual power, as if the threat that Communism posed matched the firepower and fury that they were directing toward it. On the other, this paranoia turned all citizens into suspects. Everyone was potentially up to no good, harboring within themselves a "formless banditry" waiting to take a threatening shape. The New Life Movement that the Nationalists began to promote both inside and outside of repentance camp walls aimed to address this problem amid a broader regeneration of the national spirit. As chief architects of the movement in its initial phases, the CC Clique and Blue Shirts emphasized how it would make life new while restoring enduring Confucian traditions that the Communists, and imperialism in the longer term, despoiled and endangered. Chapter 4 turns to the ways in which the New Life Movement sought to make everything and everyone perfectly legible to authorities, permanently eliminating all unknown unknowns. By treating everyone as prospective political criminals who had to rigorously monitor their own thought and behavior, the New Life Movement signaled the extension of counterinsurgency logics well beyond actual battlefields. It harkened back to an imaginary time when perfect order had prevailed and anticipated a future of synchronized industrial productivity.

4 » FIXING THE EVERYDAY
The New Life Movement and Taylorized Modernity

On March 23, 1934, the Shanghai daily *Shenbao* reported on a series of events staged the previous week in Nanchang, Jiangxi—then the main headquarters of Chiang Kai-shek's Military Affairs Council—to celebrate the recently launched New Life Movement (NLM).[1] A lantern parade converging on a sports stadium kicked off the nighttime opening ceremony, which was presided over by Blue Shirt Deng Wenyi. More than seventy thousand spectators reportedly listened to Deng announce that the NLM aimed to glorify the nation and to imbue the Chinese people with an understanding of propriety, humility, responsibility, discipline, punctuality, and hygiene. Throughout the city, venues illustrated core NLM ideas. These included pavilions dramatizing the transformation of old and degenerate ways of living into the new and wholesome, as well as a giant lantern in the shape of a tree representing the Republic of China nourished by the water of traditional morality. Trade and worker organizations participated in the events by erecting placards extolling Confucian virtues. Motorcar processions illustrated what Sun Yat-sen had named basic human necessities: clothing, food, shelter, and transportation. According to the *Shenbao* report, at the opening ceremony Deng Wenyi remarked that the spirit of unity inculcated by the NLM overcame whatever differences existed among the participants holding lanterns aloft. Nanchang's coordinated spectacles—involving the illumination of darkness by the militarized state, the representation of the Confucian nation as natural and class-cooperative, and an aestheticized response to issues of social difference—rendered Chinese fascists' national fantasy visible to all.

A kind of mobile fixity, in which capitalist dynamism was cemented by feudalistic hierarchy, was on full display in Nanchang that day. The motorcar processions were exemplary in this regard, announcing the arrival of industrial progress while also indicating that, for the masses at least, cars were not to symbolize freedom of movement. Rather, they were pedagogical reminders of the importance of punctuality and work discipline; dream objects that could symbolize personal enjoyment only to the extent that the masses should take joy in the labor process. The parade float illustrating the Three Principles' right to clothing underscored the message. Displaying an archetypal worker, peasant, student, soldier, and businessman advancing together in time, each was dressed in attire proper to their social station. The float that, seemingly redundantly, illustrated mobility conveyed not what it would feel like to ride in a motorized vehicle but instead dramatized a crowded yet orderly street scene. Spectators were thus asked to envision themselves not as passengers but as facilitating the smooth conveyance through the streets of cars carrying more important people. Nanchang's NLM activities bombarded spectators with images of dynamic progress while also interpellating them as Confucian subjects for whom a modern future would arrive if and only if they performed proper social roles.[2]

Although scholars once saw triviality in the NLM, since Arif Dirlik's pioneering 1975 essay on the NLM as counterrevolutionary scholars have recognized its importance and mined the movement for insights into the ideology and workings of the Nanjing regime.[3] The various emphases and public faces of the movement over time, from its 1934 instigation by military-based fascists to the assumption of control by Madame Chiang Kai-shek (Song Meiling) and her Anglo-American missionary supporters in 1935–36, suggests that what we know as the NLM was ultimately several intersecting movements, with varying meanings to differing proponents and differing emphases depending on where and by whom it was implemented.[4] New Life Movement promoters in Tianjin, for instance, primarily amplified long-developing hygienic discourses, which contrasted to the all-encompassing transformations implemented in postsoviet Jiangxi.[5] To fascists, the NLM's purpose centered on imbuing the population at large with militantly organized productive capacities in preparation for total war and for realizing Sun Yat-sen's vision of state-directed industrialization.[6] It presented the four Confucian bonds of *li*, *yi*, *lian*, and *chi* as intrinsically fused to the Three Principles of the People, and as providing the necessary social regulatory functions for China to modernize without generating social abnormalities. Like a scientifically managed factory or a rationalized military, the nation was to become rigidly organized and maximally efficient.

The NLM's obsession with clean lines, streamlined functions, and legible roles anticipated the high modernism in which James C. Scott saw "human needs . . . scientifically stipulated by the planner" who envisioned only "hierarchy prevail[ing] in every direction."[7] Although Scott collapsed politically varying high modernist projects into a singular type of assault on local practices, his analysis nevertheless helps to illuminate how the NLM's apparent Confucian traditionalism masked a profound reordering of the social world. As fascists envisioned it, the NLM would standardize, integrate, and coordinate the actions of the entire population, reciprocally strengthening the state domestically and on the world stage. Via campaigns to militarize, aestheticize, and productivize everyday life, the minds and bodies of Chinese citizens would become accustomed to the temporal rhythms of mechanized factory and agricultural work, and ever prepared to mobilize against domestic and foreign enemies. One CC Clique promoter called this process *zhengqihuayi*: "to organize and remake as one," or "to make uniform" in the sense of calibrating weights and measures.[8] This envisioned reorganization offered all but a select vanguard of state leaders the opportunity to affectively bond with the nation while being effectively denied the capacity to alter social relations in a manner not dictated from above.[9] The Confucianism that the NLM invoked was central to this process, as it provided a seemingly natural ground for national cohesion amid a tremendous effort toward social transformation. The NLM's idea of cooperative endeavor was deeply stratified by implicit and explicit inequalities, demanding conformity to its norms and threatening direct and indirect violence against those who did not.

This chapter addresses the ways in which the NLM, as fascists envisioned it, would fix everyday life in a twofold sense. First, its officer's- and manager's-eye view of the social world honed in on routine ideas and behavior presumed to drag on collective strength and efficiency. Bodily health had many connotations in China in the wake of imperialism, and fascists shared many assumptions with their political rivals about the relationship between individual bodies and national strength.[10] But they particularly emphasized that a strengthened body was a productive body accustomed, even before the fact, to the temporal rhythms of mechanized factory and agricultural work, and that it was an indissoluble part of an organic national collective for which it should be ever ready to sacrifice itself. Fascists therefore used militaristic and productivist metaphors interchangeably to speak about the social world: workers were soldiers in an industrial army; soldiers were expected to be as punctual as workers bound by factory whistles; and household management was conceived in terms of battlefield violence. The NLM's attention to daily life can be seen as the inverse of critical Marxist investigations into the quotidian during the interwar and postwar periods. Where the latter spotlighted the everyday as, among other things, what Harry Harootunian called "a site of practices that pointed to [modernity's] open-endedness, incompletion, contradictions, and multiaccentuality," the NLM sought to foreclose the possibility of detecting or acting upon these openings.[11] Fascists presented life's hidden corners as always already national and Confucian, as if it could not naturally give rise to anything but a militant corporatism. Revealing this underlying truth just required telling people where to look and forcing them to sweep out some accumulated dust.

The NLM also sought to fix everyday life in a second sense. Against the inevitable upheaval of bodies and aspirations implied by military mobilization and industrialization, fascists sought to assign people into legible and stable categories.[12] The Blue Shirts and CC Clique were well aware that bodies strengthened by exercise and clean living could just as easily revolt against Nanjing as fight against the Japanese or Communists. The more deeply people identified with their assigned social roles the less likely they were to act unpredictably or notice anything but what they were told to notice. When fascists of a more technocratic than militaristic bent likened society to a machine, it indexed their acute fear that anything short of rendering citizens into cogs would disrupt the nation's swift recovery of strength and prosperity. The socially integrative emphasis of the Confucianism promoted by the NLM, which organized the nation into a hierarchical unity construed as natural and eternal, aimed to foreclose the omnipresent possibility that people would choose to pursue other political paths.

The NLM's ideal of mobile fixity and the threat of violence that buttressed it was aptly expressed by banners that hung from the sides of the parade cars in Nanchang in March 1934. Reading "blockhouse," the banners referenced the military fortifications that constituted cornerstones of the Nationalists' final, successful anti-Communist encirclement campaign.[13] They unsubtly conveyed that adhering to the NLM's interpretation of Sun's Three Principles would fortify the nation against its myriad enemies. Industrialization, militarization, and Confucianism were inseparably interlinked in the creation of a stable yet dynamic new society.

Soldiers and Cogs: Rendering the Nation Militantly Productive

The NLM as implemented in Nanchang during the winter and spring of 1934 was sweeping. Sporting competitions, singing groups, street performances, and lantern parades bombarded locals with bodily experiences of new ways of being in the world.[14] Replicating the collective and dramatic forms with which Communists had experimented in their Jiangxi base areas, Nationalist propagandists supplied these forms with Confucian-nationalist content, far outdoing their Communist competitors with the amount of resources they could bring to the task of interpellating a new kind of citizen.[15] Nanchang's NLM spectacles were staged, as Guannan Li has documented, amid the city's structural revitalization.[16] Evoking Baron Haussmann's late nineteenth-century creative destruction of Paris, Nationalists brought engineers in from Shanghai to help modernize the Nanchang cityscape. These planners introduced running water and modern sewers, widened "narrow streets . . . to allow air and light to enter the houses," connected dead-end lanes, and "straightened the curves" that potentially disrupted projected traffic flows.[17] As a model city, Nanchang gave material shape to fascist convictions that a streamlined society was a manageable society. That Nanchang's transformation took place under the direction of military administrators and by pushing past local opposition only fueled Nationalist conviction that their approach was correct.[18]

Fascist writings on the NLM, penned in a context of anti-Communist military victory and escalating Japanese aggression in China's northeast, conveyed a fragile confidence that the future was theirs for the making as well as an acute fear that China would soon be demoted from a semicolony to a full colony of Japan. This precarious situation spurred their adamancy that the totality of life had to be made new all at once. At the most general level, the movement commanded the Chinese population to abide by Sun's Three Principles and the Confucian ideals of li, yi, lian, and chi—typically glossed as propriety, righteousness, integrity, and humility, though fascists themselves offered varying interpretations, discussed below.[19] It rhetorically attended to both spiritual and material dimensions of life, focusing on reforming habits of mind and behavior, and aimed to modify everything from Westernized hairstyle and clothing trends to practices perceived as subversive. A list of ninety-six rules emphasized sanitation, bodily health, public decorum, and rationalized economic behavior. This list included: "keep to the left when walking on the street"; "keep silent in meetings or at the theater"; "do not gamble or visit prostitutes"; and "salute your elders."[20] Citizens were likewise instructed to economize by being "frugal at weddings, funerals, and on festive occasions" and to "be fair in business transactions." Many rules focused on hygiene, instructing people to wash their faces, comb their hair, avoid drinking and smoking, and to keep windows open. Such stipulations were supplemented by dozens of additional rules regarding everything from the sort of shoes that rickshaw drivers should wear to methods of managerial bookkeeping. These were incorporated into campaigns to militarize, aestheticize, and productivize everyday life, whereby citizens would become accustomed to the temporal rhythms of mechanized factory and agricultural work, and ever ready to mobilize against domestic and foreign enemies.

Fascist interest in the routines of daily life constituted an extension of their own military and managerial predilections. As much as they saw "like a state" desiring legibility for the sake of control, they saw like aspirational military commanders and factory managers highly critical of Western liberalism and intensely fearful of Communism. The NLM therefore worked to establish whose and what kind of eyes could do the looking and what should and should not be looked at. It shone the light of the state into places either previously unseen or that were being seen in very different ways by novelists, left-wing activists, and the masses themselves.[21] Good soldiers are mobile and go where they are told; machine parts move but not without an external force to set them in motion, and they can also be switched off at will. Still, fascists were acutely aware that even well-trained soldiers can mutiny and that workers the world over resisted being turned into what F. W. Taylor notoriously likened to "trained gorillas."[22] The NLM therefore sought to penetrate into the deepest recesses of popular consciousness and to render political opposition an unnatural, nonnational, non-Confucian stance. As the *Future* editor Liu Bingli put it, "Revolution must enter into people's hearts, consciousness and unconscious life. . . . It must permeate the entirety of the life process."[23] Conceiving daily life as alternately a battlefield and a worksite filled with insubordinates and Luddites, the NLM aimed to keep everyone's eyes trained on a streamlined and efficient future.

SEEING LIKE AN OFFICER

Fascist concern for reconfiguring ways of being in the world animated all aspects of the movement. The NLM's frequent recourse to nighttime lantern parades was exemplary in this regard, as lantern parades claimed for the state the right to dictate how darkness could be utilized, whose bodies could move about in it, and for what purposes.[24] In certain respects, Nanchang's New Life Movement Promotion Committee's enthusiasm for nighttime lantern parades calls to mind the Nazis' contemporaneous seizure of the night for political indoctrination and violence—practices with which Guomindang militants were likely familiar. Inspirations for lantern parades were, however, doubtless closer to home. Whether conducted in barely electrified Nanchang or in neon-lit Shanghai, lantern parades suggested the power of party and state to claim the night for the nation, away from bandits who operated under the cover of darkness and away from men and women who would use its hours for individualized enjoyment or labor in degenerate professions.[25] Like the revived *baojia* community policing system, nighttime parades implied to the populace that they were always being watched.[26] This was also among the messages sent by NLM inspections of movie theaters, dance halls, and restaurants.[27] However, if a stated goal of the NLM was for the population to internalize new forms of self-discipline, its leaders nevertheless emphasized that no one could really be trusted to monitor themselves. Instead, there would always be officers and technocrats (actual and aspirational) looking over their shoulders. The officer here represented the threat of direct physical violence, and the technocrat a more abstract and impersonal control over one's capacity to simply reproduce oneself on a daily basis in a modernizing world.

Responding to critics who dismissed the NLM as "a movement unworthy of a movement," a contributor to the *Future* argued that the NLM's efforts to impose military-style discipline on the population at large constituted a vital "first step in preparing for the Second World War," in a manner that had proven necessary for "total industrial mobilization" in Europe during the first.[28] Whether or not the general populace presently recognized the importance of the movement was irrelevant to whether it should proceed. Echoing the *Future*, Xiang Ziyu, writing for *Mopping Up Thrice Monthly*'s New Life Movement special issue, argued that insofar as they were conducting "fundamental work for reviving the nation," "those of us who are knowledgeable and are leaders of the masses in various circles must shoulder this significant burden."[29] Xiang noted that turn-of-the-century "queue-cutting and foot-unbinding movements did not wait for all countrymen to become conscious" of the need to shed these outward signs of dynastic life.[30] The more the public mocked or resisted their efforts, the more convinced fascists became of the need for the movement in the first place. People who expected it to be democratic in either intent or effect misunderstood the point altogether.

In a 1934 NLM speech, Chiang Kai-shek maintained that in "the home, the factory, and the government office, regardless of place, time, or situation, everyone's activities must be the same as in the army. . . . In other words, there must be obedience, sacrifice, strictness, cleanliness, accuracy, speed, diligence, secrecy . . . and everyone together must firmly and bravely sacrifice everything for the group and for the nation."[31] Chiang's officer's-eye view of the world raised as many questions as it answered. What would it actually mean to conduct relations between friends, co-workers, or strangers on the street as if in the army? Since the army was an overwhelmingly male and entirely masculinized space—in which soldiers were expected to be politically astute but not bookish, physically assertive, and rigidly self-controlled—reshaping life in this fashion invariably had profound implications for women, children, the elderly, and so on.[32] The CC Clique preemptively provided answers in the form of pamphlets like "New Life for Peasants," "New Life for Children," "New Life for Shopkeepers," "New Life for Women," "New Life for Students," and "New Life for Musicians."[33] But the problem remained that Chiang and other New Life advocates were attempting to remake society in the image of an inherently nondemocratic organization whose temporal rhythms and mode of organization could not be easily grafted onto, for instance, the growth cycles of crops or the temporalities of child rearing.

More important, to live as if in the army meant following orders and conceptualizing daily routines as if one could participate in the most privileged and violently empowered state structure, without actually enjoying such a privilege. The NLM's exhortations to live life as if in the army at this most basic level were constant reminders that one was not and could not be at the top of the national command structure. Historian Karl Gerth has written of how NLM materials explained to women, who were categorically excluded from actual combat during the Nanjing Decade, that buying only domestically produced commodities could render them "the equivalent of someone commanding officers and soldiers on the battlefield to kill the enemy for the country."[34] For a woman to conduct a daily shopping routine as if she were setting out to "kill the enemy for the country" implied that she should relish the opportunity to issue commands to social inferiors. To whom was not clear—the vegetable seller, the tailor? While rhetorically aiming to foster social order and stability, fascist injunctions to militarize life actually encouraged people to identify and enjoy the forms of power that they could exert over others—as a corporal might enjoy climbing from the rank of private and thereby becoming empowered to give orders rather than simply receive them. It introduced antagonism into routine practices supposedly regulated by Confucian ideals of restraint. The militarized national unit envisioned by the NLM thus encouraged people to assume positions of power where they could find them, and to also abandon hope that they could exert any actual control over the structuring conditions of their own lives.

Fascists often spoke about the ways in which the NLM's coercive strictures were intended to give way to consensual self-regulation in the future. But it was equally clear that, if all aspects of life were conceptualized as battlefields, someone would always be giving orders and others would always be receiving them. Ru Chunpu, writing for the *Future* in 1935, maintained that the whole point of the NLM was to achieve a society in which young people voluntarily avoided dance halls and unauthorized movies, the average consumer felt ashamed to wear imported cloth, and otherwise experienced "improper amusements as a crime of the conscience."[35] He underscored that "the present is an age in which human life is consumed by war, [hence] the entire life of the nation-state must be devoted to developing a spirit of war." Each member of society needed to understand his or her specific role and the importance of cooperative, common effort. War and daily routines were so entwined that, Ru believed, "Life is war in the abstract, while at the same time on-the-ground combat drills one for life."[36] The average Chinese person clearly did not yet grasp this. If one examined a typical urban household, one would find that its consumption habits and ordinary activities were frivolous and purposeless. People had grown accustomed to excess comfort and were preoccupied with individual pleasures. The NLM would retrain people to take pleasure in national-collective life. In Ru's words, after "all citizens undergo military training, they will learn that present circumstances cannot permit anyone to live a life of excessive freedom. Each life will be regulated by the collective will."[37] Even if war never broke out, Ru concluded, military training was tantamount to training for life. Despite Ru's calls for individual self-regulation, he clearly did not foresee an endpoint to the militarization of mundane routines. Orders would always come from above, and these higher-ups would always be watching.

ACTING LIKE A COG

In the passage above extolling self-sacrifice for the nation, Chiang Kai-shek extended his officer's-eye view to the workplace in addition to the home. The NLM exemplified convergences between militarism and productivism in the fascist imagination: a militarized life was a life lived productively inside and outside actual places of work. In this respect, the NLM interchangeably asked people to act like soldiers (i.e., to always be receptive to orders from above) and to act like cogs in a well-oiled national machine (i.e., to have no sense of life purpose distinguishable from that determined for the nation as a whole). New Life Movement proponents therefore pondered ways to dispose the general population toward productivity and efficiency. This required retooling popular conceptions of state, society, and history, and how a given individual might best serve a higher purpose. Moral-educational suasion and direct physical force were both reasonably employed.

Some NLM promoters believed that national regeneration would occur more swiftly if people just conceptualized themselves as machine parts, as if conceptualizing themselves as soldiers—that is, as willful human beings who could potentially disobey orders—presented too many uncertainties. Arif Dirlik observed that in NLM writings "the image of society as a machine was . . . ever present."[38] Chen Lifu in particular "posited 'efficiency' as the central goal of political organization; the complexity of New Life organization was itself justified in terms of greater 'efficiency' in achieving its goals. One author explicitly suggested that the ideal social organization would be analogous to a machine in which each part performed its assigned function with witless precision, ensuring the smooth operation of the whole."[39] In an extended 1935 NLM essay, Chen elaborated on the perils of excessive individual freedom.[40] "At present," Chen wrote, "there are many who can already see liberalism's significant flaws and that humanity should not be too free. If it is, then it will remain in open strife and veiled struggle, consuming all of its strength and giving rise to problems of efficiency," writing *xiaoneng* as well as "Efficiency" in English as if to underscore its still-unassimilated aspects. It was incumbent upon "the strong, the excellent, those of great talent and knowledge" to "uplift the weak, the inferior, those who lack talent and knowledge." Sun Yat-sen promoted the division of powers and functions (the division of labor and expertise) for precisely this reason, Chen explained. Such a mode of state and social organization constituted an improvement over liberal democratic systems. As it was commonly understood that "we should increase social efficiency and enhance human life," Nanjing's single-party rule should be considered more historically progressive than backward liberal democracies.[41] The NLM thus set China on the course to realizing maximal efficiency by concentrating power in the hands of experts and ensuring that people performed their proper social functions.

Chen's justification of dictatorship in the name of efficiency was echoed by other CC Clique activists who similarly desired the industrial strength achieved by liberal democracies without their evident difficulties in controlling their citizens. The NLM was thus perceived not as retrograde but as supremely historically progressive: it could cultivate worker-citizens who stayed in their proper places and did not speak back to power. Writing for the *Periodical of the Chinese Cultural Construction Association*, a contributor named Xu Zexiang explained that the NLM opposed bourgeois culture but not industrialization as such. Xu opined that "present-day Chinese culture resembles a pell-mell pile of trash" in which capitalists, feudalists, and Communists each displayed their own malformed traits. They lacked "patriotism or love for their four hundred million brethren. Bourgeois and red culture in particular are selfish, degenerate, and completely devoid of sentiment." Out of this hodgepodge, the NLM would create unity and order. It would also combat the tendencies of ordinary people to seek comfort in the traditional and familiar when confronted with the new and unfamiliar. Their task was to "actively absorb the culture of industrial production. We must use the culture of capitalist production to overturn China's indigenous culture of predestination and nationalist culture must conquer the red culture of Communism." The Confucian ideals promoted by the NLM would help them create order out of chaos by rendering society what Xu termed *zhengqihuayi*—organized and remade as one. In his eyes, they would help recalibrate politics, finance, industrial production, agricultural prices, imports and exports, education, art, and the "thinking of the entire citizenry."[42] This would in turn facilitate the development of machinery and military preparations, and enable production and consumption to be brought under strict government control.[43] In fact, Xu optimistically reflected, "The basic spirit of Hitler's National Socialism is exactly that of Chairman Chiang's new cultural movements' efforts to zhengqihuayi."[44] Social efficiency and draconian state control were inseparably entwined.

With society as a whole conceptualized as a machine, individual members had to learn to properly promote its functioning. A contributor to the *Future*'s 1934 NLM special issue named Gu Gaoyang explained how the movement aimed "to renew the quality of life, and this means to enhance social efficiency and to enrich the content of life."[45] He pressed the Nationalist government to exert greater control over the economy and to promote "productive training to improve the material habits of the people."[46] Ordinary citizens could not remain passive spectators while the government attempted to improve their livelihoods. Their attitudes and behavior had to adapt as well. What Gu called "production education" was fundamental, as it would foster positive revaluations of productivity and enable people to grasp their roles as integral parts of a larger whole. There were still many countries in the world in which most of the population did not participate in production, Gu explained. However, rarely were people in these undeveloped countries as disdainful of productive labor as they were in China. In the ancient past, he elaborated, China's gentry had regarded themselves as superior to peasants, craftsmen, and merchants. Producers were regarded with particular derision. Though productive labor was in the midst of revaluation, it was still far from universally respected, and this was a key reason why China remained economically backward and oppressed by imperialism. The NLM therefore aimed to "break the people's bias against productive labor and establish positive views of production" and equally to "provide people with skills to discard their old methods of production and use modern machinery."[47] In Gu's analysis, the NLM would transform attitudes toward producing among elites and reskill direct producers to meet the requirements of an industrializing world.

The moral-educational initiatives against undisciplined time use at the heart of the movement could readily slide into direct physical violence against the nonconforming. Blue Shirts seem to have generally regarded the line between suasion and coercion to be thin, as suggested by a cartoon from the *Future* in which bodies labeled corrupt, selfish, and degenerate are thrown from a train "en route to national strength."[48] Failures to conform to the NLM's stringent norms were regarded as acts of national sabotage. In this vein, the modern girl was singled out by NLM promoters for particular scorn and even physical attack.[49] She was despised not only for her apparent control over her own sexuality and gender identity but also because she wasted time. She was selfish for considering her body and her capacity to labor to be her own rather than for the nation. Such generalized insubordination rendered the modern girl a partner in crime to political opposition movements. In this case especially, the NLM's positive models of proper behavior were always limned with threats of violence. One person acting out of sync could ruin the smooth functioning of the whole.

If the NLM's aestheticization of politics was clearly manifest in its expectation that citizens bond with and toil for the nation while passively receiving commands from above, its explicit campaigns for life aestheticization (*shenghuo yishuhua*) also expressed ideals of uniformity, efficiency, and order. The lack of adornment, straight lines, and spartan simplicity promoted by the NLM were modernist aesthetics as much as they were values of military men and cost-conscious managers. In certain respects, it seems surprising that men who held such ideals would have had any interest in Confucianism, whose two millennia of accreted textual exegesis and performative elaboration hardly evoked streamlined efficiency. Yet perhaps more than anything else, the NLM's Blue Shirt and CC Clique proponents understood themselves to be resuscitating an endangered native Confucian culture, which they in turn believed perfectly molded the kinds of people who grasped their cog- or soldier-like roles within a larger national machine-army advancing together into a postcolonial future.

As I examine in the following section, NLM Confucianism was as spartan and future oriented as other aspects of the movement. Its "Confucian" concern for industriousness and family values, respect for authority, and patriotism at times rang so generically authoritarian that it might have buttressed strong-armed development anywhere in the world. Such values were nevertheless touted as timelessly Chinese, and despite the fact that the industrial and corporatist character of the nation-state that they ostensibly animated was simultaneously celebrated as historically progressive. Moreover, the NLM's equation of Confucian morality with efficiency and command receptivity erased even the nominal checks on power embedded within dynastic Confucian thought.[50] This erasure meant the elimination of possibilities for political resistance: even holding the powerful accountable for their actions became a non-Confucian and hence nonnational gesture. Despite the NLM's emphasis on the responsibility of individuals to the larger national whole, the movement's concern with efficiency and top-down chains of command actually served to obviate individual responsibility. Everyone was supposed to follow orders regardless of what those orders were. People were expected to do what they were told and mind their own place in the social division of labor.

Mobile Fixity: Ritualized Subservience in a Dynamic Society

In a study of Euro-American conservatism, Corey Robin succinctly illuminates how notions of social order are renegotiated and reformulated in the process of revolutionary upheaval. The lessons that Robin sees conservatives learning from their opponents were also absorbed by interwar fascists, even as the latter recoiled with greater violence than did conservatives against their opponents and themselves clamored for sweeping social transformations. Robin observes:

> From the trauma of revolution, conservatives learn that men and women, whether through willed acts of force or some other exercise of human agency, can order social relationships and political time. In every social movement or revolutionary moment, reformers and radicals have to invent—or rediscover—the idea that inequality and social hierarchy are not natural phenomena but human creations. If hierarchy can be created by men and women, it can be uncreated by men and women, and that is what a social movement sets out to do. From these efforts, conservatives learn a version of the same lesson. Where their predecessors in the old regime thought of inequality as a naturally occurring phenomenon, an inheritance passed on from generation to generation, the conservatives' encounter with revolution teaches them that the revolutionaries were right after all: inequality is a human creation. And if it can be uncreated by men and women, it can be recreated by men and women.[51]

Robin's formulation of the uncreation and re-creation of inequality helps to illuminate the role of Confucianism in the NLM and in Chinese fascist thought more generally. As discussed in previous chapters, the dialogue that fascists had with Confucianism was largely mediated through the 1910s New Culture and May Fourth movements. Blue Shirt He Zhonghan made clear that the NLM was part of this dialogue when he stated that "the May Fourth New Cultural Movement imported foreign things to China, destroying things that are native to China. The New Life Movement that we are now promoting will foster things that are native to China."[52] To fascists, whether or not left-wing heirs of these 1910s movements even painted an accurate picture of Confucianism was of less concern than the fact that they were challenging something that ostensibly bound the nation together in a cross-class fashion. Fascists represented the social hierarchies that leftists had come to insist were reproduced by Confucianism as part of an enduring natural order of things.

CONFUCIAN NATIONAL HARMONY

In the 1930s, the struggle between right and left over Confucianism had less to do with the past as such than with what Confucianism signified in terms of social power and agency in the present.[53] Song Qingling, a prominent voice of the non-Communist left and critic of the Nanjing regime, made this clear in an essay called "Confucianism and Modern China," in which she took aim at the NLM and the "air of Confucianism" it had about it.[54] Here, Song cursorily examined the class composition of the sociohistorical context in which Confucian doctrines had first emerged in the fifth century BCE, highlighting how these were "feudal and despotic from head to toe" and prevented the development of science and social progress.[55] Her analysis of Confucianism's past was little more concerned with textual nuance than that of the rightists she was challenging. She was instead concerned with how invocations of this tradition legitimated class and gender inequalities in the present. "We don't need Confucian teachings," Song insisted, concluding that one could find "nothing new in the 'New Life Movement,' nor does it give the people anything."[56] In other words, state championing of filial piety, social propriety, and so on struck a chord so familiar that it was absurd to characterize the movement as novel in any meaningful way.

Whether Song Qingling conceded it or not, the NLM did attempt to make life new, particularly, as discussed above, by expanding foundations for industrialization and managing historically novel social dynamics. At the same time, the fact that the NLM appeared traditional to observers like Song meant that it grounded itself at least marginally convincingly in received ideas. Peter Osborne has argued with respect to fascism's historical consciousness that the "fact that the past in question is primarily imaginary" is "no impediment to its political force, but rather its very condition (myth)."[57] In this sense, the past in question is not necessarily entirely imaginary. Kernels of historical truth in fascist ideology—facts and experiences that it seizes upon before distorting to suit its own purposes—are often key to its capacity to represent itself as respectful of time-honored traditions and to thereby secure popular appeal. Confucianism, for all of its historical diversity, has certainly been persistently concerned with social order and stability. Until the collapse of China's last dynasty in 1911, the enactment of ritual (li) had been integral to the articulation and maintenance of state and social power.[58] The strict observation of ritualized practices by people who properly understood them was expected to beget harmony and prosperity. It was thus hardly an accident that Nanjing Decade fascists found in Confucianism, and in the concept of li in particular, a fertile source for instituting order within a modernizing society.[59] It is also not an accident that they ignored everything that did not fit with their visions of a new streamlined order.

Contrasting the good old days to China's fallen present helped NLM leaders distance Confucianism from undesirable aspects of the "feudal" past, while also making rigid hierarchy seem a comfortable and safe alternative to present social discord. The manner in which Song Qingling's younger sister Song Meiling (Madame Chiang Kai-shek) spoke about the NLM's core Confucian precepts is illustrative of the utility of historical imprecision. In 1935, Song recounted a story regarding the NLM's inception in which she attributed the idea for the movement to Chiang Kai-shek as he was surveying Jiangxi Province in the wake of expelling the Communists. There, Chiang

> saw that the immediate need was the development of the vitality of the people, which seemed to have been crushed. . . . He realized how much depended upon the people's consciousness of their great heritage from the past; and the conviction came to him that the four great virtues of old China, *Li*, *I*, *Lien* and *Chih* constituted a remedy that could recover the country from stagnation and ruin—because, at the time when those principles were practiced, China was indeed

a great nation. He decided there and then to base a New Life Movement upon them, to try to recover what has been lost by forgetfulness of this source of China's greatness.[60]

The vagueness of Song Meiling's remarks about "old China" and "the time when those principles were practiced" was not mere pandering to unschooled audiences. Rather, the vagueness of Song's remarks conveyed that these principles had always been foundations of Chinese life, which, if honored, begat feelings of security. She reinforced this point by criticizing popular "forgetfulness of this source of China's greatness," which implied that these principles had once been known in the manner that she and other NLM leaders understood them; that is, rather than as they may have been known to other citizens, and however differentially depending on time period or one's educational background, ethnicity, class, or gender. In Song's rendering, their collective practice had been the source of national strength; their collective revival on Nationalist terms would facilitate national regeneration and allow people to feel like their world was safe and secure again. She was speaking mythically about the way things had always been and how they should always be, rendering the myth persuasive by grounding it with familiar referents.

If Song Meiling unmoored NLM norms of propriety, righteousness, integrity, and humility from historical time, Chiang Kai-shek uprooted them from place in a manner that unwittingly highlighted their generically corporatist aspects. These timeless Chinese values, Chiang suggested in a speech recorded in *Mopping Up Thrice Monthly*, were at present more nobly honored in militant regimes elsewhere in the world than in China itself. Here, Chiang admonished his listeners that Turks, Italians, and Germans had all managed to bring their own revolutions to fruition while that of the Chinese remained stillborn. The difference, according to the Generalissimo, was that Turks, Germans, and Italians all observed li, yi, lian, and chi:

> In Italy and Germany in particular, the average citizen understands the importance of social order, observes collective discipline. . . . All of their actions are in accord with li, yi, lian, and chi, and because of this not only have their domestic enemies naturally been conquered, moreover all manner of foreigners are both awestruck and terrified by this situation. The NLM which we are now implementing aims to revive the fundamentals of the national revolution, and every comrade who participates in the movement, in particular all party, mili-

tary, academic, and police leaders, must understand that li is most important.[61]

Chiang presumably intended to express that the soldiers and citizens under his charge were alienated from their own roots, that Germans, Turks, and Italians did a better job of disciplining themselves than did the Chinese, and that the values he thought worthy of revival strongly resonated with those presently celebrated in the other three countries mentioned. However, Chiang instead revealed how non-place-specific the NLM's Confucianism actually was. Ideals of collective discipline, self-sacrifice for the nation, family cohesion, and deference to authority could be found in all fascist movements (and indeed in nonfascist polities as well) that also believed in their own radical particularity. More typically of course, Chiang was careful to stress their intrinsically Chinese-national aspects. Only by reviving such values and recognizing that the "nation's one and only revolutionary principle is the Three People's Principles" would it be possible "to restore our nation's very special standing in this world, to create a glorious and radiant world order for mankind, and in achieving this noble and great enterprise thereby save mankind and save the world."[62] While Confucian behaviors that NLM leaders touted as nation-defining might ring familiar in other national contexts, they aimed to resonate locally in a way that promised order and stability out of social collapse.

The significance of li, yi, lian, and chi in rendering social roles fixed and legible was hashed out in the pages of Blue Shirt and CC Clique publications. There, we see a dynamic tension between methodical engagements with key Confucian texts—in particular those of sixteenth-century neo-Confucianism, with its stress on self-regulation and personal cultivation—and the outright "invention of tradition" as Hobsbawm and Ranger felicitously phrased it. This tension was particularly apparent in the writings and speeches of He Zhonghan. Mr. He opened a 1934 article for the *Future*, "The Meanings of Li, Yi, Lian, and Chi," by declaring that they were ancient Chinese teachings that everyone knew were "already utterly decayed."[63] Because they had been a source of China's past greatness and because, he said, "Chairman Chiang has invoked 'li, yi, lian, chi' to discipline us, with the hope that we will utilize China's native ethics to cultivate our humanity while we utilize foreign science to handle practical matters," it was imperative to understand their meanings.[64] To illuminate each term, He Zhonghan first turned to glosses furnished by Ming

Dynasty neo-Confucian philosopher Wang Yangming. By *lizheliye*, Wang Yangming meant that observing li is to "follow a line for whatever task one undertakes."[65] But He's impatience even with reading military discipline into Wang Yangming was evident, and he quickly supplied his own "more objective" definitions. According to Mr. He, li meant to be mutually conciliatory. Yi was synonymous with performing favors without thought of repayment, or the wholesale "sacrifice of the interests of the individual." Lian meant to abide by the law and one's station in life, while chi meant to be roused to action and assert oneself. Because people were "elements of a social collective," individual failure to observe any one of these precepts would negatively influence the behavior of others. Li, yi, lian, and chi were ultimately "forces which bind society together."[66] In this way, He Zhonghan's glosses on the NLM's core terms emphasized self-sacrifice for the collective and a willingness to adhere to one's allotted role. His suggestion that people should be ready to assert themselves meant that they should be roused only when called upon, and otherwise patiently bide their time as part of a reserve army, whether military or industrial.

Chen Lifu's explanations of li, yi, lian, and chi differed somewhat from those supplied by He Zhonghan, but similarly stressed self-sacrifice, obedience, and national cohesion. Dirlik has observed that to Chen, li meant group discipline and individual politeness, yi entailed "the 'spirit of organization,' or feeling of responsibility," lian pointed to the "'division of labor,' or 'minding one's own business,'" while chi pointed to "public and individual morality."[67] Chen's seemingly contradictory injunction to "mind one's own business" while also fostering a "spirit of organization" and "responsibility" can be reconciled if we take into account Chen's managerial perspective. Chen implied that people should do what they were told without asking questions and thereby become what corporate leaders later in the twentieth century would call good team players. That Confucian values regulated a larger whole whose components had to work well together was underscored by Chen's fondness for charts and diagrams that isolated each factor and showed how they added up.[68] While doubtless inspired by Chen's training as an engineer, the inclusion of flow charts appears to have been pioneered among the Guomindang right wing by Dai Jitao. Dai had appended a "system diagram of the philosophy of popular livelihood" to his "Philosophical Foundations of the Three Principles of the People" that lined up the various components of Sun's political philosophy (the five-power system and the Three Principles of the People) with Confucian precepts.[69]

$$\text{廉}(\text{情}=\text{欲之言行})\frac{(+)\text{義}(\text{情}<\text{欲之言行})}{(-)\text{恥}(\text{情}>\text{欲之言行})}\Big\}^{\text{甲}}\longrightarrow\text{禮}^{\text{乙}}\longleftarrow-\Big\{\text{廉}(\cdots\cdots)\frac{(+)\text{義}(\cdots\cdots)}{(-)\text{恥}(\cdots\cdots)}$$

FIGURE 4.1 » Calculating *li, yi, lian,* and *chi.*

Chen Lifu's thirty-two-page essay "New Life Movement and the Principle of Livelihood in Historical Perspective" contained no less than five diagrams, including figure 4.1, which subjects li, yi, lian, and chi to the rigors of an algebraic formula.[70] Another consisted of a cluster of neatly interlocked circles illustrating a society that abided by li, yi, lian, and chi contrasted to a group of nonoverlapping, misshapen circles illustrating a collectivity that did not.[71] Visuals such as these suggested that a provable truth lay behind their cultural claims and, moreover, that they had determined with mathematical precision exactly how society best functioned. People who adhered to Confucian norms begat harmony (as represented visually by Chen's circles), while those who did not were atomizing, abnormal, and thereby harmful to the rest.

Decisions by the cc Clique (and occasionally the Blue Shirts) to include such diagrams highlight the historical specificity of the lens through which they viewed native values, in particular how Confucianism was reinterpreted to mean efficiency and obedience. China's fascists, to be sure, never succeeded in fostering the kind of rationalized social order that they perceived in Nazi Germany, nor were the Nationalists' extermination campaigns against Chinese Communists, however ruthless, executed with the industrial methods and racist fury that Nazis and their collaborators employed to carry out much of the Holocaust. But it is nevertheless important to recognize the ways in which Chinese fascists eagerly collapsed morality and efficiency, and indeed elevated efficiency to a moral imperative. Confucian morality was being repurposed in a way that could not serve as a check on abuses of power or to question orders from on high. What was efficient and served the purposes of revolutionary development was good, regardless of the human consequences. This could mean anything from a vexing but prosaic scenario of evicting a farming community to build a motorway, to the cataclysmic murder of entire populations in the name of achieving a national body free of abnormalities. Sociologist Zygmunt Bauman has drawn out the consequences of such a move:

The Holocaust is so crucial to our understanding of the modern bureaucratic mode of rationalization not only, and not primarily, because
it reminds us (as if we need such a reminder) just how formal and
ethically blind is the bureaucratic pursuit of efficiency. Its significance
is not fully expressed either once we realize to what extent mass murder on an unprecedented scale depended on the availability of well-
developed and firmly entrenched skills and habits of meticulous and
precise division of labour, of maintaining a smooth flow of command
and information, or of impersonal, well-synchronized co-ordination
of autonomous yet complementary actions: on those skills and habits,
in short, which best grow and thrive in the atmosphere of the office.[72]

The relentless division of labor that men like Chen Lifu so admired, in which
each person was supposed to carry out assigned tasks while minding his or
her own business (that is, when not being exhorted to police the neighbors),
implied a social order in which no one actually had to take responsibility
for anything. In good Confucian fashion, the NLM stressed the moral rectitude of national commanders. This was something that Chiang Kai-shek
certainly took seriously in terms of his own self-cultivation and that of his
Blue Shirt followers.[73] However, if society were organized like a military,
people at the bottom were not supposed to question those above their rank.
If it was organized like a machine, it did not matter what the machine did
as long as all of its parts were working and functioned correctly overall. In
this way, the social bonds promoted by NLM Confucianism departed from
the kinds of reciprocal obligations at least normatively expected of superiors to inferiors within a dynastic Confucian schema. Autonomous labor
unions and feminist organizations, water resources and forestry rights,
could all be razed in the name of efficiency or national emergency. People
whose behavior did not conform to norms approved by the state would find
themselves socially ostracized. Worse, they could be subjected to physical
violence in which the population at large was enjoined to participate without asking any questions because doing so, according to the NLM, was non-
Confucian and hence nonnational.

FINDING ONE'S PLACE, SERVING ONE'S PURPOSE
The NLM was, among other things, a backlash against people who either
individually or as part of an organized movement were assuming roles and
identities that did not fit into neat social equations.[74] Blue Shirt and CC

Clique activists sought to discipline the movements that had carried them to power, not to rewind history's clock altogether. Although their initiatives did not always add up coherently, we can discern a predominant logic: they did not fear modern life so much as those aspects of it that they could not control. This is clear from the White Terror's disciplining of labor unions into party-managed organizations and from the ways in which backlashes against expressions of female agency were interwoven with progressive state initiatives. During the 1927 party purge, "many women met their death on the evidence of bobbed hair, unbound feet, or their local reputation for having opposed familial authority in a marriage arrangement or demanded a divorce."[75] The Nationalist government nevertheless proceeded to promulgate a relatively progressive civil code in 1929 and 1930 that granted women (on paper at least) rights to suffrage, divorce, and inheritance.[76] Blue Shirt and CC Clique NLM sponsors likewise made a kind of peace with the idea of the modern woman, even promoting things like bobbed hair and female athleticism as long as these were controlled and circumscribed, and as long as a corresponding new masculinity regained the dominant position. In this vein, Song Meiling's emergence as a key public face of the NLM was a boon to them, as she helped to temper the overt misogyny of their own writings while still "recirculat[ing] the same strategy, leaving intact its logic of exclusions and prohibitions."[77]

The attention that the NLM bestowed upon bodies, both male and female, indexed fascist obsession with legibility and controlled modernization. Bodies coded as female have historically shouldered an undue burden of nationalist attention, and fascists intensified the nationalist gaze in the same way that they intensified other aspects of nationalism. They heaped scorn on overtly sexualized female bodies, suggesting their own fears thereof as much as an interest in crafting a chaste national image. Whether a cause or consequence of Blue Shirts' immersion in the homosocial spaces of the army and affiliated clandestine organizations, they typically subjected all but female athletes to contempt. A 1934 issue of *Sweat and Blood Weekly* ran a trio of cartoons depicting women as hopelessly self-involved and needing male discipline (fig. 4.2).[78] The cartoon at the top illustrates Hitler "corralling women back into the kitchen." That to the left shows a woman clad in a form-fitting *qipao* (a style of fashionable dress in interwar China) standing in a boudoir adorned with modern furniture, admiring herself in no less than five mirrors. The caption indicates that wealthy, housebound wives frittered away time staring at their own reflections. The drawing to its

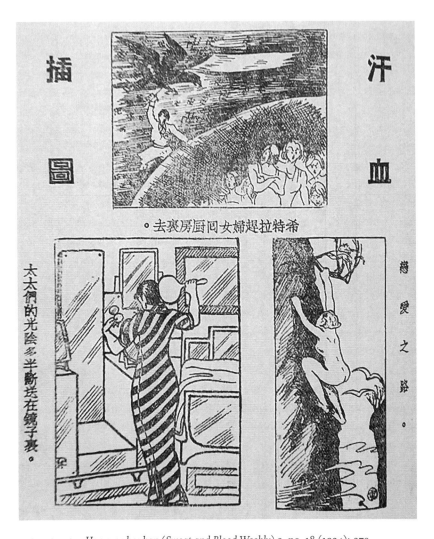

FIGURE 4.2 » *Hanxue zhoukan (Sweat and Blood Weekly)* 3, no. 18 (1934): 279.

right, which shows a naked, fair-haired woman scaling a cliff and captioned "the path of falling in love," is more ambiguous, seemingly taking aim at the notion of free love, coded here as white/Western and dangerous. Together the cartoons suggest that herding women back into the home was not a sufficient program of action. Some women were already there and, left to their own devices, squandered their time on vain indulgences. The NLM, in this respect, would show women how to behave in a domestic setting and thereby become productive members of society. Teaching modern domesticity was among the Blue Shirt–staged events in Nanchang in early 1934. Though the military men who orchestrated these events had spent their lives in the trenches, they nevertheless had specific ideas about the proper running of a household. Resembling a Möbius strip, the "inner" realm of the household was now manifestly part of the "outer" national and public world and subject to the same watchful eyes of officers and managers.[79]

Though Blue Shirts regarded home-based labor as foundational to national regeneration, they often depicted it contemptuously. Such denigration of domestic and caregiving work sharply contrasted to the positive associations with which Song Meiling and her NLM allies invested it. A cartoon in the *Future*, for instance, illuminates ways in which the NLM instructed women in their proper place, depicting this place in a decidedly unflattering light. We see a modestly dressed woman with her head cast submissively downward pushing a baby stroller labeled "the Chinese nation."[80] Three wheels of the stroller are marked li, yi, and chi (if the fourth were visible it would presumably read lian); an arrowed sign indicates that the path on which she walks is the "road to renaissance." The cartoon thus suggests that a woman's key means of observing Confucian values and contributing to national regeneration involved reproductive labor. There was nothing particularly valiant about this labor. In this rendering, women could never be among the nation's foreknower elites—they were after-knowers at best.

Such a contemptuous depiction of a body upon which the powers of li, yi, lian, and chi had acted contrasts with the NLM's oft-noted emphasis on the cultivation of bodily strength. Antonia Finanne has observed that during the Nanjing Decade female "subordination and womanliness sat in uneasy tension with an equal and opposite emphasis on physical strength."[81] These tensions were apparent in Blue Shirt and CC Clique publications as well. Chiang Kai-shek asserted in an NLM speech, "In order to become a healthy modern citizen, it is necessary first to have a strong and robust body; having a strong body, one then has a strong spirit; one can then acquire all the abilities required to strengthen the nation," and so forth.[82] Chiang's call built upon ideals of physical exercise, strength, and hygiene that had been developing in China since at least the turn of the twentieth century, many elements of which were shared across the political spectrum.[83] Alongside the overtly misogynistic images above, Blue Shirt magazines also printed laudatory photos of strong and defiant female athletes. As noted in chapter 1, athletes graced numerous covers of *Sweat and Blood Weekly* in 1935–36, in advance of the 1936 All-China Games and the Berlin Olympics. A team of adolescent girls poses defiantly in a *Sweat and Blood Weekly* cover from 1935 (fig. 4.3).[84] A far cry from the subservient mother pushing a baby carriage or the vain housewife admiring herself in innumerable mirrors, these young women are formidable. They have bobbed hair, wear clothes and shoes that enable them to move quickly and powerfully, and defiantly meet the camera's gaze. Such images suggest that Blue Shirts could be comfortable with strengthened and empowered female bodies as long as they were largely divested of feminine markings and asserted themselves in approved ways. Women who exuded sexuality or fertility were mocked and had to be corralled and contained, while those that had been properly disciplined by NLM strictures could be (on occasion) praised.

New Life Movement women's magazines provide an interesting counterpoint, as they championed similar separate and unequal roles for women but framed these roles as heroic rather than contemptible. Song Meiling's emergence as a key public face of the NLM doubtless helped to render its gender norms more palatable to elite women than they would have seemed from Blue Shirt and CC Clique writings alone. Song's refined version of the modern girl look also helped to tame its libertine, individualistic associations.[85] In this sense, among the NLM's images of ideal modern womanhood was one crafted at the expense of the modern girl that also appropriated aspects of her appeal.[86] The *Funü xinshenghuo yuekan* (*New Life Women's Monthly*), which grew from Song Meiling's endeavors rather than those of the Blue Shirts or CC Clique, reinforced the idea of good versus bad modern femininity via a cartoon of a garishly adorned woman and a gangster captioned "Nora after Leaving Home" (fig. 4.4). The caption alludes to Lu Xun's 1923 remarks on the left-liberal intelligentsia's enthusiastic reception of Henrik Ibsen's 1879 play *A Doll's House*.[87] In Ibsen's play, which was widely staged in China during the May Fourth era, the protagonist, Nora, emancipates herself from the oppressive strictures of bourgeois domesticity by walking out the front door of her home in the final scene. Lu Xun

汗血週刊

第五卷

第十八期

六屆全國女運動會子衡賽
省漫比國女運屆勝賽

FIGURE 4.3 » *Hanxue zhoukan* (*Sweat and Blood Weekly*) 5, no. 18 (1935).

FIGURE 4.4 » "Nora after Leaving Home," *Funü xinshenghuo yuekan* (*New Life Women's Monthly*) 1, no. 3 (1937).

had offered a materialist critique of Nora's decision to leave home, arguing that her emancipation meant little in the absence of structural opportunities for women to financially support themselves. The cartoon can be read as criticizing May Fourth rejections of Confucian familial norms, implying that Nora's decision to leave would lead her straight to a life in Shanghai's underworld. In the *New Life Women's Monthly*, conforming to New Life strictures and providing "home-based support for . . . men" was presented in a positive light.[88] She was encouraged to assume militant roles as long as these roles were militant in the right way. A cartoon in which a woman dressed in fatigues trades her lipstick for a dagger—the caption explains that "the blood of the enemy is better than lipstick [rouge] for moistening the lips"—fully embraces the idea of daily life as a battlefield.[89] Unlike the degenerated Nora, she would rather taste the enemy's blood than waste money on cosmetics. Her demeanor is neither retrograde nor traditionalistic, while her uniform signals a willingness to obey orders and sacrifice individual desires for the collective struggle. Akin to the ways in which the cc Clique embraced art deco as long as its meanings were channeled away from self-indulgent consumption, the NLM embraced fashion trends that could be safely disciplined and controlled.

While men were not singled out as problems to be fixed by the NLM with quite the same intensity, what modern and properly nationalistic masculinity entailed was certainly a concern, as it was for all fascist movements. The NLM embraced masculine sartorial and physical norms that had been developing since the end of the Qing. Guided by norms for modern soldiers, masculine prowess was associated with physical strength, soldierly neatness, and the readiness to fight and die for one's country.[90] Far from a traditional throwback, this masculinity bespoke accelerated historical change, providing a match and overcompensation for the approved new femininity. In *Mopping Up Thrice Monthly*'s NLM special issue, a contributor named Xia Hanhua criticized the present sickliness of Chinese bodies. Men needed to stop fearing the elements, overcome their cowardice and lack of discipline, and grasp the connections between bodily and national strength. Xia maintained, "If we turn the entire country into soldiers," people would fight on the front lines, "eliminate unequal treaties, turn a weak into a strong nation, and turn danger into peace."[91] The NLM's concern for fostering Confucian values allowed little room for the cultivated bookishness or disdain for manual labor expected of the classical Confucian scholar. Instead, movement materials constantly encouraged young men to take up productive and physically challenging work. Confucian masculinity in this rendering had little to do with command of written texts; factory workers were capable of exhibiting mastery by following shop floor instructions. This is illustrated in a *Future* cartoon in which a worker cleanses the "hearts/minds of the people" with fluid from a canister labeled li, yi, lian, chi.[92] As long as a manual laborer knew his place and kept himself tidy, his work was recognized as a noble and vital contribution to national regeneration.

In this sense, the NLM's sartorial preoccupations were as much about enabling authorities to readily identify who had conformed as about making the impoverished appear more pleasing to elite sensibilities. This took various forms in the NLM, from clarifying the sort of shoes that rickshaw drivers should wear to ensuring that students, soldiers, intellectuals, peasants, and workers outwardly distinguished themselves as such. Uniforms were not just tidy and modern styles of dress; they were also useful for fostering people's identification with their social role and for allowing authority figures to immediately know the kind of person they were dealing with. A 1934 editorial in *Cultural Construction*, "Students and Dancing," for instance, lamented the present difficulties of distinguishing students from run-of-the-mill degenerates. The nation, wrote the editors, was in crisis while loose living flourished. Students were supposed to be "model modern men and women" and were slated to become future national leaders.[93] Yet one frequently found students idling their time away in cabarets, billiard parlors, cafés, and movie theaters. Venues such as these offered opportunities for "obscene misconduct." Since most such places were in the foreign concessions and hence beyond Nanjing's jurisdiction, the editors believed that banning these activities outright was not the most expedient course of action. A more immediate solution was to require students to wear uniforms at all times, thereby outwardly distinguishing them as students. If they continued to dress like other patrons in Western clothes and leather shoes, there would be no way to tell if they were actually students and hold them accountable for their actions.[94] What this CC Clique editorial implied was that students, both male and female, should render themselves recognizably different from people whose cabaret patronage was of marginally less concern to Nanjing. Uniforms could render students more easily identified and disciplined, and also imbue them with a sense of themselves as future national leaders.

FIGURE 4.5 »
Hanxue zhoukan
(*Sweat and Blood*
Weekly) 8, no. 18
(1937).

The NLM, as Dirlik suggested, aimed to master unruly social developments. Its fascist champions sought to harness and delimit the meanings of popular trends like bobbed hair and physical fitness and to get out in front of class-conscious activity. They also sought to rationalize and coordinate practices on a national scale, accelerating the pace of change in places perceived to lag behind and remain in the grip of feudal ideologies. In the process, the NLM would teach everyone to perform their roles as instructed. Even if these roles were historically novel and enacted in new types of settings (the factory, the bus depot, the movie theater), the Confucian values by which they were animated rendered them familiar and historically continuous. Things had never been and could never be otherwise. Failing to abide by these values threatened the smooth functioning of the whole; consequences would be felt not merely by the individual and his or her family, but by the nation writ large, whose worldly survival now depended on a given person's precise performance of a specific part. The rewards of abiding by them would be equally tremendous. A 1937 cover of *Sweat and Blood Weekly*, published shortly before the fall of Nanjing to the Japanese army, shows an athletically built man (perhaps referencing the 1934 movie *The Highway* [*Da Lu*]) dressed only from the waist down in shorts worn by laborers during the hot summer months, poised on top of the world with chisel in hand, ready to sculpt a new future (fig. 4.5).[95] The vertical caption at left, which reads, "The path-breaking vanguard charts the road to rebirth," indicates that this male worker-sculptor is a collective subject that will lead the nation into a future of their own design. He has subjected himself to rigorous self-discipline and embodies a new masculinity; the rest of the nation had to follow accordingly and the future would be theirs.

Conclusion

Despite the fanfare with which the NLM was launched, it made little headway until Japan invaded in 1937, at which point its tenor became more ecumenically patriotic. Most of what the Blue Shirts and the CC Clique had originally hoped the movement would accomplish remained confined to paper. This chapter has highlighted what they wanted it to achieve rather than its concrete successes and failures in order to clarify the totalizing nature of fascist desires. Via the NLM, they articulated a program for wresting control of China's future from imperialist hands and outlined what they wanted their sovereign nation to look like. It was modern, Confucian, militantly ordered, and rigidly hierarchical. What appear on the surface to be bafflingly trivial concerns were understood by NLM promoters as ways of disciplining people for mechanized agricultural work and industrial production, of encouraging rationalized saving and spending habits, and of preparing the average citizen for war. Its relentless incantations of national unity and cohesion harbored distinct social hierarchies. Everyone would have a role and a purpose, but only a few would have a voice. The Confucianism celebrated by the NLM instructed people to mind their own places and defer to social superiors. Dai Jitao had implored the nation to follow

Sun Yat-sen's industrialization plan without germinating social diseases; the NLM would launch society on such a path, ensuring that nothing got out of hand. It would be set into motion and fixed into place at the same time.

As Chiang Kai-shek himself intimated, the NLM's militarist and collectivist injunctions could be discerned in other societies, particularly Fascist Italy, Nazi Germany, and Imperial Japan. In this respect, the NLM's self-presentation as adhering to a uniquely national Confucian cultural inheritance is belied by the global resonances of its concerns. This is not to suggest that the values NLM leaders invoked did not also have roots in the dynastic past, only that the elements of this heritage that did not accord with their ideas of a rationalized society were suppressed or ignored. The NLM's invocation of traditional values masked a profound reordering of the social world. As in a rationalized military or a Taylorized factory, commands were supposed to be relayed quickly from the top of society to the bottom. Although the NLM exhorted people to assume responsibility for their own behavior, it largely absolved people of responsibility. Reorganizing life as in the army prevented people from questioning orders given, as did insisting that authority figures had to be heeded at all costs.[96] Collapsing morality into efficiency and obedience left no room for morality to act as a check on abuses of power. And while the stated purpose of militarization was to unify society in a regimented fashion, it actually encouraged people to seek out power where they could find it and wield it against co-nationals. Although this kind of low-grade social destabilization might well have proven useful in terms of state management of society, it still ran up against fascists' professed desire for social concord on Confucian terms. Short of erasing all traces of human subjectivity, the socially leveling forces of industrial production that the NLM was supposed to foster would have expanded the objective grounds of popular claims to social equality. Only via endless state repression, which fascists were seemingly content to perpetuate, could the NLM's appeals to Confucian-grounded, cross-class cohesion, female-to-male subordination, and deference of social inferiors to superiors (like nonstudents to students) have been sustainable. The NLM's aspirations to mobile fixity, or of setting society in motion while fixing its actors into place, would have eventually run aground on its own tensions.

While the NLM focused on eliminating "formless banditry" once and for all, the Blue Shirts and CC Clique also turned their attention to artistic and literary endeavors. These complemented the NLM's attention to revitalizing thought and behavior by providing people with graspable models of what a regenerated person, nation, and world would actually look like. From the late 1920s onward, fascists had been concerned with excessive imperialist and Communist influence in what they called China's cultural enterprises, particularly in Shanghai. In chapter 5, I trace Blue Shirt and cc Clique efforts to bring these enterprises under state control. The terror that their agents waged against liberal and left-wing artists and writers during the Nanjing Decade was inseparably entwined with their own efforts to create a *minzu wenyi*, or properly nationalist literature and arts. Poetry, short stories, plays, and cinema were reconceptualized as armaments in a war for national rebirth.

5 » LITERATURE AND ARTS FOR THE NATION

In 1933, a contributor to *Sweat and Blood Weekly* parsed Nazi successes on the propaganda front. Nazi political strength could be attributed in part to the fact that they "deeply understand the psychology of the German people" and used "all manner of tactics to incite them to rise up."[1] They left nothing to chance. Even everyday consumer goods were plastered with slogans like "Followers of Marxism Have Already Reached Their Final Days!" The Nazis were seizing every opportunity to remind the people of their leaders' "correctness and greatness." Postcards of leaders like Adolf Hitler, Hermann Göring, and Joseph Goebbels circulated through German society, underscoring that "only the Nazi Party could lead the masses in recovering the native glory of the German nation of old." According to *Sweat and Blood Weekly*, the Nazis did not even have a propaganda bureau. Rather, Goebbels undertook the work himself, enlisting ordinary shopkeepers to circulate party ideas and making discipline perceptible via parades of soldiers marching through the streets in matching uniforms, singing party songs.

Nazis appeared to have already mastered what the Blue Shirt weekly called "the theatricality of propaganda."[2] They stayed abreast of new media, and with adroit use of the German language they recruited ordinary people to voice party ideas of their own accord and thereby actively participate in the construction of a new society.

Propaganda work had been taken seriously by Chinese Nationalists for many years by the time the Nazis took power in 1933. Its importance was solidified in Canton during the United Front and it remained a state priority throughout the Nanjing Decade. However, if the purpose of propaganda was to draw ever wider circles of people into the Nationalist project, Nazi successes on this front confirmed—at least to fascists within the Nationalist Party—that they themselves could be doing this work more effectively. As participants in the New Culture and May Fourth movements, and as heirs to a late Qing intellectual shift that had attributed to novelistic fiction an "unsurpassed capacity for mass education and spiritual cultivation," Nanjing Decade fascists regarded literature and the arts (wenyi)—which they invoked to designate everything from film to cartoons—as principal sites for the production and consolidation of new social meanings.[3] They invested this arena with an outsized capacity to do the work of organizing for them, particularly by imputing it with the power to draw in educated youth, who were seen as bridges to the worker and peasant masses.[4] In key respects, Chinese fascists shared the burgeoning voluntaristic belief of Chinese Marxists in the power of cultural works to moderate the pace of revolutionary change—speeding it up or slowing it down depending on the degree of progress or regress evidenced in a given work. Literature and the arts were instruments of propaganda to nestle party ideas in the crevices of everyday life; their messages needed to be clear and unambiguous lest target audiences fail to grasp their intended meanings.

In the wake of the GMD's January 1931 disappearance and execution of five leftist literary figures, the writer Lu Xun (who was by then a leader of the League of Left-Wing Writers [Zuoyi zuojia lianmeng], a CCP-backed organization founded in 1930) chided that the GMD's own artistic endeavors were sullied by the fact that they were spearheaded by "a member of the Shanghai Municipal Council and an inspector in the Secret Police, who are much more famous as 'liberators' [i.e., executioners] than as authors. If they were to write a *Methods of Murder* or *The Art of Detection*, they might find quite a few readers; but instead they will try to paint pictures and write poetry. This is as if Mr. Henry Ford in America stopped talking about cars and took up singing—people would be very surprised indeed."[5] Lu Xun understandably held the creative capacities of GMD militants in low esteem. It is, however, not surprising that they "took up singing." As we have already seen, they were not interested just in making cars and waging wars but especially in stoking affection for the nation and in rousing it to action. Literature and the arts were critical vehicles for disseminating their visions for national regeneration and rendering them collectively held. Although aspects of GMD literary and artistic initiatives can be understood as a reaction to those spearheaded by leftists, they must also be situated within a longer genealogy of Chinese efforts to create works that spoke to a postdynastic world, and within a global context of left- and right-wing revolutionary rejection of "art for art's sake."[6] It is doubtful, for instance, that Chen Guofu penned his science fiction short story "Newcomers" merely in reaction to the proliferation of "proletarian" (puluo) literature.[7] Stories like this 1930 tale—about a Nanjing man just returned via air from Liverpool who dreams about the laboratory generation of new human beings fifty years in the future—were yet other means by which GMD militants envisaged relations between modern technology and human bodies. Chen's story might not have met Lu Xun's exacting literary standards—or even the CC Clique's own strict prescriptions for minzu wenyi, as I discuss below—but the fact that Chen and his GMD comrades bothered writing stories at all suggests that they were trying to communicate sentiments and ideas inadequately captured by other forms, and that they had a specific understanding of how literature and arts operate in the world.

Dialogues concerning the power and purpose of literature and arts that took place in CC Clique and Blue Shirt circles during the Nanjing Decade pivoted around several key questions. What forms and contents could properly represent the national-revolutionary subject? In what ways could these effectively prod the people presumed to constitute this subject in a sanctioned direction? How best to convey the nation's evolution from the glorious past through the muck of the present into a renewed future? Guomindang militants also directly and indirectly grappled with challenges of inspiring the nation's varied social strata, from "foreknower" elites like themselves to the middling level of "after-knowers" to the broad masses of "ignorant and unconscious." What modes of address were suitable for whom? If a key modernist conundrum entailed finding "a balance between making demands of one's viewers" or readers "and leaving them completely behind," the tensions within fascist ideology between elitism and populism, and between creating the new and restoring the ancient, rendered such balance impossible if not ultimately undesirable.[8] From a fascist perspective, art and literature that the masses could readily appreciate in their present state of being would fail to inspire them to strive forward and would hence fail as propaganda. A leveled field of cultural consumption, moreover, might also imply to the ignorant and unconscious that their capacities for aesthetic appreciation were equal to those of foreknowers, thus eroding a basis of the latter's claims to leadership within the national frame. However, what would it mean for the GMD's insistence on national-cultural uniformity if stratifications were acknowledged? Their tradition-honoring claims were already strained by the fact that neither the Blue Shirts nor the CC Clique considered received dynastic forms like opera or ink-and-brush painting to be adequate for conveying the dynamisms of modern life. New media like film and radio, they believed—manifestly nonnative technologies that were still shockingly unfamiliar to much of the population—were far more useful and intrinsically appealing. Additional time and political strength might have papered over the tensions between estrangement and familiarity, rupture and continuity apparent in the creative endeavors of GMD fascists, as they did for more successful fascist movements. In Italy, Jeffrey T. Schnapp observed, fascists managed to generate a kind of "aesthetic *overproduction*—a surfeit of fascist signs, images, slogans, books, and buildings—in order to compensate for, fill in, and cover up [fascism's] unstable ideological core."[9] Successfully bombarding Chinese citizens with whatever state officials deemed to be properly nationalistic might have rendered mixed messages irrelevant. As it was, by the time the Nanjing regime was forcibly relocated by invading Japanese troops in 1937, the impressive volume of material produced in the vein of minzu wenyi hardly succeeded in crowding out other claims to popular attention, let alone overwhelming it. The Blue Shirts and CC Clique did, nevertheless, try.

This final chapter proceeds in two parts. The first examines what Blue Shirt and CC Clique thinkers meant when they invoked "nationalist literature and arts," as well as the conundrums that they faced in professing affinities for the visual and linguistic signs of industrial modernity while also professing commitments to preserving the native culture that industrial modernity (in its colonial guise) and the Communists were bent on relegating to the historical dustbin. Here, I spotlight Chen Lifu's 1933 booklet *The Chinese Film Industry*.[10] Chen's appreciation for film constitutes a striking example of the fascist belief that properly nationalistic arts were supposed to be faithful to the national spirit rather than to any specific dynastic inheritance. Its contents and forms were at the discretion of the requisite authorities; its purpose was to point the way to a regenerated national future. Just as the interpretive ambiguities of mass (*dazhong*) literature and arts were not officially ironed out until Mao Zedong weighed in on the matter with his 1942 Yan'an Talks, those pertaining to nationalist endeavors were not officially settled until 1936, when the CC Clique succeeded in getting a high-level state organ called the Cultural Enterprise Planning Committee off the ground. The outbreak of war with Japan meant that this committee soon became something other than envisioned, however, and the party line quickly frayed again.

In the second part of this chapter, I examine the violence with which the project to create properly nationalist literature and arts was entwined. From many angles, GMD contributions to the arts during the Nanjing Decade were wholly negative, and they seem to have compensated for the irresolvable tensions in their program by lashing out violently against their critics. They murdered leading intellectuals of the opposition, and their cultural encirclement tactics doubtless contributed, in the longer term, to the CCP's tightening of restrictions on its own cultural workers. When Mao Zedong remarked in 1940 that the Nationalists had waged two kinds of encirclement and suppression campaigns against the CCP, one military and the other cultural, he acknowledged the force of their pressure.[11] Still, Blue Shirt and CC Clique adherents understood the terror they waged to be a positive contribution to revolutionary progress and to the creation of a new national aesthetic. In particular, targeted attacks on men and women affiliated with the Shanghai-based League of Left-Wing Writers and the China League for Civil Rights (the coalition of liberals and nonaligned leftists established in 1932 to fight for freedoms of expression and the release of Nanjing's political prisoners) swiftly removed recalcitrant obstacles. It was enraging to them that "decadent," "proletarian," and "art for art's sake" works continued to proliferate in areas under Nanjing's jurisdiction, and that Nanjing lacked sovereign authority to regulate materials, especially Hollywood films, that circulated through the colonial concessions. This seemed to simultaneously mock their own authority and block the masses from perceiving the same regenerated future that they themselves saw. Attacking writers and artists cut out the sluggish middlemen of state censorship and negotiations over the unequal treaties; it efficiently removed deleterious influences from society and sped up the pace of change. Blue

Shirt and CC Clique conviction that a healthy polity could not tolerate the presence of people who produced disagreeable works, and that such works were harmful in their own right, implied that the bulk of the Chinese population was a blank, impressionable slate. Hollywood films begat citizens bereft of national-cultural pride; proletarian literature begat class-conscious activists; and most people were unlearned enough to act upon received information in exactly the manner dictated by the work or artist in question. If only the path were cleared for nationalist literature and art to exert its powers, this mass of "loose sand" (as Sun Yat-sen had termed the disunited Chinese populace) could be sculpted into a beautiful whole.

In early 1931, just as the Five Martyrs were imprisoned and executed, Chen Lifu addressed a banquet on the topic of "China's Literary and Artistic Renaissance Movement." Chen observed, "In recent years, what we have seen in China's art and literary circles are cruelty, meanness, pessimism, dispiritedness, and the din of sloganeering. . . . Comrades, storms change in an instant; it is always darkest before the dawn. The opportunity for China's literary and artistic renaissance has already presented itself to us. Let us work harder!"[12] The darkness to which Chen referred was that of an art and literary world still corrupted by leftism and imperialism. He and his comrades believed that they were poised to remake the world; art and literature was supposed to point the way to a brightened future. Works produced in the vein of minzu wenyi certainly deserve their own close literary analyses. This task has been pursued by scholars including Ni Wei and Zhang Daming and still awaits others.[13] Here, I focus on the violence that attended the production of such works. Extrapolated from context, many of the poems, stories, and plays produced in this vein might strike present-day readers as saccharine or even as progressive expressions of patriotism. The future society that nationalist literature and arts sought to disclose and consolidate, however, was far from anodyne.

Scripting the Collective Voice

Rendering the nation sensible as a historical agent and as an object of devotion was a problem that had long confronted nationalists in China and around the world. How to represent the nation, with its great diversity, as a singular unity? How might this nation effectively take shape in the minds of the people and prompt in them senses of belonging and devotion?[14] Challenged in the late 1920s and early 1930s by the increasingly salient left-wing concepts of proletarian and mass literature and art, fascists redoubled their efforts to supply their creative endeavors with coherent meaning and compelling forms. Both the Blue Shirts and the CC Clique understood themselves to be engaged in an uphill battle against Communist literary endeavors, imperialist smut, commercialist distractions, and even the inertia of other Nationalists on this front. Yet by any measure the existence of state censorship laws gave them distinct advantages, which were reinforced by the fact that their publications and cultural organizations could operate openly and secure state funding.[15] Left-wing writers, for their part, expressed concern over the progress the GMD was actually making. A pseudonymously published 1931 contribution to the League of Left-Wing Writers' flagship journal *Dazhong wenyi* (*Mass Literature and Arts*), for instance, noted the efficacy of the GMD's dissemination of wall posters, cartoons, short fiction, and popular songs aiming for mass appeal.[16] The GMD's Central Propaganda Bureau, under veteran revolutionary Ye Chucang and with Chen Lifu's cooperation, had indeed been promoting Three Principles of the People literature and arts since 1929. Sponsored publications and related societies pushed the idea that, because China did not have a clear-cut bourgeoisie or proletariat, it was wrong for creative works to highlight the travails of a particular class.[17] After 1930, the CC Clique and soon the Blue Shirts began to champion what they considered to be the more formidable concept of *minzu* (national) literature and arts.[18] That the nation was grounded in and animated by the Three Principles of the People was taken for granted by this point; renaming their project to speak to and for the nation signaled a grander world-historical mission and sense of oppositions.

Despite the ground gained by these initiatives, rage spilled out of the pages of Blue Shirt magazines regarding the inadequacy of state efforts to enforce clear cultural policies and to eradicate the art and literary endeavors of their political enemies.[19] In addition to those of the CCP, Blue Shirts saw decadence and degeneracy proliferating all around them—evidenced, they insisted, by brazen public displays of women's breasts and thighs. Treaty port entertainments like movies and cabarets continued to harm "the life of the nation."[20] Nefarious forces appeared to be entrenched and organized in ways that cultural vices had not been historically, requiring more forceful counterattacks. This, they believed, entailed establishing all-powerful propaganda organs, operating with common principles, pushing a "total mobilization for a new cultural movement" that valorized nation and state above all. Blue Shirts suggested measures like planting cultural cells among the masses, closing decadent schools, and vetting teachers for nationalist sentiments. They themselves had to muster a "sacrificial resolve to shed blood" and commit to using "unprecedented violence" to destroy national enemies.[21] Violence, in this view, was cleansing, and literature and the arts key weapons in the larger struggle.

That literature and arts necessarily had political valences echoed core assumptions of left- and right-wing revolutionary movements across the globe in the interwar years. It also echoed an intellectual tendency that historian Hsiao-t'i Li has seen developing in China from the late Qing onward, which involved conceptualizing culture (particularly that produced and consumed by nonelites) as either accelerating or retarding social change.[22] In 1930s Blue Shirt eyes, people who insisted upon artistic autonomy merely reaffirmed the bourgeois nature of their politics and failed to recognize their dependency upon the market.[23] Nothing was neutral or potentially divorced from the revolutionary process. Literature in particular was supposed to be forward striving and for the nation; pens were to be "wielded like swords."[24] Echoing the delight taken by F. T. Marinetti's 1909 *Futurist Manifesto* in the cleansing properties of violence—a tract that had been translated into Chinese by 1921—pens were likewise to be used like bombs "to blow the old society to bits." They were supposed to chart the direction in which society should change. Blue Shirts expressed paranoiac concern that most pens in China continued to "drip poison" by promoting "feudal, romantic and decadent thinking." They called on their comrades: "Use our bombs to eradicate such pens from existence, and then begin our work of whipping society into shape."[25] But the question of what constituted properly politicized, nationalistic contents and forms—and how these could actually help mold undisciplined masses into a formidably united whole—of course had no predetermined answer. It could be settled only by consensus or fiat, and fascists worked toward both over the course of the Nanjing Decade.

Answers proposed by Blue Shirt and cc Clique activists indicate that both groups were more interested in old wine (contents) than old bottles (forms). Even time-honored tales had to be altered to speak to modern problems like national mobilization against imperialist enemies—for instance a tale of the twelfth-century Han loyalist Yue Fei was turned into a serialized play distributed in a cc Clique weekly and "solemnly dedicated to the loyal and gallant officers and men resisting Japan"—inevitably changing inherited story lines in the process.[26] Stories of historical heroes like Yue Fei would ideally enjoy modernized and technologically sophisticated modes of conveyance in addition to addressing contemporary crises. In this sense, nationalistic literature and arts had to stake a positive claim to the symbols of industrial modernity, foreground people and things that seemed to signify the national collective, and demonstrate a resolute orientation toward a brighter future.

Meditating on the difficulties of "Establishing a Nationalist Literature" for *Mopping Up Thrice Monthly*, frequent contributor Xiang Ziyu settled on a definition of literature that he attributed to the Nationalist-affiliated liberal educator Luo Jialun: "Literature is something which critiques life, creates life, and idealizes life; it has feelings, it has thought, it has imagination. Using words as tools and according with artistic forms, it is something which can stir people to understanding."[27] Their revolutionary era demanded a kind of writing that motivated people to strive forward. Xiang emphasized that "all literature is propaganda," a weapon of struggle to be used for the creation of new life for the nation. As Sun Yat-sen had instructed them, the nation is "forged from natural forces," of which the most important "is blood; the second is life; the third is language; the fourth is religion; the fifth is habits and customs."[28] Literature's purpose was to "repel all thinking which hinders the nation's advance and its will to develop progressively and at the same time reveal all aspects of the nation's own glorious history."[29] Subjects that should be written about, Xiang suggested, included the nation's morality and dignity, its "spirit of ardor, fairness, diligence, and peace," good customs and habits, and historical heroes and martyrs, as well as great scholars and entrepreneurs. Writers should also expose evils of imperialism, warlords, red bandits, compradors, corrupt bureaucrats, local bullies and evil gentry, romanticism, decadence, and leisureliness.[30] While doing so, they should promote the Three Principles of the People, interclass harmony, industrial development, and science against superstition. In short, nationalist literature was to divulge the nation's collective historical formation, the forces that presently endangered it, and the ways in which the nation could achieve a renewed future together.

As among writers on the left, some on the far right vaunted realism as a favored form in which to present such ideas. This was in part due to realism's perceived capacity to objectively disclose social problems. It also involved staking a claim to a form that had historically emerged as authoritative with respect to revolutionary truth, not least because it helped to demarcate what should be considered part of reality and within the horizon of the possible. Literary scholar Marston Anderson has written that despite or perhaps because of the varied meanings with which the term *realism* was invested, in the wake of the May Fourth Movement it had come "to carry the profoundest burden of hope for cultural transformation."[31] In Xiang Ziyu's understanding, "realism is characterized by a scientific attitude and an emphasis on the problems of human life. It doesn't need fantasies; it doesn't need ornament; it has no romantic attitude of play; and it does not need to deliberately innovate. It just involves plain old, natural description and objective narration. It is a reflection of human life."[32] Though Xiang noted the utility for nationalistic literature of romanticism's stress on emotional exertion—"subjective feelings and reasonable resistance are both necessary," he observed—we can understand his expressed preference for realism, with its rejection of ornament and distraction, as in keeping with the Blue Shirts' broader political and aesthetic interests in stream-lined efficiency. Stripped of unnecessary diversions and fantastical details, literature (and art) would straightforwardly present scenarios of national significance, erasing ambiguities and spurring readers to act in accordingly controlled ways.

Still, Xiang's populist advocacy of "plain old, natural description" be-trayed an assumption that the majority of Chinese readers (or listeners) would readily recognize such a narrative form, which departed from re-ceived modes of popular storytelling, as a "reflection of human life." Did Xiang believe that the bulk of China's population would find what he termed "objective narration" to be resonant and persuasive? Or did he as-sume that they would have to be educated to become the sort of people who did? Though the answer was likely the latter, Xiang's lack of clarity on this matter bespeaks the broader problem that China's fascists faced in denying the salience of class stratifications and insisting that the nation already had a singular identifiable culture, as this ran quickly aground on problems of illiteracy and uneven social development. Blue Shirt and CC Clique theo-rists were largely beholden to the idea that the "ignorant and unconscious" needed to be at least marginally educated out of their benightedness—a stance indebted as much to Lenin as to an inherited Confucian elitism. The Blue Shirt newspaper *Society Mercury*, for instance, suggested that a power-ful state cultural committee should mandate that all organizations "adopt an open attitude which is easy for the masses to understand and to facili-tate opportunities for their participation."[33] The paper further argued that "cultural vitality must penetrate to every level" of society, that party cadres "must use cultural tools to better connect with the masses, and build close relations between the party and the people," and noted that if "upper-strata cultural organizations do not exert tight control, then organizing the lower strata will never succeed."[34] This constituted an acknowledgment of the organizing work ahead of them and of the top-down nature of their project to rectify "the low cultural level of the Chinese masses."[35] It also constituted de facto recognition that some groups within society were more firmly in possession of an ostensibly all-national culture than others.

Though their enemies on the left were simultaneously grappling with an intersecting set of problems, it is important to recognize that fascists compounded theirs by insisting that cross-class, interregional cultural unity both preceded and surmounted all extant social differences. Subjective feelings of cohesion and loyalty were more important than objective social equality. The point was to bind social inferiors and superiors together into a synchronized whole. Participants in the League of Left-Wing Writers were, by contrast, at the same time debating the audience and intelligibility of mass literature and arts with the intent to eliminate objective social inequalities.[36] To be sure, many participants in these left-wing debates were also beholden to Leninist ideas of cultural uplift, maintaining that progress toward socialism required educating people, particularly the peasantry, out of their received, backward beliefs. A few, like the Communist organizer and cultural theorist Qu Qiubai—killed in a GMD prison in 1935—were instead contributing to what would become known as the Maoist "mass line" by envisioning ways in which creative works could be scripted in a new, egalitarian language cogenerated by cadres and masses themselves, thereby pushing both to higher levels of consciousness and equality.[37] The goal for fascists was not equality but a kind of stratified national sameness, in which elites and masses felt as one and joined together in a common struggle. The purpose of national literature and arts was to effect a change in attitudes and perceptions, affectively binding the nation together. *Mopping Up Thrice Monthly* explained how nationalist literature would speak for everyone who had been massacred, trampled upon, and oppressed by imperialism, everyone who "had been massacred, oppressed, and lied to by the red bandits," everyone who had been oppressed by warlords, bureaucrats, compradors, and evil gentry. It would also speak for the unemployed and everyone who "has lost their country."[38] Everyone would speak with one voice, though the power to identify grievances would come from above and be ventriloquized from below.

With this in mind, we can better understand the expressed interest of both the CC Clique and the Blue Shirts in media that could circumvent problems of illiteracy and also bridge without actually eliminating class divides. As critics around the world were then observing, film was a particularly potent medium for seducing broad audiences and manufacturing collective sentiments. It had energizing and anesthetizing capacities in equal measure. Film's political instrumentality was widely recognized but, apart from inescapably affirming the new, the direction of its politics was not fixed, as the coexistence of films like D. W. Griffith's *The Birth of a Nation* (1915), Sergei Eisenstein's *October* (1928), and, by 1935, Leni Riefenstahl's *Triumph of the Will* attested. In *The Chinese Film Industry*, Chen Lifu parsed its potential to showcase the developmental power of the new Nationalist state and to interpellate audiences more efficiently than any medium history had yet generated. It was a technological marvel that, more directly than popular styles of singing or oral storytelling, could skirt problems of illiteracy and smooth over regional differences. It took tremendous capital and technological expertise to make a film but very little to enjoy one. Despite or perhaps because of its inescapably modern vintage and how readily social hierarchies disappeared behind the screen, cinema was considered ideal for rendering the nation broadly sensible and widely appreciated.

Historian Anson Rabinbach has written of how Nazi Germany's Beauty of Labor organization strove to "objectify the image of community in the external forms of the German industrial landscape." Aesthetic improvements including pastoral scenes painted on the walls of factories would ostensibly help "reconstitute the soul of the German worker" by providing them with images of themselves valued, nurtured, and in harmony with nature even as they became more deeply subjected to the alienating forces of industrial production.[39] In 1933, Chen Lifu wrote of film's capacity to overcome China's national alienation by presenting Chinese audiences with images of themselves hitherto denied by imperialist domination of China's silver screens. While Shanghai filmgoers protested against the screening of racist Hollywood films like *Welcome, Danger!* (dir. Clyde Bruckman, 1929, set in San Francisco's Chinatown), Chen argued that Chinese-made movies should present Chinese history and scenarios to Chinese audiences.[40] But unlike the martial arts and fairytale films churned out by the indigenous studio system at the time—which Chen acknowledged competed admirably with higher-budget and technically savvy foreign imports—the cinema that Chen envisioned would present realistic, nationalistic, and spiritually uplifting stories. He also wanted to produce newsreels to publicize state-sponsored reconstruction efforts, particularly those that required massive coordination and labor participation. Successfully harnessing this relatively new medium would enable fellow nationals to sensorily experience their connections to one another and to visualize the nation's past, present, and future precisely as the CC Clique wanted.

In *The Chinese Film Industry*, Chen Lifu expounded on ways in which film could advance the revolution. Foreign films that currently dominated China's silver screens accentuated socioeconomic differences between China and industrialized countries, but if the Nationalists could harness its power for themselves it could help surmount China's backwardness. Such foreign domination had material consequences for Chinese filmmakers as well as spiritual consequences for Chinese audiences, who were inundated by alien scenarios and denied images familiar to their own life experiences.[41] The Hollywood films that flooded Chinese screens were filled with glamour and overt sexuality. Screening such films made local audiences acutely conscious "of China's poverty and ruin; it discourages them and saps their courage to strive forward."[42] Although Chinese filmmakers recognized the material stakes of importing films from abroad, Chen doubted that they understood their spiritual toll. This was evidenced by the fact that Chinese studios, in order to turn a profit under such adverse circumstances, churned out films that appealed to the "basest of tastes," peddling licentiousness, depravity, and superstition.[43] Films like the 1928 martial arts movie *The Burning of the Red Lotus Temple* "influence[d] and lie[d] to the masses" and had deleterious effects on social morality. Chen called upon the industry to instead produce films that could "raise [popular] tastes" and respect "China's historical spirit, be appropriate to the Chinese environment, and satisfy modern Chinese needs."[44]

Paramount among these was for audiences to absorb images of the nation's glorious past, present, and future; for film to "dramatize the process of nationalist revolution."[45] "Films must not only satisfy people's senses of sight and sound," Chen argued; "they must also move the people's mind-spirit, stimulate their morality and wisdom, spur them to improve their behavior, and increase their knowledge."[46] This entailed showcasing the differences between Eastern and Western civilizations as well as China's national uniqueness.[47] Paraphrasing Sun Yat-sen on the importance of countering the foreign influences of the New Culture Movement, Chen argued that film should make "China's native old morality"—values of loyalty and filial piety, benevolence, good faith, and peacefulness—"manifest before the eyes of the audience, bolstering their beliefs, stirring their adoration, and providing them with direction."[48] As the Blue Shirt Xiang Ziyu suggested for literature, Chen argued that films should tell stories about the nation's ancient politicians, thinkers, engineers, and inventors. Chen stressed how their own ancestors had invented gunpowder, the compass, paper, and printed books. They had engineered the Great Wall and the Grand Canal, and had proved themselves masters of statecraft, science, medicine, and philosophy. They had, moreover, successfully employed propaganda to resist invasions by alien races.[49] China's filmmakers should turn their attention away from the "dull and frivolous activities of the leisure class" and away from its cities, which Chen characterized as "truly cesspools of evil, in which all manner of vile habits proliferate."[50] This, he insisted, would constitute a great boon for the Nationalist state.[51] What Chen suggested film studios do of their own accord was similar to what *Sweat and Blood Weekly* believed Joseph Goebbels had enlisted ordinary German shopkeepers to do: render party-state goals part of the fabric of everyday life. More efficiently and effectively than matchbooks and postcards, films would prompt Chinese people to feel at one with their conationals and grasp the importance of their own participation in national regeneration.

As with his nativist, Sunist developmentalism more generally, the cooperative effort that Chen Lifu wanted film to inspire harbored distinct social hierarchies. Newsreels propagating state reconstruction efforts, Chen suggested, could help mitigate "bad habits of laziness, increase the enjoyment [that people] feel in productive labor, and give them bodily experience of the construction of a new country."[52] Although the population writ large needed to acquire a higher level of scientific knowledge, Chen noted that only a select few would actually proceed to become scientists, devoting their minds to "great causes" and other things that "the masses need [not] appreciate."[53] Because the average person did not have time to study science, Chen wrote, "we can select materials for them, edit them into scripts, capture them on camera, edit this into movies, present them everywhere and allow the masses amid their enjoyment to absorb into their lives beneficial experiences and knowledge."[54] So powerful was this new technology that it could facilitate the enlightenment of "this mass of ignorant people" who did "not yet even clearly know themselves."[55] Limited electrification was a stumbling block, but film itself could broaden popular appreciation of electricity, as well as of machinery and how it is used.[56] Although film could not "rectify the chaos of modern China" of its own accord, Chen made a strong case for its value in raising educational levels just enough to make widescale industrialization possible, and to spur people to perform new kinds of labor without seeking to alter social relations or improve their conditions of labor in any unauthorized way. Perhaps most importantly, it could kindle patriotic love such that people enjoyed sacrificing themselves for the larger whole. The Nationalist revolution, Dai Jitao had earlier insisted, embraced "beautiful and elegant enjoyment," something that was categorically denied by Communism.[57] Their own revolution promised pleasure and happiness, and to make the nation a place of comfort once again.

Against the ruins into which China's dynastic system had crumbled, Chen Lifu wanted to make a version of it known and appreciated. His concern to tell its stories, via film among other media, was not merely a countermeasure against Communist cultural initiatives but also stemmed from an abiding patriotism. These sentiments took their place among what Prasenjit Duara identified as longer-germinating efforts to "[secure] for the contested and contingent nation the false unity of a self-same, national subject evolving through time."[58] What the CC Clique, and also the Blue Shirts, had in mind for a properly nationalist literature and art was for it to be faithful not to any specific dynastic inheritance or school of thought, but instead to the national spirit. It was to disclose the evolution and progressive striving of this spirit. The forms and media via which its stories were recounted did not have to be rooted in recognizably indigenous traditions. Among other things, this rendered the foreign origins of a technology like film irrelevant to considerations of its utility and import; in fact film could be seen as seamlessly merging with a native tradition of technology production and appreciation. Abiding by the national spirit enabled fascists to conjure away inconsistencies of simultaneously proclaiming themselves defenders of tradition and pioneers of the new.

Tellingly, pictures and fictional writings that circulated in their own magazines did not necessarily reflect the strict chasteness and didactic clarity that they demanded for others. This was perhaps hypocritical on their part, but it is also intelligible in terms of the competing vectors of elitism and populism in fascist politics.[59] Works that they produced for their own consumption could continue to be politically ambiguous or aesthetically estranging, as this could serve to bolster their own self-conceptions as vanguards and avant-gardes whose thinking was already correct and thus could handle things like satire, nuance, and challenge. They did not have to always be broadly intelligible, as they were only interested in narrowing the gap between leaders and led in certain ways and in certain contexts. This helps to explain why affected folkishness and dramatic experimentation mingled comfortably in the pages of their magazines, and why their own works (such as the ambiguous short story "Newcomers" by Chen Guofu) did not always adhere to the rigorous line that they prescribed for nationalist literature and arts. Although both the cc Clique and the Blue Shirts vociferously denounced the smut on display in the treaty ports, Blue Shirt magazine covers in particular frequently reproduced as critique or satire precisely the kind of images that they verbally railed against. Examples include a *Sweat and Blood Weekly* cover criticizing the manner in which Chinese men sacrificed themselves to the lustful temptations of Western imperialism—visualized here as a capitalist hanging on a cross formed by the naked body of a fair-haired woman (fig. 5.1).[60] It is also evident in a *Society Mercury* cover of a voluptuous blonde (perhaps White Russian) fan dancer performing for imperialists and fat-cat mandarins (fig. 5.2), and another of a dapperly dressed man down on his luck with the lottery slumped in front of a sexually suggestive foreign movie poster and the closed art deco doors of a movie theater (fig. 5.3).[61] Even more strikingly, the fact that they granted themselves license to enjoy images that they deemed unhealthy for others and otherwise denounced as signs of generalized Communist and treaty port debauchery is evidenced in a *Sweat and Blood Weekly* trapeze artist cover photo, which seems to serve little purpose other than titillation (fig. 5.4). Such covers suggest that they trusted themselves to read images like these in ways that did not compromise their dedication to national regeneration. They are perhaps less indicative of the failure of Blue Shirts to be proper fascists than of tensions within fascism itself. Fascists may insist that the nation share one heart and one voice, but they can always make exceptions for themselves. A unified aesthetic was, moreover, something that required a kind of discipline and state coordination toward which they aspired but did not manage to achieve.

From this brief sketch of Blue Shirt and cc Clique ideas about the proper direction of nationalist literature and arts, it is apparent that many of the subjects that they deemed suitable for popular consumption could be readily found in works generated in contemporaneous liberal polities. Movies

FIGURE 5.1 » *Hanxue zhoukan* (*Sweat and Blood Weekly*) 1, no. 10 (1933).

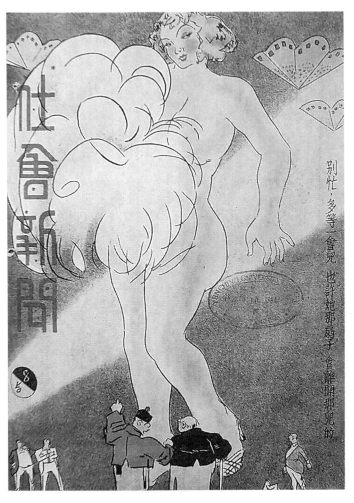

FIGURE 5.2 » *Shehui xinwen (Society Mercury)* 8, no. 5 (1934): back cover.

FIGURE 5.3 » *Shehui xinwen (Society Mercury)* 8, no. 6 (1934): back cover.

FIGURE 5.4 » *Hanxue zhoukan* (*Sweat and Blood Weekly*) 5, no. 7 (1935).

celebrating family values, the deeds of great men, and nationalistic sacrifice would have passed through Hollywood's Production Code, as long as the heroic roles were written for white people. It is, therefore, important to not extrapolate the kinds of creative works that Chinese fascists promoted from their context of production. It is difficult to discern a distinctly fascist aesthetic in Nanjing Decade China, to the extent that one existed anywhere. The political valences of minzu wenyi are instead discernible in relation to the actions and aspirations with and for which it was generated. Works of nationalist literature and arts were, on the one hand, to be strictly prescribed by the state and produced to the exclusion of everything else. On the other, the Blue Shirts and CC Clique killed and terrorized people who produced works that did not accord with their understandings of what literature and arts should do. This terror revealed the depth of their assumptions regarding elite cultural influence on impressionable masses and their confidence that violent direct action could accelerate the pace of national consolidation.

Removing Obstacles and Sculpting Loose Sand

Attacks on left-wing cultural elites—including the execution of the Five Martyrs in 1931, the 1933 kidnapping of the writer Ding Ling, the subsequent assassination of League for Civil Rights director Yang Xingfo after publicizing her disappearance, and the 1934 murder of the *Shenbao*'s Shi Liangcai for, among other things, criticizing the assassination of Yang—garnered negative domestic and international attention for the Nanjing regime. Blue Shirt and CC Clique agents waged this terror while other Nationalist officials, including those with the Ministry of Foreign Affairs, worked to overturn the unequal treaties. Since overturning the treaties required evidence that the Nationalist government had a modernized legal system to which imperialists would be willing to subject themselves, kidnapping and assassinating citizens (non-Communists at least) was undermining the regime's credibility in significant ways. Chiang Kai-shek, who as a head of state straddled the worlds of the Ministry of Foreign Affairs and the party's fascist organizations, would certainly have been aware of the cross purposes at which their respective endeavors were working. Terror attacks nevertheless proceeded apace. Though it is possible to interpret this terror as indicative of insufficiently modernized mentalities and a lack of understanding of the democratic procedures by which other members of the Nanjing regime were trying to operate, it is more apt to interpret it as stemming from a belief in its efficiency and efficacy. Some, like the Blue Shirt Dai Li, who has been described as a "sadist addicted to killing," also evidently enjoyed it.[62] Not unlike their contemporaries Adolf Hitler and Benito Mussolini, who regarded themselves as artists charged with reworking the raw material of the masses, China's fascists understood themselves to have inherited Liang Qichao's late Qing call to "make the people new."[63] The Nationalists' particular historical problem was that, despite having achieved state power, they did not yet have what they imagined to be unobstructed access to said people. Obstacles including opposition artists, writers, and journalists, as well as civil rights campaigners who emerged to defend them, continued to flout Nanjing's laws and block their capacity to sculpt the national people into a singular mass.

When, as discussed in chapter 1, Dai Jitao visited Song Qingling's French Concession home in 1929, he had insinuated that her criticism of the Nanjing government was aiding and abetting the Communists. Although Dai's accusation collapsed varied strains of political activism into an all-encompassing Communist menace, it was partially grounded in the fact that GMD terror had been driving non-Communist leftists and even self-identified liberals further leftward, or at least into alliances in keeping with the global rise of an antifascist Popular Front. Men like Dai Jitao did not see these alliances as forming because of the state's repressive tactics. Rather, they perceived groups like the League of Left-Wing Writers and the China League for Civil Rights as products of the CCP's omnipresence and general nefariousness. Alternately, they perceived emergent liberal discourses of civil rights and press freedoms as coconspirators with red imperialism, working in tandem to sabotage the state and erode the nation's unity. Either way, by the early 1930s prominent non-Communists like civil rights campaigner Yang Xingfo and *Shenbao* managing editor Shi Liangcai became caught in their crosshairs, while names including Lu Xun and *Eastern Miscellany* editor Hu Yuzhi appeared on a long list of Blue Shirt assassination targets.[64] In good paranoid fashion, dissent of any kind suggested conspiracy that served to drive the GMD farther away from the masses.

In this vein, fascists feared the Communist Party was pressuring non-aligned artists and writers into joining the CCP's cause and thereby expanding its own sway over said masses. The CC Clique's Xu Enceng was under the impression that by the early 1930s the CCP was actively coercing skeptics into their ranks of cultural workers.[65] After the CCP had been forced underground in 1927, Xu observed, it had followed the precedent set by centuries of literati social leadership and established cultural groups to continue its organizing work. Its epicenter was Shanghai's League of Left-Wing Writers. They employed all manner of tactics to force non-Communist writers to join them, such as preventing the latter from finding publishing outlets for their work unless they supported the Communist cause. To Xu, the writer Lu Xun was a case in point.[66] Lu Xun, he believed, had been pressured by the American leftist Agnes Smedley into joining the League of Left-Wing Writers despite his obvious disdain for Communism. By exerting such pressure, the CCP swiftly "occupied several of Shanghai's most important cultural camps, including newspaper supplements, bookstores, and newspaper editorships." Activists in the CCP, Xu insisted, also penned articles in other people's names, including social commentary in the *Shenbao*. Xu's fears resonated with those of the Blue Shirts, who characterized the CCP as a kind of hydra whose cultural heads continually regenerated after severing. A *Socialism Monthly* piece, "Past and Present of Left-Wing Cultural Movements," maintained that all left-wing cultural organizations, regardless of what they called themselves, were under the control of the Communist Party.[67] Even in the face of repression its partisans had formed and reformed organizations such as the Creation Society, the Proletarian Poetry Alliance, the Left-Wing Playwrights Association, the League of Left-Wing Writers, and the General Left-Wing Cultural Alliance.[68] *Society Mercury*, meanwhile, complained, "Although [the left] has been severely repressed on all fronts and is internally divided, it is nevertheless slowly rising again."[69] The author feared that even historically moderate magazines like the *Eastern Miscellany* were veering leftward, while *Shenbao*'s "Ziyoutan" (Free Talk) supplement was "now under the control of the League of Left-Wing Writers," as were a number of other smaller publishing houses.[70] Despite their own efforts to counterbalance left-wing cultural activism by founding competing magazines, the influence of the right remained slight by comparison.[71] This was not due to any innate appeal of left-wing ideas, they insisted, but rather to the fact that the Nationalists were not striking back hard enough against nefarious forces.

While the entire point of producing "nationalist literature and arts" was to help rectify this situation, it was clear that they would get nowhere without taking direct action. Targeted force would accelerate the glacial temporality of creating new works of art and literature, forming state committees to sponsor them, banning undesirable publications, and eventually securing a monopoly on mass attention. A 1933 front-page *Society Mercury* story noted that the Nazis were "burning and proscribing communist books and periodicals," stressing that the "chaos in China is a thousand times greater than it was in Germany [before the Nazis took power]." The lesson here was to follow Nazi initiative and destroy Communist literature, and likewise to learn from the example set by China's first emperor, Qin Shi Huang, in his draconian approach to both books and scholars—his reputation as a ruthless tyrant here apparently trumped the fact that he victimized Confucians. "We must eradicate all periodicals that damage the minds and bodies of the young, and strike against all disloyal movements. . . . Indeed, while China remains mired in chaos it makes one yearn for the salvation that Germany has attained."[72] Blue Shirts took the Nazis' theatrical destruction of books and bodies to heart, as these actions seemingly affirmed the efficacy of such measures in clearing the slate for the new.

Lu Xun, for his part, seemed to give GMD militants more credit than they gave themselves for the effectiveness of their destructive endeavors. "In November 1933," wrote Lu Xun, "the Yihua Film Company in Shanghai was suddenly attacked by a band of men and left in utter shambles. The attackers were well organized. When a whistle blew, they set to work; when another whistle blew, they stopped and scattered."[73] The assailants, the writer noted, took care to leave pamphlets explaining that they had acted in retribution for the company's alleged Communist ties. Such connections were also named as reasons for their more widespread assaults on left-wing bookstores. "In some cases a whole band rushed in to smash everything," Lu Xun explained; "in others stones were thrown at windows breaking panes of plate glass worth two hundred dollars apiece."[74] As the writer well knew, this work of destruction extended to the bodies of artists themselves and to the people who had emerged to defend them.

With Lu Xun as a member, the China League for Civil Rights had formed in October 1932, publishing its manifesto in the *Shenbao*. Led by prominent non-Communist intellectuals including Cai Yuanpei, Song Qingling, and Yang Xingfo, the league's stated purpose was to "fight for the liberation of political prisoners in China and to fight the system of imprisonment, torture and execution now prevailing," to provide legal assistance to said prisoners, and also to "assist in the struggle for civil rights, i.e., rights of organization, free speech, press and assembly."[75] In addition to such aims, the fact that the league's work involved defending Communists, and the fact that the *Shenbao* had been brazen enough to publish its manifesto, suggested to fascists a rapidly expanding and politically undifferentiated menace. Blue Shirt Dai Li reportedly discussed plans to assassinate league leader Yang Xingfo in detail with Chiang Kai-shek. According to Frederic Wakeman, Chiang persuaded Dai that "Yang should be killed in the French Concession, where his death would have a greater impact on [Sun Yat-sen's widow] Song Qingling."[76] Yang was gunned down on June 18, 1933, near the Academia Sinica offices and died of his wounds shortly thereafter.[77] That this attack occurred in the French Concession indicated unconcern for imperialist opinions of the Nationalist justice system as well as the belief that the concession areas were in fact spaces within which Nationalist authorities could do as they pleased with respect to Chinese citizens. That the location chosen was the premier state educational institution Academia Sinica was presumably also intended to have a chilling effect on nationwide campus organizing in addition to the stated purpose of silencing civil rights activists.

Based on the writings of the Blue Shirt and CC Clique partisans involved with these attacks, there is little doubt that they intended to quell dissent. But their chosen targets—bookstores, film studios, editors, and writers—also indicate that these attacks were entwined with the project of creating a new nationalist literature and arts. This is evidenced, for instance, by Xu Enceng's recollection of the kidnapping and detention of the female, Communist partisan writer Ding Ling. One of the issues to which the murdered civil rights activist Yang Xingfo had called public attention shortly before his death was Ding Ling's April 1933 disappearance. While fascists regarded Yang and the Civil Rights League as opponents to be crushed, Ding Ling's case was somewhat different. As recalled by Xu Enceng, who had ordered her kidnapping and oversaw her nearly three-year detention, the purpose of disappearing her was less to silence her voice than to harness it for the Nationalist cause. To be sure, kidnapping Ding Ling served to frighten and silence her comrades, who assumed that she had been killed just as the GMD had killed Ding Ling's former husband Hu Yepin alongside other martyred writers in 1931.[78] But Xu stressed that her detention had a constructive in addition to a destructive rationale. He had ordered her kidnapping, Xu explained in his memoir, with the hope of persuading her to defect to the Nationalist camp, anticipating that she could become "a powerful cultural worker" for the GMD.[79] Xu's account of Ding Ling's detention—written nearly twenty years after she escaped from house arrest in Nanjing and made her way to the northwest Communist stronghold Yan'an in 1936—conveyed no trace of remorse. Xu instead characterized the kidnapping as a reasonable means of turning Ding Ling into a writer for the Nationalists.

Details of Xu's account line up with narrations that Ding Ling herself provided after escaping from captivity, but Xu's own telling projects onto the writer a kind of Stockholm syndrome, intimating her gratitude for the potential salvation that her captors offered.[80] At the time of her arrest, Xu recalled, Ding Ling had already joined the CCP and was a leader of the League of Left-Wing Writers, conducting organizing work in schools. In contrast to her dismal underground life in Shanghai, she lived comfortably under house arrest in Nanjing, where she enjoyed Nationalist hospitality and freedom to roam around the city, as well as the company of her partner, mother, and captivity-born daughter. Xu and Ding Ling developed something like a friendship, he recalled, exchanging visits to each other's homes. When he saw that she was depressed following the birth of her daughter, he gave her permission to travel on her own to Beiping. And after she returned from Beiping and explained that she was ill and wanted to go to Shanghai to see a Japanese doctor, he agreed to let her go. Thereupon, Xu recalled, she bid goodbye to her baby, mother, and tubercular husband, and never returned.[81]

Reflecting on Ding Ling's decision to leave Nanjing and return to the Communist fold, Xu mused, "To this day I cannot say for certain" why she chose to do so. Mulling the possible reasons why she left—Xu used the word *chuzou*, which connotes leaving home as much as breaking free from captivity (as per Nora in *A Doll's House*)—he did not raise the possibility that being disappeared and held prisoner for several years, under whatever conditions, might have been a harrowing or embittering experience. Instead, Xu speculated that he had witnessed a Communist returning to her true nature, by which he seems to have meant that she could not have been saved after all, despite his best efforts to turn her. His superiors subsequently reprimanded him for his leniency with a political enemy, but Xu defended his treatment of Ding Ling, as he believed that it helped put the lie to critics of the Nationalists, and of his bureau in particular, by demonstrating that they in fact treated their enemies well. In this sense, Xu presented kidnapping and indefinite detention as a reasonable and compassionate means of capturing Ding Ling's talents for the Nationalists. It was a way of simultaneously eliminating a Communist obstacle and contributing to the creation of a new nationalist literature. The ends were justified and the means efficient.

From such a perspective, the November 1934 Blue Shirt assassination of Shi Liangcai—whose newspaper, the *Shenbao*, had run advertisements for the *Future* just a year earlier—would have been seen as an expedient means of press control. Members of China's press during the Nanjing Decade had consistently resisted state control efforts; *Shenbao* was proving a particularly sharp thorn in the Nationalists' side. Shi's killing has been linked to his decision to print stories about the murder of Yang Xingfo and to the fact that *Shenbao*'s "Free Talk" supplement had connected dots "between internal persecution of liberal human rights proponents and external appeasement of the Japanese" in a manner that reportedly infuriated Chiang Kai-shek.[82] Blue Shirts killed Shi Liangcai in front of Shi's family as they drove home to Shanghai from vacation. Also killed in the roadside ordeal was Shi's chauffer and a school-age friend of his son. His wife and niece were wounded.[83] Murdering Shi silenced a prominent non-Communist critic of the Nanjing regime; it also bespoke a worldview that prized efficiency and obedience and expected all nationals to speak with a single authorized voice. The domestic outcry that this action sparked seems to have merely confirmed their belief in the need to proceed more swiftly and effectively with the work of remolding popular consciousness.

It is easy to spot cruelty and hypocrisy in the implementation of the White Terror, to the point where it seems too obvious to note. Killing Shi Liangcai in front of his wife and children made a mockery of any reasonable conception of filial piety or social concord; kidnapping Ding Ling with the expectation that she would agree to become a cultural worker for the Guomindang suggested a flagrant disrespect for an otherwise-championed law and order. Harder to see than hypocrisy is how these violent acts were considered necessary to speed the national regenerative process along. Writers whose pens "dripped poison" and who were not properly responsive to censorship measures could be eliminated from the scene altogether. Likewise, film studios that churned out movies that did not accord with nationalistic visions of what cinema should do could be ransacked, as could bookstores that carried subversive or degenerate literatures. Unity was strength, and the nation's chances for worldly survival were too precarious to allow for any kind of internal dissent. With cacophonous voices silenced or harmonized, nationalist literature and arts would gain an undistracted captive audience, and China's vast population could be reformed into a singular mass capable of thriving in a ruthlessly competitive world.

Conclusion

When formulating plans for the creation of a new nationalist literature and arts, neither the Blue Shirts nor the CC Clique were particularly concerned with reviving or protecting received dynastic forms. Reproductions of centuries-old creative works seldom appeared in the pages of their magazines. When they did they were framed in distinctly modern terms—for instance, the stark black-and-white photographs of dynastic art and engineering treasures in the pages of *Cultural Construction* arranged to suggest past national greatness and the imperative of recuperating its spirit. Blue Shirt papers like the *Future*, *Sweat and Blood Weekly*, and *Society Mercury* favored abstract graphics, photographs of modern subjects like sports teams, and figurative drawings that were formally distinct from popular cartoon arts of the past. Their literary sections were not filled with Tang poems or Ming vernacular fiction. Rather, they contained new kinds of stories, plays, and screenplays with titles like "Sparks of the Future" and "Sketches before the Camera."[84] Such works seem to have been primarily produced for their own consumption, with the expectation that one day illiterate peasants and workers could be raised to a cultural and educational level at which they might appreciate them, while in the meantime the latter would be fed easily graspable films about electrification and Confucian values. The intent was to inundate people with images and stories that accorded with the national spirit and pointed to national regeneration, rather than to revive and popularize any particular dynastic art form.

While Blue Shirts called in 1933 for establishing an all-powerful cultural committee and cultural commissar, the CC Clique actually succeeded in inaugurating a state committee along these lines in 1936 called the Cultural Enterprise Planning Committee. Decided upon at the 1935 Fifth Party Congress and headed by Chen Guofu, this committee was to regulate customs, education, history and geography, language, the publishing industry, news media, broadcasting, the film industry, theater, music, fine arts, and everything else under the heading "other."[85] It worked in conjunction with committees established in May 1935 and February 1936 to exert specific control over film and broadcasting, respectively.[86] The committee's statement of purpose reiterated common CC Clique concerns: the need to rectify the dissipation of the national spirit, to "unite the masses behind a common goal," and to resist the "invasion of foreign culture." It would promote Sun's Three Principles as well as Confucian values.[87] In October 1936, Chen delivered a report on the committee's efforts thus far, stressing how they constituted a kind of spiritual national defense preparation on par with ongoing material efforts to bolster the nation's military strength. At the time, he expected that the committee would "henceforth determine China's cultural policy."[88] In other words, it would set the party-state line for what was properly nationalistic, officially settling discussions that had taken place within party ranks over the previous decade.

Despite their best efforts, however, reality remained considerably less amenable to engineering. Less than a year after the Cultural Enterprise Planning Committee got off the ground, Chiang Kai-shek was himself kidnapped and detained in Xi'an by two of his own generals and forced into agreeing to a Second United Front with the Communist Party to fight against Japan. While Blue Shirt Dai Li's successful advocacy on Chiang's behalf in Xi'an meant that his own political fortunes rose in the ensuing years, those of other Blue Shirts (like He Zhonghan and Deng Wenyi) waned.[89] As a concession to the Communists for their renewed alliance, Chiang agreed to disband the Blue Shirts altogether. Its members were mostly redeployed in less overtly anti-Communist directions, for instance toward the new Three Principles of the People Youth Corps in 1938, with which Chen Lifu was also involved.[90] There is little evidence to suggest that their anti-Communism abated during the war, though their nationalistic fervor could now be openly channeled toward the Japanese. The specificity of their interpretation of Sun's Three Principles of the People left little room for compromise even as it served as a doctrinal basis for GMD-CCP cooperation, and war against Japan provided added rationale for fostering material strength and spiritual unity. While Nanjing's fractured intelligence agencies, previously divided between the Blue Shirts and the CC Clique, were consolidated under Dai Li's notorious direction, Chen Lifu emerged to even greater public prominence as the wartime minister of education from 1938 to 1944. Chen Guofu resumed his work selecting and training party personnel at the Central Political Institute in Chongqing after 1939, where, "acting directly under Chiang Kai-shek, [he] was able to wield personal influence that could hardly be matched by any other official in the wartime capital," and also served as a member of the Supreme National Defense Council.[91] Despite Chen Guofu's 1936 expectation that his Cultural Enterprise Planning Committee would set cultural policy going forward, the conditions of the Second United Front and total defensive war against Japan meant that it never garnered the authority that Mao's wartime talks at Yan'an on mass literature and arts would after the Communist victory in 1949.

Aspects of nationalist literature and arts as proposed by the Blue Shirts and cc Clique during the Nanjing Decade certainly developed in dialogue with Communist cultural initiatives, but they were not merely reactive. And though the writer Lu Xun might have been surprised that men better known as soldiers and executioners took up singing, the fact that they worked to set cultural policy, and that the pages of their periodicals were filled with cartoons, stories, and plays is indicative of the totalizing nature of their political project. One's entire being was part of the struggle; there was to be no such thing as privatized enjoyment. They were products of the New Culture and May Fourth movements, enmeshed in the cultural idioms of the treaty ports, and above all wanted to demonstrate that they loved the nation more than anyone. Literature and the arts were critical components of the process of national rebirth. As good soldiers and meticulous engineers, nothing could be overlooked or left to chance.

There is a particular perversity to assessing a fascist movement in terms of its success. How many people had to be killed, how much destruction wrought, in order for a movement to count as successful? Even the most powerful were of course militarily defeated by August 1945 and therefore failed on their own terms. Still, scholars must recognize and account for differences between fascist movements that succeeded in capturing states and securing the consent of targeted populations and those that, as in 1930s China, saw their energies and organizing capacities dissipated before making much headway toward their desired futures. The weak and fractured nature of the Nanjing regime and the socioeconomic unevenness of the vast territory that they claimed—especially the preponderance of isolated rural areas where fascist rhetorics of Confucianism as a national spirit that promoted efficiency would have rung particularly hollow—stymied their efforts as much as the Nanjing regime's abrupt 1937 southwestward removal. Guomindang fascism may have been largely defused soon after it emerged, but it nevertheless left important legacies. Identifying these legacies is not akin to suggesting that fascism has reappeared in the Chinese-speaking world since the heyday of the Blue Shirts and CC Clique or that it necessarily will, only that they need to be considered when evaluating its historical significance.

This book has treaded and retreaded the years between 1925 and 1937 to explain the rise of fascist organizations in China as well as their cultural preoccupations—how groups within the GMD came to espouse what I have called a revolutionary nativism that cast Confucianism as the timeless core of Chinese national belonging and potentially animated its postdynastic resurgence. From the merged crucibles of the 1910s May Fourth Movement and 1920s United Front Canton, militant young nationalists narrowed the means and ends of their desired revolutionary path. Squaring off against the legacies and present threats of imperialism as well as a burgeoning Communist movement, men who trained as soldiers and in technical professions articulated ever more extreme theories of national unity and renaissance. Political liberalism appeared to them weak-willed and historically passé, unbridled capitalism precisely what ruined the Chinese dynastic system in the first place, and Communist internationalism a nail in the nation's coffin. Amid labor, feminist, and anti-imperialist mobilizations, amid the parceling of former Qing territory into warlord-ruled areas and Japanese puppet states, and amid the unraveling of the Anglo-French-dominated League of Nations in the face of an ascendant Japan, Germany, and Italy, lockstep national unity appeared to them key to resolving China's protracted crises. For the nation to rise from the ashes of postdynastic ruin required the industrial and agrarian development called for by Sun Yat-sen before his 1925 death, and for this program to advance at all required the resuscitation of ancient Confucian values that fostered social cohesion and rendered the nation uniquely formidable.

To regard either the Blue Shirts or the CC Clique—the two fascist factions within the Nationalist Party on which this book has focused—as merely imitators of metropolitan fascist movements causes us to miss and misunderstand their contributions to social, political, and cultural praxis. The crises that they sought to resolve and the politico-intellectual debates into which they intervened were local ones. It is also the case that their specific localities (the Yangzi delta, Shanghai, and Canton) were important nodes of global imperialism, and that they understood China's crises as relating, in one way or another, to its now-subordinated position on the world stage. It was hardly happenstance that the Comintern chose Canton as a key base of operations in its fight against a world-enmeshing capitalism, located as the city was in close proximity to French Indochina, the Dutch East Indies, British Hong Kong, and Japanese Taiwan. Nationalist theorist Dai Jitao emerged from this crucible with little interest in seeing postdynastic China become like what liberal Western powers had revealed themselves to be in Asia or elsewhere in the colonized world, or like what the Soviet Union and its apparent Chinese pawns seemed to be prescribing. In the wake of Sun

Yat-sen's death and amid the social upheavals of United Front Canton, Dai Jitao recast Sun as a machine-age Confucian sage who had authored a revolutionary course that flowed from China's unique cultural inheritance and promised to abide by it. China would industrialize in a class-harmonious fashion; new social actors would be tamed and disciplined; and the national people would proudly reclaim their millennia-old Confucian inheritance.

Had the objective local, regional, and global situations been less volatile, Dai Jitao's ideas might have fallen on deaf ears. As it was, they resonated strongly with young Chinese nationalists who had emerged from the New Culture and May Fourth movements, were conversant with various strains of socialist thought, and convened in mid-1920s Canton with the intent to engage in combat for new state and social structures. Soldiers who trained in Japan and the USSR, and budding technocrats who trained in the United States, heard in Dai Jitao's rendition of Sun Yat-sen the siren song of a truer revolutionary path, one that conceded as little as possible to the West and seemed to honor received traditions in a way that liberal and Communist heirs of the May Fourth Movement did not. These soldiers and technocrats can certainly be understood as developmental nationalists. But the development that they desired was not a static thing, isolable from the historical flux in which it was envisioned and implemented. They came to understand China's industrial development as a historical destiny to be achieved regardless of domestic and international opposition, and in a manner that avoided social abnormalities like class conflict and feminist activism evident in industrialized, imperialist countries as well as their colonies and semicolonies. Seemingly authorized after 1927 by an unraveling global order and the imperative to bind the nation together to survive in such a ruthlessly competitive world, they vowed to destroy remnants of the old regime and clear away the rubble so that the nation's ancient spirit could rise again. In the process they summoned an increasingly mythical history to suture the violent ruptures of their postdynastic present and to steer the nation into the industrial age.[1]

The GMD right-wing turn to Confucianism constituted an engagement with the New Culture and May Fourth movements' critiques of the social dynamics bequeathed by this heritage as much as an engagement with tradition as such. The issue is not whether their interest in Confucianism was genuine—there is no reason to doubt their seriousness of purpose, and all interpretations of Confucian texts are better and worse interpretations— but why they interpreted it in the way that they did and what they believed that it authorized. Eager to distance their promotion of key Confucian tenets from the feudal or generally conservative labels that fellow May Fourth activists had assigned to them, GMD militants insisted that they were not interested in returning to the past or in shoring up feudal remnants but rather in resuscitating an ancient spirit for the sake of binding the nation together and hurtling it into the future. In this sense, what emerged was less a "Confucian fascism"—a fascism that flowed from an ingrained cultural disposition onto which a fascist militarism was grafted, as Frederic Wakeman suggested with a jab at Chiang Kai-shek's ostensibly "self-righteous mother," as if she were to blame for his politics—than a regional variant of fascism that, for reasons particular to the political and intellectual landscape of interwar China, named Confucianism as the nation's cultural core.[2] Chinese fascist defense of this heritage resonated with tendencies of anticolonial nationalist movements elsewhere in the world concerned to protect aspects of received traditions that had been denigrated by imperialism. Insofar as liberal and left-wing heirs of the May Fourth Movement were vehemently challenging the mentalities and social relations apparently bequeathed by Confucianism, those on the right claimed this ground and positioned themselves as protectors of the nation against its myriad domestic and foreign enemies. Communism was quickly recast as a red imperialism and as something utterly alien to the national ethos.

Invoking Confucianism as a kind of national spirit was one way by which Blue Shirt and CC Clique thinkers skirted tensions of simultaneously figuring themselves as revolutionaries angling to destroy remnants of the old regime and as protectors of native values then under attack from imperialists and leftists. As they understood it, this national spirit superseded time and place, binding the diverse body of people that Blue Shirt and CC Clique activists claimed as Chinese together through history and across China's vast territory. Many of the nation's present ills, they believed, stemmed from the fact that it was presently lapsed and endangered. With shrill paranoia they saw this spirit and its potential resuscitation particularly threatened by Communists, whose flagrant repudiation of native values meant that they did not deserve to be understood as fellow nationals or even as fellow humans. Communists were to be exterminated or, if possible, rehabilitated in concentration camps geared toward repentance. Repentance in the Chinese fascist imagination meant coming to appreciate that Confucian values and Sunist productivity were inseparably fused, and that deviating from either spelled national-revolutionary sabotage. The New Life Movement launched in 1934 and spearheaded by the Blue Shirts and CC Clique approached the nation as a repentance camp writ large, seeking to render popular attitudes and behavior legible to authorities as noncriminal. Their NLM entailed subjecting people to the rationalized rhythms of factory work and soldierly mobilization, presenting efficiency and self-sacrifice for the nation as lapsed and endangered Confucian norms. Beneath the NLM's championing of norms that would recalibrate the nation as a cohesive, cooperative entity was a distinctly competitive ethos that pushed people to be more nationalistic, productive, and self-sacrificial than their compatriots. The movement's positive valuation of hierarchical rationalization, as well as its interest in disciplining rather than eliminating newly classed and gendered social actors, bespoke its leaders' embrace of modern life and the capitalistic orientation of the Confucian values that they claimed as ancient.

The CC Clique's and Blue Shirts' enthusiasm for modern technologies and modernist aesthetics further underscores how these groups were not conservative in any meaningful sense. They were attuned to cutting-edge artistic and decorative trends, appreciated the power of technologies like radio and film, and thought about these things in terms of their capacity to mobilize the national masses. As we have seen, China's fascists made their own unique contributions to trends of graphic abstraction popular in Nanjing Decade Shanghai, embracing in particular industrial motifs that helped to publicly position them as champions of dynamic progress. They strove to integrate such futuristic imagery with emergent national symbols (such as the Temple of Heaven and the Great Wall), assembling dynastic engineering feats into visual narratives of historical continuity with Nanjing's new construction efforts—suggesting that the GMD was effectively suturing the indigenous past with a renewed future across the morass of the present. Whereas contemporary nonpartisan magazines like *The Young Companion* presented "kaleidoscopic" windows onto modern life that suggested diversity and open-endedness, fascist magazines embraced signs and symbols of modernity like express trains and fighter planes with the intent to eliminate ambiguities of meaning. Meaning as well as pleasure were for the nation; people were to find joy in hard work, self-sacrifice, and performing their allotted roles for the good of national rebirth. Fascists theorized and produced "nationalist literature and arts" to this end—as instruments of propaganda to mobilize the masses in a singular direction, to speak with one authorized voice.

China's fascism may have been minor in the monstrous perspective of those that thrived in Europe and Japan from the 1920s to the 1940s, but it nevertheless animated the very center of Chinese party politics during this period—and the center of a party that has left an indelible imprint on greater China's twentieth and twenty-first centuries. Interpreting the politics of key GMD factions as fascist prompts us to reckon with several historical as well as enduring problems. If scholars are now eager to see pre-1949 China as an "age of openness," and signs of modern life flourishing in cities like Shanghai from the late nineteenth century onward, then we should not be surprised that this virulently nationalistic variant of socialism—desperately desiring industrial strength without attendant social dislocations—emerged there as well.[3] The long twentieth century witnessed multiple epochal transformations in China, with revolutionaries of all sorts emerging at one point or another. That militant nationalists on the eve of World War II pushed, and allowed their agenda to be pushed, to right-wing extremes signals that a multiplicity of revolutionary paths were possible and hence that none of these paths were inevitable. Industrial development, moreover, is never a politically or socially neutral process, nor is it isolable from the local, regional, and global context in which it occurs. For all of its promise to liberate humanity from constraints, social stratification is inevitably generated in the process and only politics can determine its magnitude. In this sense, arguments that a given culture naturally dictates a particular development path or specific forms of state-society and workplace relations should always be interrogated to understand who is making the argument and why. Who stands to gain and lose by defining culture in a particular way, or by insisting that society is naturally parceled into elites and masses who should abide by their allotted roles for the good of the whole? There is no reason to believe that what was being promoted by the GMD during the Nanjing Decade would have naturally evolved into something more democratic, especially as the fascist groups focused on here, largely ascendant within the GMD party structure by 1935, had actively worked to render opposition of any kind into a nonnational, non-Confucian act that could easily get one killed, as the assassinations of Shi Liangcai and Yang Xingfo made clear. In the 1920s and 1930s, it was not a conservative move to name Confucianism as buttressing corporatist development—corporatism was a historically novel form of state-society relations—but rather a simultaneously revolutionary and counterrevolutionary one seeking to promote dramatic change in one direction and preclude it in others.

The potential for exclusionary violence is inherent in all nationalisms past and present, and the case of the pre–World War II GMD exemplifies how anti-imperialist nationalisms can take sharply rightward turns. The Second United Front, cemented in late 1936, forced the GMD (at least those who opted to flee from rather than ally with Japan) into championing a more ecumenical and inclusive version thereof. Chiang Kai-shek's wartime elevation to one of the major Allies fighting a world war against fascism further necessitated a kind of political and rhetorical positioning considerably different than what he had, for instance, presented to counterinsurgency officers in training at Mt. Lu in the summer of 1933. After World War II concluded, the GMD did not become demonstrably more democratic or less anti-Communist, but voices within the party calling for a totalizing revolution to resuscitate an ancient spirit quelled and accommodated themselves to a new, U.S.-led Cold War order that rested much of its legitimacy on having militarily defeated wartime fascist regimes. *Fascism* became a term with which few people anywhere wanted to be associated, and scholarly efforts to explain ever more precisely its various pre-1945 instantiations accompanied those declaring it safely confined to a defeated era.[4] In addition to a dramatic shift in global political winds, it became advantageous for the GMD to radiate conservative values of stability and order amid Communist upheavals across Cold War Asia to ensure its own longevity and U.S. patronage.

It is difficult not to hear echoes of 1930s Blue Shirt and CC Clique rhetoric in campaigns launched by the Communist Party after its 1949 victory. The demands of GMD fascists for hyperproductivity, self-sacrifice, and the speeding up of historical time via collective effort resonated strongly in the Great Leap Forward of 1958–59. The chaste proscriptions of the Maoist regime had much in common with the Blue Shirt and CC Clique's own, however much these jarred against the wanton licentiousness that the latter ascribed to the former. More strikingly, the Maoist Great Proletarian Cultural Revolution (GPCR) was launched in 1966 by factions within a party that had already achieved state power and sought to deepen a revolution already in motion, penetrating into every possible recess of everyday life. Citizens during the GPCR were enjoined to struggle against compatriots exhibiting unacceptable thought and behavior. Yet these surface similarities suggest less the symmetry of GMD and CCP agendas (as two sides of one totalitarian coin) than their ongoing, albeit indirect in the 1960s, arguments about the role of culture in social transformation, whose key terms dated back to the 1910s and 1920s. The GPCR especially appears as a challenge to the notions of cultural revolution proposed by fascists in the 1930s, in its concern to root out old habits, to upend social hierarchies, and to question relations between knowledge and power (the authority of experts) that GMD fascists sought to solidify and naturalize. Although domestic developments in Taiwan were perhaps not a top concern of CCP leaders during the GPCR, the GMD was certainly paying close attention to events on the mainland. On November 12, 1966, GMD leaders including Chiang Kai-shek and Chen Lifu inaugurated a Chinese Cultural Renaissance Movement (Zhongguo wenhua fuxing yundong) from the Sun Yat-sen Memorial Hall in Taibei.[5] As their worst nightmares seemed to be realized on the mainland, this GMD movement registered an attempt to counteract the GPCR's excesses. It echoed the NLM of the 1930s but had a more pronounced preservationist thrust, eschewing the futurist modernism of the interwar years and announcing the Republic of China as a site of heritage conservation against the destruction being wrought in the People's Republic.[6]

As this oblique argument between the GMD and CCP continued, another afterlife of the GMD's interwar revolutionary nativism gained force. This book has underscored that right-radicalized GMD theorists during the 1920s and 1930s contributed to a great twentieth-century reversal in the historical fortunes of Confucianism. Their intellectual labor constituted the Sinophone world's first organized effort to render this heritage compatible with a form of state-led industrialization averse to ostensibly Western things like autonomous labor unions, unfettered media, and individual rights. Seemingly unwittingly, late Cold War champions of Asian values echoed ideas pioneered by GMD fascists in the 1930s in their attempts to advance state-led development agendas, maintaining that a unique cultural inheritance fostered social obedience, diligent toil, and nonconflictual workplace relations.[7] In more recent years, the CCP has itself assumed a dramatic about-face with respect to a Confucian heritage that it previously decried as feudal. It now brands itself overseas via Confucius Institutes and celebrates ideals of a harmonious society in ways that resonate with the class-cooperative efforts lauded by the 1930s GMD. There may not be direct connections between the intellectual labors of interwar GMD fascists, late Cold War champions of Asian values, and present-day CCP espousals of social harmony, but it is nevertheless important to acknowledge the role of right-radicalized Nationalists in laying the foundations of, and generally making available, a discourse that rendered certain Confucian tenets compatible with a specific path of modernization.

My intent in this book has not been to suggest that fascisms across the world prior to 1945 were exactly the same as one another, or even that emphases other than those that I have focused on here cannot be found in interwar China. Future researchers might productively examine Blue Shirt and CC Clique agrarian ideals, their notions of race and eugenics, of masculinity and femininity, their ties to educational institutions, their mass outreach efforts via such organizations as the Boy Scouts, and the turns in their thinking and activities during World War II.[8] Researchers might also explore what their insistence on Confucianism as the exclusive heart of Chinese national belonging meant for the ethnic minority–inhabited borderland areas that they claimed within the national-territorial fold—and in the process provide new perspective on the present-day problems of representing the People's Republic of China on the world stage via the image of Confucius. Such a wider field of inquiry might yield a more comprehensive picture of Chinese fascist ideology and practice, as well as explanations of their successes, failures, and legacies.

List of Characters for Selected Romanized Terms

biedongdui
別動隊

buzhibujue
不知不覺

CC Clique
CC 系

Chen Guofu
陳果夫

Chen Lifu
陳立夫

Chiang Kai-shek (Jiang Jieshi) / Jiang Zhongzheng
蔣介石 / 蔣中正

Dai Jitao
戴季陶

Deng Wenyi
鄧文儀

Ding Ling
丁玲

fanxingyuan
反省院

fugu
復古

Funü xinshenghuo yuekan
婦女新生活月刊

fuxing
復興

Fuxingshe
復興社

Ganzai huikan
贛災彙刊

guyou wenhua
固有文化

Guomindang zhongyang zhixing weiyuanhui wenhua shiye jihua weiyuanhui
國民黨中央執行委員會文化事業計劃委員會

Hanxue zhoukan
汗血周刊

He Zhonghan
賀衷寒

houzhihoujue
後知後覺

jiaofei
剿匪

Jingbao
京報

Jingcheng yuekan
精誠月刊

Junshiweiyuanhui
軍事委員會

Lanyishe
藍衣社

Lixingshe
力行社

li, yi, lian, chi
禮義廉恥

Lushan junguan xunliantuan
廬山軍官訓練團

Lu Xun
魯迅

minzu jingshen
民族精神

minzu wenyi
民族文藝

puluo wenyi
普羅文藝

Qiantu
前途

Qu Qiubai
瞿秋白

Sanminzhuyi
三民主義

Saodang huabao
掃蕩畫報

Saodang xunkan
掃蕩旬刊

Shehui xinwen
社會新聞

Shehuizhuyi yuekan
社會主義月刊

Shenbao
申報

Shidai gonglun
時代公論

Shi Liangcai
史量才

Song Meiling (Soong May-ling / Madame Chiang Kai-shek)
宋美齡

Song Qingling
宋慶齡

Sunwenzhuyi xuehui
孫文主義學會

Sun Yat-sen (Sun Zhongshan)
孫中山

Tiexue yuekan
鐵血月刊

xianzhixianjue
先知先覺

Xinshenghuo cujin zonghui huikan
新生活促進總會會刊

Xinshenghuo yundong
新生活運動

Xinshengming
新生命

Xu Enceng
徐恩曾

Yang Xingfo (Yang Quan)
楊杏佛 (楊銓)

yi, shi, zhu, xing
衣食住行

yibeishuizhuyi
一杯水主義

zhengqihuayi
整齊劃一

Zhongguo minquan baozhang tongmeng
中國民權保障同盟

Zhongguo wenhua xuehui
中國文化學會

Zhongguo wenhua jianshe xiehui
中國文化建設協會

Zhongguo zuoyi zuojia lianmeng
中國左翼作家聯盟

zishou zixin
自首自新

INTRODUCTION

Epigraph: Chiang Kai-shek quoted in Deng, *Guomindang hexin zhuzhi zhenxiang*, 322.

1 Chan, "A Turning Point in the Modern Chinese Revolution," 224–41; Gilmartin, *Engendering the Chinese Revolution*, 131–41; Kwan, *Marxist Intellectuals and the Chinese Labor Movement*, esp. ch. 2; Tsin, *Nation, Governance, and Modernity in China*, 143–68.

2 The city was also called Red Canton by Western journalists. Gilmartin, *Engendering the Chinese Revolution*, 152; Ho Chi Minh, then known as Ngyuen Ai Quoc, was dispatched by Moscow to Canton in 1925 to assist with local peasant organization and to work with representatives from China, Korea, the Dutch East Indies, and India in forming the Society of the Oppressed Peoples of Asia. Ho remained in Canton until Chiang Kai-shek's 1927 party purge. Duiker, *Ho Chi Minh*, 122, 141–45.

3 Murdock, *Disarming the Allies of Imperialism*, 188–93; Perry, *Shanghai on Strike*, 91; Wilson, "Principles and Profits," 628.

4 Tsin, *Nation, Governance, and Modernity in China*, 103–9.

5 Tsui, "China's Forgotten Revolution," esp. introduction and ch. 1. Also Tsui, *China's Conservative Revolution*.

6 Dai, *Sanminzhuyi zhi zhexue de jichu*, 15. Slavoj Žižek has identified this as a desire for "capitalism without capitalism," or a system of industrial production grounded in capitalist social relations without concomitant alienation or class strife in *Organs without Bodies*, 165; also see Harry Harootunian's extended historical elaboration on this idea in *Overcome by Modernity*.

7 Sun Yat-sen [Sun Zhongshan], *Sanminzhuyi*, 52–53.

8 This book uses the terms *semicolonialism* and *colonial modernity* to describe the circumstances that Chinese fascists sought to overcome and to prevent from

being overcome by Communism and Japanese imperialism. For an inventory of the forms of imperialist violence and control to which China was subjected during the pre-Maoist period, see Osterhammel, "Semi-colonialism and Informal Empire in Twentieth-Century China," 290–314; also the introduction to Hevia, *English Lessons*. Though semicolonialism and colonial modernity are contested terms, I find both useful for describing China's global predicament, as they recognize China's difference from territories directly ruled by a single colonial power while also acknowledging the forms of racialized violence and external control to which China was subjected by European, American, and Japanese powers. For a review of recent debates, see Barlow, "Debates over Colonial Modernity in East Asia and Another Alternative," 617–44.

9 E.g., Mann, *Fascists*; Mosse, *The Fascist Revolution*.

10 On the Janus-faced nature of nationalism, see Benedict Anderson's discussion of Walter Benjamin's "Angel of History" in *Imagined Communities*, 161–62; McClintock, *Imperial Leather*, 358–60; Nairn, *The Break-Up of Britain*, ch. 9. On the ways in which fascism intensifies the temporal contradictions of nationalism, see Neocleous, *Fascism*.

11 *Qiantu* 1, no. 8 (1933): front cover.

12 Yao, *An Introduction to Confucianism*, 18–25.

13 Griffin, *The Nature of Fascism*, 47; also Griffin, *Modernism and Fascism*, 2. Such a worldview in the German context has also been identified by Jeffrey Herf as a reactionary modernism that eschewed "backward looking pastoralism, pointing instead to the outlines of a beautiful new order replacing the formless chaos due to capitalism in a united, technologically advanced nation." Herf, *Reactionary Modernism*, 2. Peter Osborne has in turn challenged Herf's identification of fascism's modernism with its affirmation of technology, rather than with its paradoxical and "rigourously futural" temporality as such. Osborne, *The Politics of Time*, 163–68.

14 Letter reprinted in Jo-Anne Danzker, "Shanghai Modern," in Danzker, Lum, and Zheng, *Shanghai Modern*, 51–52.

15 Danzker, "Shanghai Modern," 52.

16 Wakeman, *Spymaster*, 175–82.

17 On Shanghai's "mediasphere," see DesForges, *Mediasphere Shanghai*.

18 Dooeum Chung notes that "the Blueshirts founded a variety of mass media, opened bookstores, published periodicals, while propaganda work was performed by publishing newspapers, journals, and books." Chung estimates that between "1932 and 1935 approximately two hundred different periodicals with publications about Fascist propaganda were supervised by the Blueshirts." Chung, *Élitist Fascism*, 146–47; Wakeman, *Spymaster*, 102–4.

19 Key works include Eastman, *The Abortive Revolution*; Chang, *The Chinese Blue Shirt Society*; Chung, *Élitist Fascism*; Deng, *Guomindang hexin zuzhi zhenxiang*; Li, "Culture, Revolution, and Modernity"; Kirby, *Germany and Republican China*; Tsui, "China's Forgotten Revolution"; Wakeman, "A Revisionist View of the

Nanjing Decade"; Wakeman, *Spymaster*; Xu, "1930 niandai Lixingshe yanzhong de Yidali faxisizhuyi."

20 Deng, *Guomindang hexin zhuzhi zhenxiang*, 155.

21 Judge, *Print and Politics*; Fitzgerald, *Awakening China*.

22 Mark Neocleous succinctly observes how "it is fascist *nationalism* which facilitates the break with liberal and Marxist universalism, and, in the case of the latter, its identification of internationalism as the key to class struggle." Neocleous, *Fascism*, 19.

23 Wang, *Geming yu fangeming*, esp. 67, 118–19.

24 Mayer, *Dynamics of Counterrevolution in Europe*, 5.

25 The coup that brought the Nationalists to power, writes Peter Zarrow, was regarded as such by the CCP, for it "had eliminated the peasant and worker movements that represented anti-imperialism, anti-feudalism, and social justice"—the oppressed classes in whose name the Communist revolution was being organized. Yet the GMD also "saw themselves as loyal to the revolution—whose goal was to build a strong state—because the White Terror had saved the nation from class struggle." Zarrow, *China in War and Revolution*, 245–46.

26 Mao Zedong and the Chinese Communists would invoke the struggles of the "national people" (*quanguo renmin*) during the Second United Front, but this concept never elided class conflicts within China but instead recast these conflicts as contradictions temporarily subordinated to the more pressing contradiction of local and global struggles against imperialism and fascism.

27 As Guannan Li has emphasized, "Ideological battles were constantly fought [among Sun's followers] for an 'original' and thus authoritative explanation of his ideology." Li, "Culture, Revolution, and Modernity," 119. Also Wells, *The Political Thought of Sun Yat-sen*, 122–40; Harrison, *The Making of the Republican Citizen*, 207–39.

28 Deng, *Guomindang hexin zuzhi zhenxiang*, 50–52; van de Ven, *From Friend to Comrade*, 171–73; Fitzgerald, *Awakening China*, 241; Wilbur and How, *Missionaries of Revolution*, 188–93, 245–46, 714.

29 Gibson with Chen, *The Secret Army*; Peralta, "Central America between Two Dragons," 168.

30 Roy, *Revolution and Counterrevolution in China*, 283; also quoted in Chang, *The Chinese Blue Shirt Society*, 30; Gregor, *A Place in the Sun*, 75.

31 Gregor, *A Place in the Sun*, 81.

32 Chang's analysis aimed to rebut Lloyd Eastman's bold but thinly substantiated claims about fascist tendencies within the GMD. Chang, *The Chinese Blue Shirt Society*, 135. As I elaborate in chapter 1, the Renaissance Society (Fuxingshe) was a Blue Shirt front organization.

33 The argument that the interwar GMD were merely developmental nationalists also sidesteps the extensive literature on European and Japanese fascisms as products of "late development," e.g., Mann, *Fascists*, 48–64.

34 E.g., Yang, *Jiang Jieshi yu Nanjing guomin zheng fu*; Yang, *Guomindang de "lian-gong" yu "fangong"*; Wang, *Geming yu fangeming*.

35 Zanasi, *Saving the Nation*.

36 Mayer, *Dynamics of Counterrevolution in Europe*, 9.

37 As Brian Tsui has written, "the GMD held dearly to the rhetoric of revolution. . . . Inasmuch as the GMD claimed a monopoly on China's revolutionary course, the rightwing party-state was a reaction against the ascendant Communist movement." Tsui, "China's Forgotten Revolution," 2.

38 William C. Kirby, for instance, characterized Chinese fascism as a "vogue that coincided with the emergence of a close Sino-German friendship," in *Germany and Republican China*, 175. This characterization is restated in Kirby, "Images and Realities of Chinese Fascism," 267. The sense that fascism was a force external to Chinese social conditions also appears in analyses specifically concerned with the extremes of Nationalist nationalism, e.g., Ni, *"Minzu" xiangxiang yu guojia tongzhi*, 168–73, 299. See also Clinton, "Fascism, Cultural Revolution, and National Sovereignty in 1930s China," introduction.

39 Chang, for instance, in *The Chinese Blue Shirt Society*, 25–54, based much of her argument against regarding the Blue Shirts as fascist on the fact that they preferred not to use the term *fascism* to describe their own politics.

40 On Chinese fascist analyses of the Italy-Ethiopia conflict, see Clinton, "Ends of the Universal," 1740–68.

41 E.g., Xia Dianren, "Deren yanmu zhong zhi Zhonggruoren" [Chinese people in German eyes], *Qiantu* 1, no. 5 (1933): 1–5.

42 Dai was a longtime comrade of Sun who reluctantly joined the United Front in 1924, serving on the Soviet-reorganized GMD Central Executive Committee and heading the party's propaganda department, during which time Dai helped create its Central News Agency. Boorman and Howard, *Biographical Diction-ary of Republican China*, vol. 3, 201; also Mast and Saywell, "Revolution out of Tradition," 73–98; Bai, "Jiang Jieshi ruhua sanminzhuyi zhi pingxi," 76–79; Tsui, "China's Forgotten Revolution," introduction and ch. 1; Yang, *Guomindang de "liangong" yu "fangong,"* 79–87.

43 Audrey Wells characterized Dai's neglect to mention the influence of Western political and economic theories on Sun Yat-sen as "difficult to fathom" and likely due to Dai's noted mental instability. Wells, *The Political Thought of Sun Yat-sen*, 136. As the scholars cited above have emphasized, Dai's rereading of Sun was a political rather than a psychological move. Historian Yan Lu aptly termed it an effort to "nativize" Sun's thought in *Re-understanding Japan*, 148–51.

44 Taylor, *The Generalissimo*, 18, 35. Dai's son was raised as Chiang Wei-kuo.

45 For instance, Chiang and Chen Guofu formed a Shanghai investment firm in 1920 with the soon-disappointed idea of speculating in stocks to fund the revolution. Taylor, *The Generalissimo*, 35.

46 Chung, *Élitist Fascism*, 133; van de Ven, *From Friend to Comrade*, 171–73; Zhang, Fang, and Huang, *Zhonghua minguoshi dacidian*, 833–34.

47 Wakeman, "Confucian Fascism," 420.

48 Van de Ven, *War and Nationalism in China*, 119.

49 Ho Chi Minh, for instance, was in Canton at the time of the purge and immediately recognized the imperative to leave China before being handed over to
French police. See Duiker, *Ho Chi Minh*, 144–45. Writings that soon appeared on
the events of 1927 included M. N. Roy's *Revolution and Counterrevolution in China*,
Leon Trotsky's writings collected in *Leon Trotsky on China*, and André Malraux's
novel *Man's Fate*.

50 Peter Zarrow has underscored the importance of separating the New Culture and May Fourth movements historically and conceptually, as the former
constituted a series of intellectual discussions and the latter a mass social movement. See chapters 7 and 8 of Zarrow, *China in War and Revolution*. However,
Revolutionary Nativism follows convention by using "May Fourth" to denote the
comprehensive intellectual and social ferment of the years 1915 to 1922. Chow,
The May Fourth Movement; Schwarcz, *The Chinese Enlightenment*.

51 Liu, *Translingual Practice*, 256.

52 Liu, *Translingual Practice*, 239.

53 Chan, "A Turning Point in the Modern Chinese Revolution," 230–31.

54 Ko, *Teachers of the Inner Chambers*, 3–4. As Prasenjit Duara summarized, people
during this period engaged with something that was "not an inert inheritance
from the past, but equally a range of responses to this inheritance in the contemporary scene." Duara, *Rescuing History from the Nation*, 90.

55 Luo, *Inheritance within Rupture*. This is a translation of Luo Zhitian, *Liebianzhong
de chuancheng: Ershi shiji qianqi de Zhongguo wenhua yu xueshu* (Beijing: Zhonghua shuju, 2003).

56 Levenson, *Confucian China and Its Modern Fate*, 99–104, 116.

57 E.g., Chatterjee, *The Nation and Its Fragments*.

58 Lionel Jensen has argued that the narrowing of this heritage into something
bequeathed by Confucius was itself a product of Chinese encounters with European, particularly Jesuit, intellectuals beginning in the sixteenth century. Jensen,
Manufacturing Confucianism, introduction.

59 Fanon, *The Wretched of the Earth*, 41.

60 Chen, *Zhongguo wenhua jianshe xiehui gaikuang yilan*, 1.

61 Yang, *Jiang Jieshi yu Nanjing guomin zhengfu*, 5–6.

62 Deng, *Guomindang de hexin zuzhi zhenxiang*, 322.

63 As Parks Coble has noted, this was the general thrust of a 1937 report issued
by the Research Division of Japan's Foreign Ministry (Iwai, *Ran'isha ni kansuru
chōsa*). Coble, *Facing Japan*, 226. The report was translated into English during
World War II and can be found here: U.S. State Department, Confidential Central Files, China, Internal Affairs, 1945–1949, 893.00/3-3045. See esp. p. 76 of the
English translation.

64 Herzstein, *Henry R. Luce, Time, and the American Crusade in Asia*; also Mao, *Asia
First*, ch. 2.

65 Jay Taylor's English-language biography of Chiang, *The Generalissimo*, maintains
that the absence of clear discussions of fascism in Chiang's diaries, coupled with

Chiang's disinterest in replicating Nazi ideology in China, meant that "Chiang was fascist in neither ends nor means." Taylor, *The Generalissimo*, 101–2. I argue throughout this book that Chinese disinterest in replicating metropolitan fascisms on Chinese soil was consistent with their extreme nationalist position, sharing a logic with what Reto Hofmann has identified as a concomitant "fascist critique of fascism" in Japan. Joseph Esherick has compellingly questioned Taylor's portrayal, noting not only that Chiang had "many faces" but also that the biography's generally "apologetic tone is most pronounced in Taylor's discussion of fascism." Esherick, "The Many Faces of Chiang Kai-shek," 22. Also Hofmann, *The Fascist Effect*.

66 Dirlik, "Ideological Foundations of the New Life Movement," 968.

67 Griffin, *The Nature of Fascism*, 41.

1 » HIDING IN PLAIN SIGHT

1 Bloch, *Heritage of Our Times*, 64–68.

2 Griffin, *The Nature of Fascism*, 48.

3 Dagmar Herzog, for instance, has argued that "Nazism has been misremembered and misrepresented as sexually repressive for everyone"—as merely affirming long-standing bourgeois morals—"what Nazism actually did was to redefine who could have sex with whom." Herzog, *Sex after Fascism*, 18.

4 The literature on Chinese Communist ideology is vast. For comparative reference, see, for example, Dirlik, *The Origins of Chinese Communism*; Chen, *Zhongguo gongchan geming qishinian*.

5 Sun, *The International Development of China*, 195.

6 E.g., Bodenhorn, *Defining Modernity*; Eastman, *The Abortive Revolution*; Musgrove, *China's Contested Capital*; Strauss, *Strong Institutions in Weak Polities*; Yeh, *Becoming Chinese*.

7 Wei, *Counterrevolution in China*; Coble, *The Shanghai Capitalists and the Nationalist Government*.

8 Fitzgerald, *Awakening China*; Gilmartin, *Engendering the Chinese Revolution*, 149–50.

9 Harvey, *The Condition of Postmodernity*, 127; Maier, "Between Taylorism and Technocracy," 36; Rabinbach, *The Human Motor*, 272.

10 Boorman and Howard, *Biographical Dictionary of Republican China*, vol. 3, 203.

11 Song Qingling, "Tongchi Dai Jitao" [A bitter account of Dai Jitao], in *Song Qingling xuanji*, 43–49.

12 Song, "Tongchi Dai Jitao," 48. Their discussion of popular rule refers to Nanjing's decision to indefinitely extend what was sketched by Sun Yat-sen as an interim period of "political tutelage," with the idea that the nation was not yet ready to participate in state-level politics and that emergency conditions demanded popular exclusion.

13 Song, "Tongchi Dai Jitao," 45–46.

14 Song, "Tongchi Dai Jitao," 44.

15 Yang, *Guomindang de "lian gong" yu "fangong,"* 266.

16   Sun, *Sanminzhuyi*, 124. See also Bergère, *Sun Yat-sen*, 374–77.

17   Yang, *Guomindang de "liangong" yu "fangong,"* 273.

18   Chan, *Historiography of the Chinese Labor Movement*, 103; also Perry, *Shanghai on Strike*, 88–108.

19   Chan, *Historiography of the Chinese Labor Movement*, 103.

20   Chan, *Historiography of the Chinese Labor Movement*, 105.

21   Hung-Mao Tien, for instance, read Chiang Kai-shek's "dependence on loyal stooges" of the CC and Whampoa cliques (some of whom went on to form the Blue Shirts) as having "severely undermined the Nationalists' revolutionary legacy and his own claim to inherit it." Tien, *Government and Politics in Kuomintang China*, 4; Elizabeth J. Perry has also observed how the "factional battles that wracked the Shanghai labor scene [in the wake of the 1927 party purge] were but a harbinger of the endless intragovernment disputes that would eventually sap the Nationalist state of its capacity to rule." Perry, *Shanghai on Strike*, 93.

22   Ming K. Chan and Arif Dirlik underscored that, until 1927, the GMD was far from politically unified, containing "under its political umbrella the whole spectrum of politics from anarchists to radical Marxists to hidebound conservatives and militarists." Chan and Dirlik, *Schools into Fields and Factories*, 7. On the GMD left, see So, *The Kuomintang Left in the National Revolution*; also Zanasi, *Saving the Nation*.

23   Zanasi, *Saving the Nation*.

24   Discussions of rivalries between these factions, as well as their development and memberships, can be found in Chung, *Élitist Fascism*, 111–15; Li, "Culture, Revolution, and Modernity in China," ch. 2; Wakeman, *Spymaster*, passim; Wakeman, *Policing Shanghai*, 236–38.

25   Even the main Japanese intelligence officer charged with investigating the Blue Shirts in the 1930s believed that there was "no reason for opposition between the LAN I SHE [Blue Shirts] and the CC Band [CC Clique] as far as essential nature is concerned . . . but so far they have continued their opposition to each other." "The Chinese Lan-i-she Society," U.S. State Department, Confidential Central Files, China, Internal Affairs, 1945–1949, 893.00/3-3045, 76 (microfilm p. 00718).

26   Tien, *Government and Politics in Kuomintang China*, 49.

27   Tien, *Government and Politics in Kuomintang China*; Wakeman, *Spymaster*, 91.

28   Guo, *Zhonghua minguo shiqi junzheng zhiguan zhi*, 506–7; Li, "Culture, Revolution, and Modernity in China," 43; Tien, *Government and Politics in Kuomintang China*, 49.

29   Tien, *Government and Politics in Kuomintang China*, 50.

30   Li, "Culture, Revolution, and Modernity in China," 45; also Tien, *Government and Politics in Kuomintang China*, 51.

31   Li and Zhang, *Minguo liang xiongdi*, 82.

32   Chen Lifu quoted in Li and Zhang, *Minguo liang xiongdi*, 82; also Chen, *Chengbai zhi jian*, 105.

33   Chen, *Chengbai zhi jian*, 106; Li and Zhang, *Minguo liang xiongdi*, 82–83.

34 Li and Zhang, *Minguo liang xiongdi*, 19.

35 Li and Zhang, *Minguo liang xiongdi*, 20–23.

36 Boorman and Howard, *Biographical Dictionary of Republican China*, vol. 1, 202.

37 Boorman and Howard, *Biographical Dictionary of Republican China*, vol. 1; on Nationalist involvement in speculation, see Goodman, "Things Unheard of East or West," 57–76.

38 Boorman and Howard, *Biographical Dictionary of Republican China*, vol. 1, 203.

39 Yergin, *The Prize*, part I.

40 Chen, *The Storm Clouds Clear over China*, 18.

41 Chen, *Chengbai zhi jian*, 33; Chen, *The Storm Clouds Clear over China*, 16–17.

42 Chen, *The Storm Clouds Clear over China*, 16–17.

43 Chen, *The Storm Clouds Clear over China*, 19–20.

44 Chen, *The Storm Clouds Clear over China*, 21.

45 Chen Lifu quoted in Li and Zhang, *Minguo liang xiongdi*, 47.

46 Chen, *The Storm Clouds Clear over China*, 21.

47 Chen, *The Storm Clouds Clear over China*, 21.

48 Taylor, *The Principles of Scientific Management*.

49 Chen, "Application of Mechanical and Electrical Devices to Coal Mining in China," 25.

50 Chen, *The Storm Clouds Clear over China*, 21.

51 Perry, *Shanghai on Strike*, 90–91, fn.

52 Perry, *Shanghai on Strike*, 91.

53 The methods Chiang's men employed to subjugate labor unions were brutal; they were also quickly followed by unprecedented waves of legislation to regulate factories and organizing conditions. While these new laws were difficult to enforce because most of China's factories were located in colonial concessions, they nevertheless signaled a concerted effort to manage modern forms of class conflict. Perry, *Shanghai on Strike*, 92; Chan, *Historiography of the Chinese Labor Movement*, 10–11.

54 On corporatism and the Nanjing regime, see Zanasi, *Saving the Nation*.

55 Chen, *The Storm Clouds Clear over China*, 25.

56 Marx and Engels, *The Communist Manifesto*, 43.

57 Sayer, *Capitalism and Modernity*, 98; Gerth and Mills, *From Max Weber*, 261.

58 Foucault, *Discipline and Punish*, 151, 152, 157.

59 J. Edgar Hoover to Frederick B. Lyon, letter, March 30, 1945, "The Chinese Lan-i-she Society," U.S. State Department, Confidential Central Files, China, Internal Affairs, 1945–1949, 893.00/3-3045.

60 Historian Deng Yuanzhong, son of Blue Shirt founder Deng Wenyi, discussed methodological challenges of reconstructing Blue Shirt activities. As a secret organization, they were not subject to official state record-keeping practices, and many relevant documents were lost during the GMD flight from Nanjing before advancing Japanese armies in 1937. Deng, *Guomindang hexin zuzhi zhenxiang*, 12–13.

61 Chung, *Élitist Fascism*, 89–92.

62 Liu, *Fuxing Zhongguo geming zhi lu*.

63 Chung, *Élitist Fascism*, 115–16.

64 Chung, *Élitist Fascism*, 92–93.

65 On the origins of the name Blue Shirts, see Chung, *Élitist Fascism*, 105–9.

66 Deng, *Guomindang hexin zuzhi zhenxiang*, 2.

67 Chung, *Élitist Fascism*, 95.

68 Chung, *Élitist Fascism*, 97.

69 Chiang's removal from centralized power gave Wang Jingwei's faction room to pursue corporatist economic development strategies while Chiang pursued military campaigns against the Communists—and left Wang's faction to face the brunt of public scrutiny for what seemed to be weakness vis-à-vis Japanese aggression. See Coble, *Facing Japan*; Zanasi, *Saving the Nation*.

70 Chung, *Élitist Fascism*, 98. According to Hung-Mao Tien, Blue Shirt "funds came either from Chiang's personal financial sources or from institutions that he directly controlled. Thus the Military Council, its branch offices, and most military schools connected with Nanking allocated money for Blue Shirt activities." Tien, *Government and Politics in Kuomintang China*, 63; also Wakeman, *Spymaster*, 82.

71 Coble, *Facing Japan*, 226–28.

72 Chung, *Élitist Fascism*, 140.

73 Chang, *The Chinese Blue Shirt Society*, 3–4; Deng, *Guomindang hexin zuzhi zhenxiang*, 40–41.

74 Deng, *Guomindang hexin zuzhi zhenxiang*, 54.

75 Tien, *Government and Politics in Kuomintang China*, 61–62.

76 Though by 1936 He Zhonghan had attained the army rank of lieutenant general, he is typically identified as "Mr. He" in sympathetic contemporaneous and posthumous writings, so I follow this convention. Zhang, Fang, and Huang, *Zhonghua minguoshi dacidian*, 1444.

77 Deng, *Guomindang hexin zuzhi zhenxiang*, 43–44; He Zhonghan xiansheng zhisang weiyuanhui, *He Zhonghan xiansheng shilüe*, 1; Wakeman, *Spymaster*, 49–50.

78 "The Training of the National Revolutionary Army for War," in Wilbur and How, *Missionaries of Revolution*, 623.

79 "The Training of the National Revolutionary Army for War."

80 Deng, *Guomindang hexin zuzhi zhenxiang*, 53–54.

81 Reese, *The Soviet Military Experience*, 53, 55–59.

82 Reese, *The Soviet Military Experience*, 57. Soviet advisers at Whampoa were likewise concerned with political consciousness and sanitation. E.g., "Report on Sanitary Conditions in the National Revolutionary Army of the Canton Government as of March 15, 1926," in Wilbur and How, *Missionaries of Revolution*, 636–39.

83 Chung, *Élitist Fascism*, 64–66; Wakeman, *Spymaster*, 48, 89.

84 Teng Jie quoted in Wakeman, *Spymaster*, 48.

85 He Zhonghan xiansheng zhisang weiyuanhui, *He Zhonghan xiansheng shilüe*, 1.

86 Wakeman, *Spymaster*, 41, 213.

87 Deng, *Guomindang hexin zuzhi zhenxiang*, 53; Wakeman, *Spymaster*, 41, 81.

88 Chang, *The Chinese Blue Shirt Society*, 74–78.

89 Chang, *The Chinese Blue Shirt Society*, 64.

90 Chang, *The Chinese Blue Shirt Society*, 64.

91 Chang, *The Chinese Blue Shirt Society*, 65.

92 Chang, *The Chinese Blue Shirt Society*, 69–74.

93 Eley, *Nazism as Fascism*, 203.

94 Tien, *Government and Politics in Kuomintang China*, 52.

95 Mayer, *The Furies*, 34.

96 Legal text quoted from Yang, *Guomindang de "liangong" yu "fangong,"* 266.

97 Deng, *Guomindang hexin zuzhi zhenxiang*, 414–17.

98 This picture took the form of a five-hundred-page chapter on "works and publications" in the 1936 *Domestic Affairs Almanac* (*Neizheng nianjian*), which recorded nearly one thousand distinct newspapers (printed daily or every other day) and roughly eighteen hundred magazines (which ran every three days and upward) in circulation. The almanac classified every publication as either having or lacking government approval. Li, *Zhongguo baokan tushi*, 123; Neizhengbu nianjian bianzuan weiyuanhui, "Di shiyi zhang: zhuzuowu ji chubanpin," in *Neizheng nianjian*, c798–c1304.

99 For a comparative analysis of fascist visual cultures across the world during the interwar and wartime years, see essays in Thomas and Eley, *Visualizing Fascism in East Asia and Europe*.

100 On the competition between the Blue Shirt and cc Clique cultural organizations, see Li, "Culture, Revolution, and Modernity," 199–202; Xiong, *Nanchang xingying*, 155–57.

101 "Guomindang zhongyang zhixing weiyuanhui wenhua shiye jihua weiyuanhui zuzhi tiaolie; 1936 nian 3 yue 3 ri" [Organizational regulations of the Cultural Enterprise Planning Committee of the Guomindang Central Executive Committee, March 3, 1936], in Zhongguo di'er lishi dang'an guan, *Zhonghua minguoshi dang'an ziliao huibian*, 1.

102 Zhao Shu, "cc de kuozhang huodong" [The cc Clique's broader activities], in Chai, *cc Neimu*, 92–95.

103 Text accompanying photograph in Wan et al., *Zhongguo jindai zhencang tupianku*, 75.

104 Photograph from Wan et al., *Zhongguo jindai zhencang tupianku*, 75.

105 Photograph from Wan et al., *Zhongguo jindai zhencang tupianku*, 94.

106 "Benkan qishi (er)" [Announcements, 2], *Wenhua jianshe* 1, no. 1 (1934): frontmatter.

107 "Zhongguo wenhua de jiejing" [Crystallizations of Chinese culture], *Wenhua jianshe* 1, no. 1 (1934).

108 "Suturing a historical rupture" is paraphrased from Buck-Morss, *Dreamworld and Catastrophe*, 43. Buck-Morss writes, "The suturing of history's narrative discourse transforms the violent rupture of the present into a continuity of meaning."

109 *Wenhua jianshe* 1, no. 5 (1935). On the Union Pacific train design, see Maffei, "The Search for an American Design Aesthetic," 361–69; see also Jackson, "Art Deco in East Asia," 371–81.

110 Pickowicz, Shen, and Zhang, *Liangyou*, passim.

111 Wu, "Wenhua tongzhi yu guojia suzao," 16.

112 Wu, "Wenhua tongzhi yu guojia suzao."

113 Chen, *Zhongguo dianying shiye*.

114 Chen, *Zhongguo dianying shiye*, 42.

115 Deng, *Guomindang hexin zuzhi zhenxiang*, 150–51. Blue Shirt leader Deng Wenyi, who Frederic Wakeman reports "had a longtime commercial interest in cultural affairs," founded the Tiba Shudian, which "published collections of Chiang Kai-shek's speeches and a series of handbooks for the military man." It was reportedly quite "successful in attracting customers eager to better themselves." Wakeman, *Spymaster*, 103.

116 Wakeman, *Spymaster*, 102.

117 Chung, *Élitist Fascism*, 146.

118 Deng, *Guomindang hexinzuzhi zhenxiang*, 148.

119 Deng, *Guomindang hexinzuzhi zhenxiang*, 151.

120 William C. Kirby suggested that the phrases "Blood and Iron" and "Blood and Sweat" were inspired by Bismarck and Churchill, respectively. Kirby, *Germany and Republican China*, 149–50.

121 The 1933 first issue went through three separate printings. By 1935 it reportedly had twenty thousand subscribers. It was edited by a hometown associate of He Zhonghan's named Liu Bingli (a secondary school teacher in Shanghai); He provided start-up funds for the magazine and frequently contributed his own essays. Each issue was thematically organized and totaled some hundred pages of essays, cartoons, advertisements, short stories, poetry, and plays. Deng, *Guomindang hexinzuzhi zhenxiang*, 154–55; Wakeman, *Spymaster*, 98–99; Xu, "1930 niandai Lixingshe yanzhong de Yidali faxisizhuyi," 147.

122 Pan, *Shanghai Style*, 97–99.

123 *Hanxue zhoukan* was listed in the *Domestic Affairs Almanac* as registered in Jiangxi, but its own pages indicated that its offices moved to Shanghai after the conclusion of the counterinsurgency campaigns in 1934. Neizhengbu nianjian bianzuan weiyuanhui, "Di shiyi zhang: Zhuzuowu ji chubanpin," in *Neizheng nianjian*, c1102. Wang Xiaohua identified *Hanxue zhoukan* as initiated under the auspices of the Blue Shirts' Nanchang-based Zhongguo wenhua xuehui (Chinese Culture Study Society), which was founded in December 1933 by Deng Wenyi, He Zhonghan, and Xiong Shihui at Chiang Kai-shek's suggestion. Wang, *"Mofan" Nanchang*, 5.

124 *Hanxue zhoukan* 1, no. 2 (1933): front cover; e.g., *Hanxue zhoukan* 5, no. 3 (1935): front cover.

125 *Hanxue zhoukan* 2, no. 10 (1934); an image of Qian Juntao's *Shidai funü* cover can be found in Minick and Ping, *Chinese Graphic Design in the Twentieth Century*, 61. Cover designs of fascist magazines were rarely attributed. Shanghai's limited

number of graphic designers possibly moonlighted for far right publications to support themselves.

126 *Hanxue zhoukan* 5, no. 1 (1936).

127 See Tang, *Origins of the Chinese Avant-Garde*.

128 *Jingcheng yuekan* 1, no. 3 (1933): front cover. The word *monthly* (*yuekan*) occasionally appears in *Jingcheng*'s title. I therefore include it in references to the magazine, as it also helps to distinguish this publication from the related *Jingcheng zazhi*.

129 Kirby has documented how both the Blue Shirts and the CC Clique were vocal admirers of Nazi Germany, using the pages of their publications to introduce readers to aspects of National Socialist thought and practice. Chen Lifu, for his part, "sent a party commission to Europe to investigate fascist party organization and edited [this commission's] study of the ruling parties of Germany, Italy, and Turkey, which gave particularly high marks to NSDAP organization, Leadership Principle, and recruitment of youth," while the clique more broadly admired the Nazis' "*volkisch* and Germanic ideology" as it suggested how "regeneration was rooted in a people's cultural heritage"; Kirby, *Germany and Republican China*, 163, 158–65.

130 "A-li-an minzu zhi zaixing" [Revival of the Aryan race], *Hanxue zhoukan* 5, no. 21 (1935): inside front cover.

131 Clinton, "Ends of the Universal."

132 "Jiu minzu shengcun, A-guo wuli ziwei" [For the survival of the nation, Ethiopians use armed force to defend themselves], *Hanxue zhoukan* 5, no. 21 (1935): back cover.

2 » SPIRIT IS ETERNAL

1 E.g., Anderson, *Imagined Communities*; McClintock, *Imperial Leather*; Nairn, *The Break-Up of Britain*.

2 Hobsbawm and Ranger, *The Invention of Tradition*.

3 Karl Marx, "The Eighteenth Brumaire of Louis Bonaparte," trans. Terrell Carver, in Cowling and Martin, *Marx's "Eighteenth Brumaire*," 22.

4 Fung, "Nationalism and Modernity," 800.

5 Fung, *The Intellectual Foundations of Chinese Modernity*, 62. Charlotte Furth stated this another way when she wrote, "In China, as elsewhere, modern conservatism has been a response to new issues, a response in which reevaluations of tradition have gone hand in hand with competing models for change. . . . Similarly, in China modern conservatism like its rivals was a reaction to imperialism and the introduction of Western ideas." Furth, "Culture and Politics in Modern Chinese Conservatism," 24.

6 Fung, drawing on Edmund Burke, has written of how the conservative position is necessarily historically and contextually specific, but that one can detect a common assumption that "civilized society requires order and class, that prudent change is the means of social preservation and that society is joined in perpetuity by a moral bond among the dead, the living and those yet to be born.

Additionally, conservatism is opposed to economic and political levelling." Fung, *The Intellectual Foundations of Chinese Modernity*, 64.

7   On "creative destruction" as a core element of aesthetic modernism as well as processes of capitalist modernization, see Harvey, *The Condition of Postmodernity*, 16–38; also Berman, *All That Is Solid Melts into Air*, esp. 87–129.

8   "Guomindang de wenhua zhengce pipan" [A critique of Guomindang cultural policy], *Shehuizhuyi yuekan* 1, no. 7 (1933): 99.

9   Terry Bodenhorn has noted the imprint of Chen Lifu's education in mine engineering on Chen's tract *Weishenglun* (*Vitalism*), "Chen Lifu's Vitalism: A Guomindang Vision of Modernity circa 1934," in Bodenhorn, *Defining Modernity*, 104n16.

10 Bodenhorn, "Chen Lifu's Vitalism," 98–99.

11 Levenson, *Confucian China and Its Modern Fate*, 116.

12 A summary of the movements' key arguments re: Confucianism can be found in Chow, *The May Fourth Movement*, 300–313.

13 Chen Lifu, "Zhongguo wenhua jianshe lun" [On Chinese cultural construction], *Wenhua jianshe* 1, no. 1 (1935): 15. Arif Dirlik underscored that GMD promoters of the New Life Movement were keen on emphasizing the distinction between fuxing and fugu. Dirlik, "Ideological Foundations of the New Life Movement," 961.

14 Dirlik, *Anarchism in the Chinese Revolution*, 158.

15 Wang, *Women in the Chinese Enlightenment*, 11–12. In her work on Republican-era family reform, Susan Glosser has written of how many New Culture advocates focused on "family reform as the key to unlocking the potential of China's youth and rebuilding their shattered nation. They accused the traditional patriarchal family of sacrificing China's youth on the altar of filial obligation, teaching them dependency, slavishness, and insularity, and robbing them of their creative energy. In its place they advocated the Western conjugal family ideal (xiao jiating, literally 'small family'), an ideal that promoted free marriage choice, companionate marriage, and economic and emotional independence from the family (da jiazu, literally the 'large family')." Glosser, *Chinese Visions of Family and State*, 3.

16 Dirlik, *Anarchism in the Chinese Revolution*, 156.

17 Wang Hui, "The Fate of 'Mr. Science' in China: The Concept of Science and Its Application in Modern Chinese Thought," in Barlow, *Formations of Colonial Modernity in East Asia*, 21–82.

18 Kwan, *Marxist Intellectuals and the Chinese Labor Movement*, 7.

19 He Zhonghan xiansheng zhisang weiyuanhui, *He Zhonghan xiansheng shilüe*, 1; Wakeman, *Spymaster*, 49–52.

20 Chen, *The Storm Clouds Clear over China*, 14.

21 Chen, *The Storm Clouds Clear over China*, 14. According to Tse-tsung Chow, "Aided by Mr. Te and Mr. Sai, the new intellectual leaders set out to attack traditional ethics. They aimed first of all at dethroning what became known in Hu Shih's catch phrase as 'Confucius and Sons' (K'ung-chia-tian) from its undisputed sway over ethics and ideas in China which had lasted two thousand years." Chow, *The May Fourth Movement*, 300.

22 Deng discusses the May Fourth educational milieu experienced by Blue Shirts such as Teng Jie, Kang Ze, and He Zhonghan in *Guomindang hexin zuzhi zhenxiang*, 41–47.

23 Chen, *The Storm Clouds Clear over China*, 14.

24 Chen, *The Storm Clouds Clear over China*, 16–22.

25 David Harvey's felicitous phrase "accumulation by dispossession," which emphasizes the ways in which Marx's notion of primitive accumulation (of separating producers from means of production) is an ongoing and intrinsic dimension of capitalism, is readily relatable to imperialism's cultural violence. This is perhaps most evident in the looting of art and artifacts for metropolitan museums, but it is also discernible in the ways in which denigrating indigenous traditions as backward and unsuited for modernity was instrumental to colonial rule. On "accumulation by dispossession," see Harvey, *The New Imperialism*, 137–82. On these practices in the colonized world, see, e.g., Cohn, *Colonialism and Its Forms of Knowledge*; Hevia, *English Lessons*.

26 E.g., Chatterjee, *Nationalist Thought and the Colonial World*; Fanon, *The Wretched of the Earth*.

27 On the folk studies movement that emerged from the May Fourth injunction to "go to the people," see Hung, *Going to the People*; on labor mobilization, see Kwan, *Marxist Intellectuals and the Chinese Labor Movement*.

28 Lam, *A Passion for Facts*.

29 Bergère, *Sun Yat-sen*, 89. Bergère continued that "his initiation into Christian values and Western civilization combined with his rejection by dominant Chinese elites, did not dispose him favorably to the relations of subordination (of a son to a father, a subject to his prince) taught by Confucianism," 89–90. By the time Sun delivered his last version of the Three Principles lectures in 1924, however, he had clearly become comfortable with modern forms of social hierarchy.

30 Guannan Li, drawing upon the work of Yu Ying-shih, has noted how Sun Yat-sen's long-standing recourse to Confucian categories marked "a common tendency among late Qing scholars who tended to address contemporary matters by reorienting Confucianism toward reform and change." Li, "Culture, Revolution, and Modernity," 193n20; also Yu, "Sun Yat-sen's Doctrine and Traditional Chinese Culture," 92.

31 Li, "Culture, Revolution, and Modernity," 192.

32 Sun, *Sanminzhuyi*, 52–53.

33 Sun, *Sanminzhuyi*, 48–49. Family and clan organizations, Sun maintained, were deeply inscribed in China's social structure. In their capacity to function as mediators between the individual and the state, they were to be regarded as assets in the construction of nationalism.

34 Sun, *Sanminzhuyi*, 29.

35 Sun, *Sanminzhuyi*, 29, 32–33; Fitzgerald, *Awakening China*, 86–87.

36 Sun, *Sanminzhuyi*, 169.

37 Sun, *Sanminzhuyi*, 164.

38 Sun, *Sanminzhuyi*, 131–32.

39 See also Bergère on Sun's approach to questions of equality, *Sun Yat-sen*, 374–77. In certain respects, Sun's view of the buzhibujue echoed F. W. Taylor's notorious observation in his 1911 *Principles of Scientific Management* that the "work of [pig-iron handling] is so crude and elementary in nature that . . . it would be possible to train an intelligent gorilla so as to become a more efficient pig-iron handler than any man could be." Taylor, *The Principles of Scientific Management*, 18. Antonio Gramsci in turn observed that "Taylor was in fact expressing with brutal cynicism the purpose of American society—developing in the worker to the highest degree automatic and mechanical attitudes, breaking up the old psycho-physical nexus of qualified professional work, which demands a certain active participation on the part of the worker, and reducing productive operations to the mechanical, physical aspect." Antonio Gramsci, "Americanism and Fordism," in Gramsci, *Selections from the Prison Notebooks*, 302. The same might be said of the ways in which Chinese fascists came to characterize the role of laborers in China's development.

40 Sun, *Sanminzhuyi*, 124.

41 Sun, *Sanminzhuyi*, 124.

42 Sun, *Sanminzhuyi*, 124.

43 Sun, *Sanminzhuyi*, 124.

44 Sun, *Sanminzhuyi*, 125.

45 Sun, *Sanminzhuyi*, 132–33. See also Bergère's discussion of this example in *Sun Yat-sen*, 375.

46 Sun, *Sanminzhuyi*, 133.

47 Lenin, "Can the Bolsheviks Retain State Power?"

48 Sun, *Sanminzhuyi*, 126.

49 Sun, *Sanminzhuyi*, 133–51.

50 Tsui, "China's Forgotten Revolution," 46–52.

51 Mast and Saywell, "Revolution out of Tradition," 75.

52 Boorman and Howard, *Biographical Dictionary of Republican China*, vol. 3, 201; Zhang, Fang, and Huang, *Zhonghua minguoshi dacidian*, 1910.

53 Dirlik, *The Origins of Chinese Communism*, 123.

54 Boorman and Howard, *Biographical Dictionary of Republican China*, vol. 3, 201–2; Zhang, Fang, and Huang, *Zhonghua minguoshi dacidian*, 1910.

55 Tsui, "China's Forgotten Revolution," 46–52.

56 Tani E. Barlow, "Introduction: On 'Colonial Modernity,'" in Barlow, *Formations of Colonial Modernity in East Asia*, 8. Etienne Balibar also maintained that, in "a sense, every modern nation is a product of colonization: it has always been to some degree colonized or colonizing, and sometimes both at the same time." Etienne Balibar, "The Nation Form," in Balibar and Wallerstein, *Race, Nation, Class*, 89. In other words, no nation is hermetically sealed.

57 Mast and Saywell, "Revolution out of Tradition," 88.

58 Dai, *Sanminzhuyi zhi zhexue de jichu*, 28.

59 Dai, *Sanminzhuyi zhi zhexue de jichu*, 13, 20–21.

60 Dai, *Sanminzhuyi zhi zhexue de jichu*, 21.

61   Dai, *Sanminzhuyi zhi zhexue de jichu*, 15.

62   Dai, *Sanminzhuyi zhi zhexue de jichu*, 24–25.

63   Dai, *Sanminzhuyi zhi zhexue de jichu*, 25.

64   Qu and Chen, *Fan Dai Jitao de guomin geming guan*, 2.

65   Under pressure from the Soviets and from Chiang Kai-shek (who was then trying to maintain unity among his troops), the society's founding manifesto upheld the principles of the Hong Kong Canton strike-boycott, and rejected the declared anti-Communism of the conservative Western Hills group as well as that of GMD activists (including Dai Jitao) who had decamped to Shanghai after Sun's passing. However, the Western Hills group, Chiang Kai-shek, and Dai Jitao all supported the Sun Yat-senism Study Society behind the scenes, and the society's professed concern to distill the truth of Sun's thought pointed in a decidedly counterrevolutionary direction. Wilbur and How, *Missionaries of Revolution*, 192–93, 245–47, 251; Deng, *Guomindang hexin zuzhi zhenxiang*, 50–51.

66   Zhang, Fang, and Huang, *Zhonghua minguoshi dacidian*, 833–34.

67   An article in Shanghai's *Geming daobao* (Revolutionary guide) insisted that the purpose of the organization was not anti-Communist but rather to propagate the true meaning of Sun's thought, and that the revolution aimed to "destroy the old and construct the new." Pan Shuzi, *Geming daobao*, January 4, 1926, 7; a Peking University paper, meanwhile, claimed that its branch already had over seven hundred members, that it was propagating true Sun Yat-senism, and that "other foreign isms are unsuited to the national character." "Beijing Sunwenzhuyi xuehui Beida fenhui yuelanshi chengli tongbao" [Notice of the establishment of the Sun Yat-senism Study Society Peking University Branch Reading Room], *Beijing daxue ribao* [Peking University Daily News], February 6, 1926, di'er ban. On the CC Clique's later absorption of Sun Yat-senism Study Society members, see Tien, *Government and Politics in Kuomintang China*, 49.

68   Deng, *Guomindang de hexin zuzhi zhenxiang*, 117.

69   Koonz, *The Nazi Conscience*, 6.

70   This problem as it pertains to the Nanjing regime's approach to religion and superstition has been traced in Duara, *Rescuing History from the Nation*, ch. 3; Nedostup, *Superstitious Regimes*. Guannan Li has also illuminated subtle but decisive modern transformations in state Confucian rituals in "Culture, Revolution, and Modernity," ch. 7.

71   Chen Bulei, "Fakanci" [Introductory remarks], *Xinshengming* 1, no. 1 (1928): 1–3.

72   Jiang Zhongzheng (Chiang Kai-shek), "Geming yu bugeming" [Revolution and not-revolution], *Xinshengming* 2, no. 3 (1929): 1–7; Sa Mengwu, "Minshengzhuyi shixian de qianti" [Prerequisites for the realization of Sun's principle of popular livelihood], *Xinshengming* 2, no. 3 (1929): 1–11; Fang Yue, "Zhongguo fengjian zhidu de xiaomie (shang)" [The elimination of China's feudal system, part 1], *Xinshengming* 2, no. 3 (1929); Fang Yue, "Kongzi xueshuo de jinzhan" [The progress of Confucian doctrine], *Xinshengming* 2, no. 9 (1929): 1–17.

73   Deng Wenyi, "Yijiusanlingnian de Zhongguo wenti" [China's problems in 1930], *Zhongguo wenhua* 1, no. 1 (1930): 21–22.

74 Jiang Zhongzheng (Chiang Kai-shek), "Yi liyilianchi wei dang wei guo zhi ben" [Propriety, righteousness, integrity, and humility as bases for party and state], *Zhongguo wenhua* 1, no. 1 (1930): 1–4.

75 He Zhonghan, "Guomin yinggai jiaozheng liangzhong wangguo guannian" [Citizens must rectify two kinds of lost-nation views], in *He Zhonghan xiansheng jiangshu xuanlu*, 170.

76 He, "Guomin yinggai jiaozheng liangzhong wangguo guannian," 165–66.

77 He, "Guomin yinggai jiaozheng liangzhong wangguo guannian," 166.

78 He, "Guomin yinggai jiaozheng liangzhong wangguo guannian," 169.

79 He, "Guomin yinggai jiaozheng liangzhong wangguo guannian," 168.

80 He Zhonghan, "Li, yi, lian, chi de yiyi" [The significance of propriety, righteousness, integrity, and humility], *Qiantu* 2, no. 5 (1934): 1–4.

81 *Shehuizhuyi yuekan* was published in Shanghai by the Socialism Monthly Society (Shehuizhuyi yuekan she), with Gu Xiujian named as the principal publisher, the Socialism Study Society as the general editor, and the Xinguang (New Light) Bookstore as its primary distributor to sellers in Wuhan, Beiping, Hangzhou, Nanjing, Kaifeng, and elsewhere. *Shehuizhuyi yuekan* 1, no. 7 (1933): backmatter.

82 "Women xuyao zenyang wenhua? (shelun shang)" [What kind of culture do we need? Editorial part 1], *Shehui xinwen* 3, no. 21 (1933): 322–23. This series of editorials was reprinted as a single article with further editorial commentary under the title "Geming yu wenhua wenti" [Problems of culture and revolution], in *Shehuizhuyi yuekan* 1, no. 5 (1933): 5–21.

83 "Women xuyao zenyang wenhua? (shelun shang)," 323.

84 "Women xuyao zenyang wenhua? (shelun shang)," 323.

85 "Women xuyao zenyang wenhua? (shelun zhong)" [What kind of culture do we need? Editorial part 2], *Shehui xinwen* 3, no. 22 (1933): 338.

86 "Women xuyao zenyang wenhua? (shelun zhong)," 338.

87 "Women xuyao zenyang wenhua? (shelun zhong)," 338–39.

88 "Women xuyao zenyang wenhua? (shelun xia)" [What kind of culture do we need? Editorial part 3], *Shehui xinwen* 3, no. 23 (1933): 354–55.

89 Kirby, *Germany and Republican China*, 163.

90 "Women xuyao zenyang wenhua? (shelun shang)," 322.

91 Chiang Kai-shek quoted in Deng, *Guomindang hexin zuzhi zhenxiang*, 322.

92 *Hanxue zhoukan* 8, no. 23 (1937): front cover.

93 Ru Chunpu, "Wenhua tongzhi de genben yiyi yu minzu qiantu" [The fundamental significance of cultural control and the future of the nation], *Qiantu* 2, no. 8 (1934): 10.

94 "Guomindang de wenhua zhengce pipan (shelun er)" [A critique of Guomindang cultural policy: Part 2], *Shehui xinwen* 4, no. 14 (1933): 210–11.

95 Ye Fawu, "Wenhua geming lun" [On cultural revolution], *Hanxue zhoukan* 2, no. 5 (1934): 7.

96 Ye, "Wenhua geming lun."

97 Ye, "Wenhua geming lun."

98 Ye, "Wenhua geming lun," 9.

99 Sun Xiyu, "Sanminzhuyi zhi wenhua yanjiu" [An investigation into the culture of the Three Principles of the People], *Qiantu* 2, no. 5 (1934): 3.

100 Sun Xiyu, "Sanminzhuyi zhi wenhua yanjiu," 4.

101 Sun Xiyu, "Sanminzhuyi zhi wenhua yanjiu," 2.

102 Sun Xiyu, "Sanminzhuyi zhi wenhua yanjiu," 8.

103 Sun Xiyu, "Sanminzhuyi zhi wenhua yanjiu," 10–11.

104 Sun Xiyu, "Sanminzhuyi zhi wenhua yanjiu," 2.

105 "Fakanci" [Introductory remarks], *Wenhua jianshe* 1, no. 1 (1934): 1–2.

106 Chen Lifu, "Zhongguo wenhua jianshe lun" [On Chinese cultural construction], *Wenhua jianshe* 1, no. 1 (1934): 11–15.

107 Chen, "Zhongguo wenhua jianshe lun," 13.

108 Bodenhorn, "Chen Lifu's Vitalism," 98n8.

109 Bodenhorn, "Chen Lifu's Vitalism," 98.

110 Bodenhorn, "Chen Lifu's Vitalism," 99.

111 Bodenhorn, "Chen Lifu's Vitalism," 103.

112 Ru, "Wenhua tongzhi de genben yiyi yu minzu qiantu," 11–12.

113 Ru, "Wenhua tongzhi de genben yiyi yu minzu qiantu," 11.

114 Sa Mengwu et al., "Zhongguo benwei de wenhua jianshe xuanyan" [A manifesto for cultural construction on a Chinese basis], *Zhongguo wenhua jianshe xiehui huibao* 1, no. 6 (1935): 1–4. A partial translation of the manifesto can be found in de Bary, Chan, and Lufrano, *Sources of Chinese Tradition*, 387–88; see also Ma, *Zhongguo benwei wenhua jianshe taolunji*.

115 Li, "Culture, Revolution, and Modernity," 23, 219, for an extended discussion of the manifesto's origins and contents; also Fung, *The Intellectual Foundations of Chinese Modernity*, 113–16.

116 Sa et al., "Zhongguo benwei de wenhua jianshe xuanyan," 1.

117 De Bary, Chan, and Lufrano, *Sources of Chinese Tradition*, 388.

3 » SPIRITUAL OFFENSES

1 Zhang, "Ruijin zhan zai jingshenshang fanggong diyi xian," 11–16. After the 1927 GMD party purge, Communist activists regrouped in the remote Jinggang Mountains straddling Hunan and Jiangxi provinces and soon organized self-governing soviets in the region, from which they were militarily ousted by GMD forces in late 1934, embarking on what became known as the Long March. See Stephen Averill's posthumously published *Revolution in the Highlands*. On the Nationalist military campaigns, see Wei, *Counterrevolution in China*.

2 Zhang, "Ruijin zhan zai jingshenshang fanggong diyi xian," 11.

3 Zhang, "Ruijin zhan zai jingshenshang fanggong diyi xian," 14.

4 Zhang, "Ruijin zhan zai jingshenshang fanggong diyi xian," 15.

5 On Zhang's political development, see Jeans, *Democracy and Socialism in Republican China*.

6 Xu, *Wo he gongdang douzheng de huiyi*, 11.5. Each numbered page of this book runs the length of two printed pages. This and future citations of Xu's book therefore use ".5" to indicate the second side of a numbered page.

7 Barbara Evans Clements maintained that the specific phrase "drink of water theory" was Lenin's rather than Kollontai's. Clements, "Emancipation through Communism," 323n1.

8 The quoted phrase is from Barlow, *The Question of Women in Chinese Feminism*, 101.

9 Ranajit Guha, "The Prose of Counter-insurgency," in Guha and Spivak, *Selected Subaltern Studies*, 59.

10 This is not to say that the CCP was somehow pure or innocent, only that historical research has revealed their gender and sexual politics, as well as their engagements with tradition, to have often differed from what GMD propagandists attributed to them. E.g., Gilmartin, *Engendering the Chinese Revolution*, ch. 4.

11 Jing Wang and Tani E. Barlow, introduction to Dai, *Cinema and Desire*, 2; Schoenhals, *China's Cultural Revolution*, 17.

12 Khalili, "Gendered Practices of Counterinsurgency," 1473n13. Here, Khalili builds on the idea of "telling" elaborated in Feldman, *Formations of Violence*, 56–59.

13 He Zhonghan, "Guomin yinggai jiaozheng liangzhong wangguo guannian" [Citizens must rectify two kinds of lost-nation views], in *He Zhonghan xiansheng jiangshu xuanlu*, 171. For names of the various positions and offices that He Zhonghan held from the 1920s to the 1960s, see Zhang, Fang, and Huang, *Zhonghua minguoshi dacidian*, 1444.

14 The first campaign, directed by war minister He Yingqin against Communist strongholds in Jiangxi, Hubei, and Hunan, lasted from December 1930 to January 1931. Wei, *Counterrevolution in China*, 36.

15 Wei, *Counterrevolution in China*, ch. 3.

16 Wei, *Counterrevolution in China*, 46–47.

17 Van de Ven, *War and Nationalism in China*, 140. Chiang's Nanchang, Jiangxi, field headquarters in particular emerged as a powerful counterweight to Wang's authority in Nanjing, even as the Wang faction–controlled National Economic Council remained involved in the economic redevelopment of areas militarily wrested from the CCP.

18 The MAC did in fact begin clandestinely preparing for war against Japan, but it maintained a public anti-Communist focus. Van de Ven, *War and Nationalism in China*, esp. 151–52.

19 Chen Guofu, "Dui dangzheng gongzuo tongzhi de qimian; (liu) Yao gaibian gongwuyuan de duoxing" [Expectations of cadres for party and government work: (Six) We must change the inertia of public servants], in *Chen Guofu xiansheng quanji, di er ce: Zhengzhi jingji*, 139–40.

20 The July 1933 "Lushan junguan xunliantuan" followed on a higher-profile conference at Lushan the preceding summer that was attended by top military commanders including He Yingqin and Chen Cheng, as well as the civilian leader Wang Jingwei, to discuss strategy for the Fourth Encirclement campaign. Zhang, Fang, and Huang, *Zhonghua minguoshi dacidian*, 991–92, estimates that, by the time the war broke out in 1937, some 25,000 officers had gone through these training sessions.

21   Wakeman, *Spymaster*, 112.

22   The *Jingcheng yuekan* 1933 inaugural issue reproduced that of Executive Branch member Chu Minyi exhorting readers to be "all-conquering." *Jingcheng yuekan* 1, no. 1 (1933).

23   *Saodang huabao* was published by the MAC's Political Training Bureau (Junshi weiyuanhui zhengzhi xunlian chu). I have seen only three issues of this publication (nos. 3–6, 1933), the first of which addresses the Japanese invasion. The others tie Japanese imperialism and Communism together as twin national enemies. See also Wu, *Zhongwen qikan dacidian*, 1303.

24   He Zhonghan, "Jiaofei yingyou de renshi he nuli: Ershi er nian shi yue niansan ri zhongyang junxiao zongli jinian zhou yanjiang" [The effort and consciousness required for bandit suppression: A speech given on October 23, 1933, during Sun Yat-sen Memorial Week at the Central Military Academy], recorded by Lin Mu in *Saodang xunkan* 2, no. 32 (1933): 8.

25   He Zhonghan, "Jundui zhengxun gongzuo de luxian" [The line for political training work among soldiers], in *He Zhonghan xiansheng jiangshu xuanlu*, 94.

26   He Zhonghan, "Jundui zhengzhi gongzuo de yiyi" [The significance of political training for soldiers], in *He Zhonghan xiansheng jiangshu xuanlu*, 75–78.

27   "Lushan junguantuan yu Huangpu junxiao zhi qianhou liangda shiming" [Two great missions of the Lushan Officer's Group and the Whampoa Military Academy], in Deng, *Lushan xunlian ji*, 4.

28   Shahar, "Violence in Chinese Religious Traditions," 192.

29   Now that they had secured positions of state power, Chinese fascists seemed unwilling to concede even popular associations of banditry with the exaction of justice under unjust conditions. On meanings of banditry, see Perry, "Social Banditry Revisited," 355–82.

30   "Bubing caodian cao'an gangling" [Infantry drill regulations draft principles], *Jingcheng yuekan jiaofei zhuanhao* [Bandit eradication special issue] 2, nos. 2 and 3 (1933): 1.

31   "Jiang weiyuanzhang xunci (san)" [Admonitions from Chairman Chiang (3)], *Jingcheng yuekan jiaofei zhuanhao*, 32.

32   Chen Guofu, "Tongzhijian ying goutong yijian zenggao gongzuo xiaolü" [Comrades must communicate ideas for increasing work efficiency], in *Chen Guofu xiansheng quanji, di er ce: Zhengzhi jingji*, 132. Drawing on the work of Julia Strauss, Robert Culp has observed that Nationalist Party conceptions of training (*xunlian*) entailed the "attempt to transform the thought and behavior of individuals and groups through compartmentalized and repeated practice that we justified by reference to an articulated sociopolitical ideology"; also that the content of xunlian varied depending on the target audience. See Culp, "Rethinking Governmentality," 531n4.

33   Chen Guofu, "Gongwuyuan bujin yao 'xiushen' erqie yao 'qijia'" [Civil servants must not only "cultivate themselves" they must also "put their homes in order"], in *Chen Guofu xiansheng quanji, di er ce: Zhengzhi jingji* 2, 142–43. With what was perhaps a jab at Song Meiling, Chen also noted that women were welcome to

enter politics on their own, but admonished they should not attempt to wield influence via their politician husbands.

34 See Wyatt, "Confucian Ethical Action and the Boundaries of Peace and War," 237–48.

35 "Lushan junguantuan yu Huangpu junxiao zhi qianhou liangda shiming," in Deng, *Lushan xunlian ji*, 3.

36 "Lushan junguantuan yu Huangpu junxiao zhi qianhou liangda shiming," 4–5.

37 "Lushan xunlian zhi yiyi yu geming qiantu" [The significance of Lushan officer training to the future of the revolution], in Deng, *Lushan xunlian ji*, 10.

38 "Lushan xunlian zhi yiyi yu geming qiantu," 11.

39 "Lushan xunlian zhi yiyi yu geming qiantu," 11.

40 "Jiaofei junguan xuzhi" [What bandit suppression officers must know], in Deng, *Lushan xunlian ji*, 31.

41 "Xiandai junren xuzhi" [What modern soldiers must know], in Deng, *Lushan xunlian ji*, 43.

42 Ding Wenyan, "Fuxing Zhonghua minzu yu tichang minzu jingshen" [Reviving the Chinese nation and promoting the national spirit], *Saodang xunkan* 2, no. 28 (1933): 30.

43 Ding, "Fuxing Zhonghua minzu yu tichang minzu jingshen," 31.

44 Ding, "Fuxing Zhonghua minzu yu tichang minzu jingshen," 35–36.

45 Huang Lisen, "Xiamian shi dui tufei yi feng gongkai de xin" [The following is an open letter to the bandits], *Saodang xunkan* 2, no. 28 (1933): 183.

46 Huang, "Xiamian shi dui tufei yi feng gongkai de xin," 181–82.

47 Huang, "Xiamian shi dui tufei yi feng gongkai de xin," 178.

48 Huang, "Xiamian shi dui tufei yi feng gongkai de xin," 178–79.

49 Dai Jitao paraphrased and quoted in Lu, *Re-understanding Japan*, 147.

50 Silverberg, *Erotic Grotesque Nonsense*, 59.

51 Wakeman, *Policing Shanghai*, 133.

52 Duus, *The Abacus and the Sword*, 16; Berke et al., *Even Paranoids Have Real Enemies*.

53 Xu, *Wo he gongdang douzheng de huiyi*, 48; Wakeman, *Policing Shanghai*, 133–34.

54 Xu, *Wo he gongdang douzheng de huiyi*, 48.

55 Xu, *Wo he gongdang douzheng de huiyi*, 47.

56 Xu, *Wo he gongdang douzheng de huiyi*, 12.

57 Xu, *Wo he gongdang douzheng de huiyi*, 11–12.

58 Xu, *Wo he gongdang douzheng de huiyi*, 6.

59 Liu Baichuan, "Wenhua jiaofei de zhongren" [The heavy responsibility of cultural anti-banditry], *Hanxue zhoukan* 2, no. 1 (1934): 1.

60 *Shehui xinwen* 8, no. 2 (1934).

61 The propaganda brigade reported, "The Communist bandit party advocates the nationalization of wives. . . . They completely lack human moral conceptions of integrity and shame; wives can casually commit adultery with others; husbands cannot keep track of them; husbands also casually commit adultery and have extramarital sex; their wives also cannot keep track of them; and moreover fathers

and daughters; brothers and sisters can all be indiscriminately promiscuous. . . . Every day they start fires; every day they kill people. . . . Is it any wonder that they seek to kill people all over the world?" "Xuanchuan dadui gao tongbao shu" [Letter to brethren from the propaganda team], *Ganzai huikan* 1, no. 1 (1930): 17.

62 "Xuanchuan dadui gao tongbao shu."

63 "Xuanchuan dadui gao tongbao shu."

64 Jiang Zhongzheng (Chiang Kai-shek), "Jiaofei de yiyi yu zuoren de daoli" [The significance of bandit extermination and reasonable human conduct], *Saodang xunkan* 2, no. 28 (1934): 6–7.

65 "Jiang siling gao wuru gongchan feidang de minzhong shu" [Message from Commander Chiang to the masses who mistakenly joined the Communist Bandit Party], *Ganzai huikan* 1, no. 1 (1930): 13.

66 "Jiang siling gao wuru gongchan feidang de minzhong shu."

67 Lipkin, *Useless to the State*; Chen, *Guilty of Indigence*.

68 Cheng Tianfang, "Geming de mudi—jianshe" [The goal of revolution: Construction], *Jingbao* (*Nanking Times*), April 23, 1928 (diyi zhang, diyiban).

69 He Zhonghan, "Feiqu minzhong bei fei xiepo de zhenxiang" [True facts about bandit oppression of the people in the bandit areas], in *He Zhonghan xiansheng jiangshu xuanlu*, 199.

70 He, "Feiqu minzhong bei fei xiepo de zhenxiang," 200.

71 Lu, "The Renaissance of Rural Kiangsi," 20.

72 Wei, *Counterrevolution in China*, 110–19; Tan Binxun, "Shinian lai zhi Jiangxi gonglu" [Jiangxi public roads during the past decade], in Hu, *Ganzheng shinian*, section 22, 1–12. By March 1934, nearly fifteen hundred miles of roads had been built in Jiangxi, with another six hundred planned or under construction. In this way, the encirclement campaigns established foundations for the region's socioeconomic integration into the Nanjing-centered state, while absorbing the labor—and potentially the hostility—of displaced agricultural workers.

73 Wei, *Counterrevolution in China*, 137–51.

74 Kiangsi Rural Welfare Centers, *New Life Centers in Rural Kiangsi*, 6.

75 Li, "Reviving China," 106–13.

76 To highlight Lu Xun's use of the terms *repentance* (chanhui) and *spirit* (jingshen), I have slightly modified Gladys and Hsien-Yi Yang's rendering of this passage: "Yes, there are gallows. But gallows are not so bad. Simply to have a noose put round your neck is preferential treatment. Moreover not everyone ends up on the gallows, for some find a way out by pulling hard on the legs of those friends being hanged. This gives concrete evidence of their true repentance, and those who can repent are noble souls." Lu Hsun (Lu Xun), "Spooks and Spectres in the Chinese World of Letters" (1935), in *Selected Works of Lu Hsun*, vol. 4, 146. The Chinese text can be found here: Lu Xun, "Zhongguo wentanshang de guimei," in *Lu Xun quanji*, vol. 6, 156–64.

77 Frederic Wakeman detailed these techniques in *Policing Shanghai* and *Spymaster*.

78 On new truths produced by thought reform in interwar Japan, see Ward, "The Problem of 'Thought.'"

79 "Jiang siling gao wuru gongchan feidang de minzhong shu," 13.

80 "Jiang siling gao wuru gongchan feidang de minzhong shu."

81 The first term promised that "anyone who sincerely repents, surrenders, and pledges to live in a law-abiding manner will be fully pardoned and will receive the guarantee that they will be permitted to live in peace." The other terms promised a full pardon to anyone who recanted their views along with surrendering arms, or captured or killed an important bandit leader. "Jiang siling gao wuru gongchan feidang de minzhong shu," 14.

82 "Guomin zhengfu junshiweiyuanhui weiyuanzhang Nanchang xingying banfa 'Jiaofei qunei zhaofu toucheng chifei zanxing banfa, 1933 nian 7 yue'" [Promulgation by the chair of the Nationalist Government Military Affairs Council: "Temporary provisions for the negotiated amnesty of surrendered red bandits, July 1933"], in Zhongguo di'er lishi dang'an guan, *Guomindang zhengfu zhengzhi zhidu dang'an shiliao xuanbian (shang ce)*, 472–74.

83 Chen, *Guilty of Indigence*, 2.

84 Chen, *Guilty of Indigence*, chs. 1–2.

85 Dikötter, *Crime, Punishment, and the Prison in Modern China*, introduction.

86 Dikötter, *Crime, Punishment, and the Prison in Modern China*, 185–86.

87 Chen, *Guilty of Indigence*, 29.

88 Dikötter, *Crime, Punishment, and the Prison in Modern China*, 280.

89 Memoirs of imprisoned CCP activists recall their success in prison organizing. Dikötter, *Crime, Punishment, and the Prison in Modern China*, 289.

90 "Reform Measures for Reds," *North-China Herald and Supreme Court and Consular Gazette*, April 26, 1933, 122, ProQuest document ID: 1371407849.

91 Dikötter, *Crime, Punishment, and the Prison in Modern China*, 283.

92 Durkheim, *The Rules of Sociological Method*, ch. 3, "Rules for the Distinction of the Normal from the Pathological."

93 Dikötter, *Crime, Punishment, and the Prison in Modern China*, 280–83.

94 Young, *New Life for Kiangsi*, 103–8.

95 Young, *New Life for Kiangsi*, 104, 106.

96 Dr. A. Kapelle, "Kiangsi-Bericht eines deutschen Journalisten" [Jiangxi-Report of a German Journalist], in Tang, *Chinas Kampf gegen den Kommunismus*, 87–92. Neither the English nor the French version of Tang's book mentions the camps; the French version is attributed to Clarence Kuangson Young and titled *Vers la fin du communism et du banditisme en Chine* (Paris: Agence Chekai, 1934). Tang Leang-li, a close associate and foreign-language publicist for Wang Jingwei, worked tirelessly to communicate Nationalist undertakings to foreign imperialists in China. He took particular care to convey the gravity of the Communist threat in China, and hence the potential consequences to foreign powers if they did not concede Nationalist demands for greater autonomy from imperialist dictates. As Tang wrote in English, "Nowhere in Europe, America, or Asia—outside of Republican China—does the problem of dealing with communism take the peculiar form it has assumed in this country." Unlike in Europe, where Communists had accommodated themselves to parliamentary procedures, in China the

Communist Party operated in an extralegal fashion and was actively working to overthrow or, as Tang put it, "sovietize" the legitimately ruling Nanjing regime. Tang, *Suppressing Communist Banditry in China*, 3.

97   Kapelle, "Kiangsi-Bericht eines deutschen Journalisten," 87.

98   Kapelle, "Kiangsi-Bericht eines deutschen Journalisten," 106.

99   Gellately, *Backing Hitler*, 54, and ch. 3 passim.

100 Yang, *Guomindang de "liangong" yu "fangong,"* 249–64.

101 Jiang, "Jiaofei de yiyi yu zuoren de daoli," 5.

4 » FIXING THE EVERYDAY

1   "Nanchang tideng dahui; cujin xinshenghuo yundong; canjiazhe qiwan yuren" [Mass lantern rally in Nanchang promotes New Life Movement; more than seventy thousand people attend], *Shenbao*, March 23, 1934 (09 ban; 21884 qi); also Wang, *"Mofan" Nanchang*, ch. 4.

2   See Wang, *"Mofan" Nanchang*, for an extended discussion of these activities.

3   For instance, in *Public Passions* Eugenia Lean characterized the 1930s Nanjing regime as the "New Life regime," designating the NLM as an official ideology that influenced Nanjing's legal system as well as public expectations of state actions. Lean, *Public Passions*, 16. Other key studies include Averill, "The New Life in Action," 594–628; Ferlanti, "The New Life Movement in Jiangxi Province," 961–1000; Oldstone-Moore, "The New Life Movement of Nationalist China; Wang, *"Mofan" Nanchang*; Yen, "Body Politics, Modernity, and National Salvation," 165–86.

4   Deng Yuanzhong suggested that Blue Shirts' direct leadership of the movement ended by the second half of 1934, though they did not sever ties to the movement altogether. Deng, *Guomindang hexin zuzhi zhenxiang*, 326–28; Arif Dirlik saw "militaristic elements in the Kuomintang" as dominating the movement through 1936, after which control was assumed by Song Meiling. Dirlik, "Ideological Foundations of the New Life Movement," 948.

5   Rogaski, *Hygienic Modernity*, 238–39.

6   Deng, *Guomindang hexin zuzhi zhenxiang*, 316.

7   Scott, *Seeing Like a State*, 112, 115.

8   Xu Zexiang, "Ruhe jianshe Zhongguo minzu wenhua" [How to construct China's national culture], *Zhongguo wenhua jianshe xiehui huibao* 1, no. 4 (1935): 24.

9   Walter Benjamin discussed this tendency as fascism's aestheticization of politics, which offered the masses "not their right, but instead a chance to express themselves." Benjamin, "The Work of Art in the Age of Mechanical Reproduction," in *Illuminations*, 241.

10 Esp. Rogaski, *Hygienic Modernity*; Morris, *Marrow of the Nation*.

11 Harootunian, *History's Disquiet*, 6.

12 Works on social legibility and designated social roles that have informed this chapter include Lanza, *Behind the Gate*; Marotti, "Japan 1968," 97–135; Ross, *May '68 and Its Afterlives*; Scott, *Seeing Like a State*.

13 "Nanchang tideng dahui."

14 Wang, *"Mofan" Nanchang*, esp. 30–49.

15 Judd, "Revolutionary Drama and Song in the Jiangxi Soviet," 127–60. What Nationalists served as old wine in new bottles was in fact new wine in new bottles, insofar as the national-future orientation of all of Nanchang's activities invariably impinged upon the Confucian content offered.

16 Li, "Reviving China," 106–35.

17 Li, "Reviving China," 111, 117, 119–20.

18 Li, "Reviving China," 123–26.

19 New Life Movement documents and organizational details comprise nearly five hundred pages of volume 68 of the *Xinshenghuo yundong shiliao* [Historical materials on the New Life Movement] (ed. Xiao Jizong). Details about its founding and goals can be found in the introduction to this volume; also Dirlik, "Ideological Foundations of the New Life Movement."

20 A translated list of ninety-six NLM behavioral rules can be found in Chang and Leszt, *The Search for Modern China*, 298–300.

21 Qian Zhu has traced the quotidian investigations of China's nonparty leftists during the 1920s and 1930s, whose projects, like the 1936 China's One Day (Zhongguo de yi ri) investigations, revealed precisely the kinds of diverging life rhythms and aspirations that fascists sought to render unthinkable. Zhu, "The Politics of Everyday Life."

22 Taylor, *The Principles of Scientific Management*, 18. See also ch. 2, note 39, above.

23 Liu Bingli, "Xinshenghuo yundong—yige geming fangfa" [The New Life Movement: A revolutionary method], *Qiantu* 2, no. 5 (1934): 1.

24 Wang Xiaohua notes that lantern parades were a novel development of the Republican era. With daylight hours allocated to work and other activities, Wang writes, the night emerged as a preferred time for public congregation, while shortage of street lights coupled with the festive symbolism of lanterns meant that they were favored means of illuminating nighttime gatherings. Slogans could moreover be readily inscribed on them, radiating their messages into the night sky. Wang, *"Mofan" Nanchang*, 37–39.

25 On Shanghai's lantern parades, see Wakeman, *Policing Shanghai*, 233.

26 Wei, *Counterrevolution in China*, 96–100.

27 Examples of Nanchang inspection reports can be found in the *Xinshenghuo cujin zonghui huikan* 1, no. 3 (1934): 38–47. A report on the Mingxing Movie Theater, for instance, observed, "Movie theater order passable. Cigarette ashes, butts, and snack particles behind back row of seats. Restrooms undergoing renovation. Hat and coat check also in midst of improvements." The Desheng dance hall fared less well: "Venue disorderly. Refreshments room needs cleaning. Garments unbuttoned, phlegm spit everywhere, dancers making a ruckus, smoking and snacking freely."

28 He Haoruo, "Xinshenghuo yundong piping zhi piping" [A critique of criticism of the New Life Movement], *Qiantu* 2, no. 6 (1934): 2.

29 Xiang Ziyu, "Xinshenghuo shi fuxing minzu de jiben gongzuo" [The New Life Movement is fundamental work for reviving the nation], *Saodang xunkan*

Xinshenghuo yundong zhuanhao [*Mopping Up Thrice Monthly*, New Life Movement Special Issue] 2, no. 37 (1934): 41.

30 Xiang, "Xinshenghuo shi fuxing minzu de jiben gongzuo."

31 Chiang Kai-shek as quoted by Hong, "Blue Shirts, Nationalists, and Nationalism," 215.

32 These were ideals cultivated at Whampoa. Chen, *Huangpu junxiao wanquan dang'an*, 27–34; Wilbur and How, *Missionaries of Revolution*, passim.

33 Fan, "Nongmin de xinshenghuo"; Wang, "Dianyuan de xinshenghuo"; Xiao, "Yinyuejia de xinshenghuo"; Hu, "Ertong de Xinshenghuo"; Yan and Ye, "Funü de xinshenghuo"; Ye and Pan, "Xuesheng de Xinshenghuo." Others in this CC Clique press series included Zhang, "Yinhangyuan de xinshenghuo"; Zhou, "Jingcha de xinshenghuo."

34 Gerth has sketched what running a household "as in the army" meant in practice. Although during the Nanjing Decade women were not considered strong enough to participate in actual combat, militarization nevertheless "reached into the family and to the way women were expected to connect their roles as housewives to national salvation." Gerth, *China Made*, 296.

35 Ru Chunpu, "Xinshenghuo yundong de yibufen jiancha" [A partial examination of the New Life Movement], *Qiantu* 3, no. 3 (1935): 5.

36 Ru, "Xinshenghuo yundong de yibufen jiancha."

37 Ru, "Xinshenghuo yundong de yibufen jiancha," 6.

38 Dirlik, "Ideological Foundations of the New Life Movement," 971.

39 Dirlik, "Ideological Foundations of the New Life Movement," 971–72.

40 Chen Lifu, "Xinshenghuo yu minsheng shiguan," in Chen and Yang, *Xinshenghuo yundong zhi lilun yu shiji*, 1–32.

41 Chen, "Xinshenghuo yu minsheng shiguan," 10–11.

42 Xu, "Ruhe jianshe Zhongguo minzu wenhua," 22–24.

43 Xu, "Ruhe jianshe Zhongguo minzu wenhua," 26–27.

44 Xu, "Ruhe jianshe Zhongguo minzu wenhua," 25.

45 Gu Gaoyang, "Xinshenghuo yundong zhong zhi jingji wenti" [Economic problems in the New Life Movement], *Qiantu* 2, no. 5 (1934): 2.

46 Gu, "Xinshenghuo yundong zhong zhi jingji wenti," 3–4.

47 Gu, "Xinshenghuo yundong zhong zhi jingji wenti," 4.

48 Cartoon, *Qiantu* 2, no. 4 (1934).

49 Soon after the NLM was launched, men and women wearing Western clothes or cosmetics found themselves under physical attack in major cities. "Men who called themselves the Smashing Modernity Gang," Yen reports, "poured acid on people in theatres and amusement [centers]. Although some young men dressed in Western attire were also attacked, the victims were mostly Modern Girls." Yen, "Body Politics, Modernity, and National Salvation," 173. That contributors to *Libailiu* approved the actions of the acid throwers suggests the readiness of some to conform to NLM norms.

50 Dirlik noted how dynastic Confucian schemas "rested moral responsibility with the ruler, employing it to restrict the power of the state. New Life ideology

placed the burden of proof on the population: it was the people who were expected to prove their worthiness to their rulers." Dirlik, "Ideological Foundations of the New Life Movement," 971.

51 Robin, *The Reactionary Mind*, 53.

52 He Zhonghan quoted in Deng, *Guomindang hexin zuzhi zhenxiang*, 322.

53 Vera Schwarcz argued this point with an emphasis on the relationship between Confucianism and the emancipation of the individual in *The Chinese Enlightenment*, ch. 5.

54 Song Qingling, "Rujiao yu xiandai Zhongguo" [Confucianism and modern China], *Song Qingling xuanji*, 103.

55 Song, "Rujiao yu xiandai Zhongguo," 106.

56 Song, "Rujiao yu xiandai Zhongguo," 110–11.

57 Osborne, *The Politics of Time*, 164, emphasis in original.

58 In her study of imperial rituals during the high Qing period, Angela Zito emphasized how "the study and practice of *li*, both its texts and performances, formed a particularly supple arena for the display and construction of gentry power." Zito, *Of Body and Brush*, 71. On the role of li in the NLM, see Oldstone-Moore, "The New Life Movement of Nationalist China," 208–9.

59 Dirlik, "Ideological Foundations of the New Life Movement," 967.

60 Chiang, *War Messages and Other Selections by May-ling Soong Chiang*, 305.

61 Jiang Zhongzheng (Chiang Kai-shek), "Xinshenghuo yundong ying zhuzhong liyue yu shijian" [The New Life Movement must emphasize rites, music, and time], *Saodang xunkan* 2, no. 37 (1934): 3.

62 Chiang Kai-shek quoted in and translated by Wakeman, "A Revisionist View of the Nanjing Decade," 424.

63 He Zhonghan, "Li, yi, lian, chi zhi yiyi" [The meanings of propriety, righteousness, integrity, and humility], *Qiantu* 2, no. 5 (1934): 1.

64 He, "Li, yi, lian, chi zhi yiyi," 1.

65 He, "Li, yi, lian, chi zhi yiyi," 1.

66 He, "Li, yi, lian, chi zhi yiyi," 1.

67 Dirlik, "Ideological Foundations of the New Life Movement," 965–66.

68 Terry Bodenhorn has observed that Chen "provided charts and algebraic diagrams to show his audience how various permutations of *chengji* (perfection of the self) and *chengwu* (perfection of others) fitted into the grand advancement of *cheng*." Bodenhorn, "Chen Lifu's Vitalism," in *Defining Modernity*, 111.

69 Dai, *Sanminzhuyi zhi zhexue de jichu*, appendix, "Minsheng zhexue xitong biao."

70 Chen, "Xinshenghuo yu minsheng shiguan," 26.

71 Chen, "Xinshenghuo yu minsheng shiguan," 28.

72 Bauman, *Modernity and the Holocaust*, 14–15.

73 On Chiang's concern for his own and Blue Shirts' mind and bodily cultivation, see Deng, *Guomindang hexin zuzhi zhenxiang*, esp. 117–29.

74 Diamond, "Women under Kuomintang Rule."

75 Diamond, "Women under Kuomintang Rule," 7.

76 Diamond, "Women under Kuomintang Rule," 214.

77 Spackman, *Fascist Virilities*, xiii.

78 Cartoon, *Hanxue zhoukan* 3, no. 18 (1934): 279.

79 Wendy Larson and Bryna Goodman have observed that "the call for gendered divisions of labor and of space is marked clearly in classical texts from early China, which later scholars intoned like mantras." Women's actual confinement to "inner" quarters nevertheless varied widely depending on region, class, and the historical era in question. Larson and Goodman, "Introduction: Axes of Gender: Divisions of Labor and Spatial Separation," in Goodman and Larson, *Gender in Motion*, 1.

80 Cartoon, *Qiantu* 2, no. 6 (1934).

81 Finnane, "What Should Women Wear?," 118.

82 Chiang Kai-shek quoted in Hong, "Blue Shirts, Nationalists, and Nationalism," 215–16.

83 Morris, *Marrow of the Nation*; Rogaski, *Hygienic Modernity*. In this sense, there was no uniquely fascist aesthetic of the body—like all aspects of fascist politics, bodily expectations were part of a larger ensemble of beliefs and practices, none of which can be taken in isolation, in the same way that Nazism had no exclusive lock on racism.

84 *Hanxue zhoukan* 5, no. 18 (1935): front cover.

85 Madeleine Y. Dong has observed that this look, "with its painted face, bobbed or permed hair, fashionable qipao, and high-heeled shoes, was so widely adopted by women of diverse social groups, including high school and college students, professionals, young wives of the upper and middle classes, and prostitutes, that by the 1930s it had become a passport to opportunity and a dress code of necessity for young female city dwellers." Dong, "Who Is Afraid of the Chinese Modern Girl?," 196.

86 Yen, "Body Politics, Modernity, and National Salvation," esp. 172–73.

87 *Funü xinshenghuo yuekan* 1, no. 3 (1937). On Lu Xun's assessment of Nora's predicament, see Schwarcz, "Ibsen's Nora," 3–5.

88 Zarrow, *China in War and Revolution*, 263.

89 Cartoon, *Funü xinshenghuo yuekan* 1, no. 3 (1937).

90 On shifting historical associations of masculinity with literary erudition and martial valor, see Louie, *Theorising Chinese Masculinity*; also Wang, "Mr. Butterfly in *Defunct Capital*," 41–58.

91 Xia Hanhua, "Xinshenghuo yundong de diyi yaojian—junshihua" [The New Life Movement's first prerequisite—militarization], *Saodang xunkan* 2, no. 37 (1934): 26–27.

92 Cartoon, *Qiantu* 2, no. 4 (1934).

93 "Xuesheng yu tiaowu" [Students and dancing], *Wenhua jianshe* 1, no. 2 (1934): 2–3.

94 "Xuesheng yu tiaowu," 3–4.

95 *Hanxue zhoukan* 8, no. 18 (1937): front cover. I thank students in Brian Tsui's spring 2016 master of arts seminar at the Hong Kong Polytechnic University for

pointing out the connection between this cover image and the film *Da Lu* (dir. Sun Yu, 1935).

96 Eugenia Lean has traced a tangled logical consequence of Nanjing's promotion of filial piety in the revenge killing enacted by Shi Jianqiao. The Nationalist state, Lean reveals, could reconcile its sanction of Shi's actions with its own desire for a monopoly on the use of violence only by convicting and then pardoning her. Lean, *Public Passions*, esp. 146–58.

5 » LITERATURE AND ARTS FOR THE NATION

1 Liang Yu, "Deguo Nuoxisi de xuanchuan gongzuo" [Propaganda work of German Nazis], *Hanxue zhoukan* 1, no. 6 (1933): 19.

2 Liang, "Deguo Nuoxisi de xuanchuan gongzuo," 20.

3 Tang, *Chinese Modern*, 11. "Spiritual" here points to the fostering of human character, not to the cultivation of a transhistorical national essence, as fascists used the term.

4 Xu, *Wo he gongdang douzheng de huiyi*, 12.5.

5 Lu Hsun (Lu Xun), "The Present Condition of Art in Darkest China," in *Selected Works of Lu Hsun*, vol. 3, 111. This essay was written at the behest of Agnes Smedley for the U.S. magazine the *New Masses*, though according to Gloria Davies it remained unpublished. Davies, *Lu Xun's Revolution*, xix.

6 Zhang Daming's study and painstaking transcription of examples of "Three Principles of the People" and "nationalist" literature and arts frames both as reactions against left-wing initiatives. Zhang, *Guomindang wenyi sichao*. Ni Wei, by contrast, has framed them as part of broader Nationalist efforts to establish a new hegemony in *"Minzu" xiangxiang yu guojia tongzhi*.

7 Chen Guofu, "Xin Renwu" [Newcomers], *Xinshengming* 3, no. 1 (1930): 1–3.

8 Clark, *Farewell to an Idea*, 248.

9 Schnapp, *Staging Fascism*, 6.

10 Chen, *Zhongguo dianying shiye*.

11 Mao Zedong, "On New Democracy," in Cheek, *Mao Zedong and China's Revolutions*, 107–8; see also Wu, "Kangzhan shiqi Zhongguo Guomindang de wenyi zhengce jiqi yunzuo," 69–74, for a discussion of the GMD's "cultural encirclement" tactics.

12 Chen Lifu quoted in Zhang, *Guomindang wenyi sichao*, 25–26.

13 Ni, *"Minzu" xiangxiang yu guojia tongzhi*; Zhang, *Guomindang wenyi sichao*.

14 E.g., Anderson, *Imagined Communities*; Duara, *Rescuing History from the Nation*.

15 Ni, *"Minzu" xiangxiang yu guojia tongzhi*, 5–6; Wu, "Kangzhan shiqi," 64–68.

16 Li, "Making a Name and a Culture for the Masses," 53–54.

17 Zhang, *Guomindang wenyi sichao*, 18–21, 55.

18 Wu, "Kangzhan shiqi," 42–43.

19 E.g., "Guomindang de wenhua zhengce pipan: Shelun yi" [A critique of Guomindang cultural policy: Editorial part 1], *Shehui xinwen* 4, no. 13 (1933): 194–95.

20 "Women xuyao zenyang wenhua? Shelun xia," *Shehui xinwen* 3, no. 23 (1933), 354.

21 SW, "Geming yu wenhua wenti" [Problems of revolution and culture], *Shehuizhuyi yuekan* 1, no. 5 (1933): 7–9.

22 Li, "Making a Name and a Culture for the Masses," 30–31.

23 Xu Yin, "Ping tuifei pai wenxue" [A critique of decadent literature], *Hanxue zhoukan* 1, no. 2 (1933): 9–12.

24 Da Huang, "You bi ru dao" [Wielding pens like swords], *Hanxue zhoukan* 3, no. 13 (1934): 207–8. The "Futurist Manifesto" appeared in full translation in the journal of the Shanghai Art Academy in 1921. Pan, *Shanghai Style*, 69.

25 Da, "You bi ru dao," 208.

26 Gu Yiqiao, "Yue Fei (Si mu ju)" [Yue Fei (A play in four acts)], *Shidai gonglun* 1, no. 1 (1932): 31.

27 Xiang Ziyu, "Jianli minzuzhuyi de wenxue" [Establishing a nationalist literature], *Saodang xunkan* 2, no. 35 (1934): 87–88.

28 Xiang, "Jianli minzuzhuyi de wenxue," 88.

29 Xiang, "Jianli minzuzhuyi de wenxue," 89.

30 Xiang, "Jianli minzuzhuyi de wenxue," 90–91.

31 Anderson, *The Limits of Realism*, 3.

32 Xiang, "Jianli minzu zhuyi wenxue," 92.

33 "Guomindang de wenhua zhengce pipan, shelun san," 227.

34 "Guomindang de wenhua zhengce pipan, shelun san."

35 SW, "Geming yu wenhua wenti," 6.

36 Li, "Making a Name and a Culture for the Masses," esp. 52–58.

37 Qu Qiubai, "Dazhong wenhua zhi wenti" [Problems of mass art and literature], in Qu, *Qu Qiubai xuanji*, 488–98. Qu's position bore similarities with that of his imprisoned Marxist contemporary Antonio Gramsci in its identification of contradictory progressive and regressive tendencies in popular thought, which indicated that the Communist Party's program of cultural revolution had to identify and invigorate existing progressive elements while overcoming regressive ones, such as those that shored up patriarchy, promoted peasant deference to landlord authority, and so on.

38 Xiang, "Jianli minzuzhuyi de wenxue," 92.

39 Rabinbach, "The Aesthetics of Production in the Third Reich," 51.

40 On protests against the screening of this film, see Xiao, "Anti-imperialism and Film Censorship during the Nanjing Decade," 39.

41 Chen, *Zhongguo dianying shiye*, 2. Zhiwei Xiao has sketched the objective situation shaping Chen's concern: "During the 1920s and 1930s, foreign films, especially Hollywood movies, dominated China's film market. Ninety percent of the films being shown were of foreign origin. This situation lasted until 1949. During the 1920s all of Shanghai's first-class theaters were foreign owned. . . . According to one estimate, during the decade from the mid-1910s to the mid-1920s, more than twenty million *yuan* of Chinese money went into the hands of foreigners on movies alone each year. Chinese filmmakers had long complained about the government's lack of control over the tremendous influx of foreign films." Xiao, "Anti-imperialism and Film Censorship," 43.

42 Chen, *Zhongguo dianying shiye*, 2–3.

43 Chen, *Zhongguo dianying shiye*, 3.

44 Chen, *Zhongguo dianying shiye*, 3–4. Chen's Educational Film Association aimed to raise industry tastes, improve the content of their films, and direct the criteria by which the success of a film was measured away from commercial considerations. Xiao describes this association as "quasi-governmental" and mentions that it included CC Clique member and Shanghai GMD education bureau chief Pan Gongzhan. Xiao, "Anti-imperialism and Film Censorship," 50.

45 Chen, *Zhongguo dianying shiye*, 12.

46 Chen, *Zhongguo dianying shiye*, 4.

47 Chen, *Zhongguo dianying shiye*, 7–8.

48 Chen, *Zhongguo dianying shiye*, 9–10.

49 Chen, *Zhongguo dianying shiye*, 11–14.

50 Chen, *Zhongguo dianying shiye*, 16.

51 Chen, *Zhongguo dianying shiye*, 17–18.

52 Chen, *Zhongguo dianying shiye*, 18–19.

53 Chen, *Zhongguo dianying shiye*, 23.

54 Chen, *Zhongguo dianying shiye*, 24.

55 Chen, *Zhongguo dianying shiye*, 29.

56 Chen, *Zhongguo dianying shiye*, 32–33.

57 Dai Jitao quoted in Tsui, *China's Conservative Revolution*, 22.

58 Duara, *Rescuing History from the Nation*, 4.

59 Griffin, *The Nature of Fascism*, 41.

60 Cartoon, *Hanxue zhoukan* 1, no. 10 (1933).

61 Cartoon, *Shehui xinwen* 8, no. 5 (1934): back cover; *Shehui xinwen* 8, no. 6 (1934): back cover.

62 Wakeman, *Spymaster*, 168.

63 Michaud, *The Cult of Art in Nazi Germany*, chs. 1 and 2.

64 Chung, *Élitist Fascism*, 269–71 (appendix 2).

65 Xu, *Wo he gongdang douzheng de huiyi*, 13.5.

66 Chung, *Élitist Fascism*, 269–71 (appendix 2).

67 Jian, "Zuoyi wenhua yundong zhi jinxi" [The past and present of the left-wing cultural movement], *Shehui xinwen* 2, no. 15 (1933): 196–97.

68 Jian, "Zuoyi wenhua yundong zhi jinxi," 197.

69 Shui Shou, "Zuoyi wenhua yundong zhi taitou" [The left-wing cultural movement rears its head], *Shehui xinwen* 2, no. 21 (1933): 294.

70 Shui, "Zuoyi wenhua yundong zhi taitou."

71 Shui, "Zuoyi wenhua yundong zhi taitou," 295.

72 "Deguo fenjin gongchan shubao" [Germany burns and proscribes Communist books and newspapers], *Shehui xinwen* 3, no. 17 (1933): 257; *Socialism Monthly* also celebrated the precedent that Qin Shi Huang had set by "fenshu kengru" [burning books and burying scholars], literally destroying the old culture as did Lenin, Stalin, Hitler, and Mussolini. SW, "Geming yu wenhua wenti," 19.

73 Lu Hsun (Lu Xun), "Spooks and Spectres in the Chinese World of Letters," in *Selected Works of Lu Hsun*, vol. 4, 149.

74   Lu, "Spooks and Spectres," 149–50.

75   Chen, "The Rise and Fall of the China League for Civil Rights," 128.

76   Wakeman, *Spymaster*, 176.

77   Wakeman, *Spymaster*.

78   Alber, *Enduring the Revolution*, 92.

79   Xu, *Wo he gongdang douzheng de huiyi*, 36.5.

80   See Alber, *Enduring the Revolution*, 89–105; Chung, *Ting Ling*, 56–71, which contains a partial translation of Xu Enceng's memoir.

81   Xu, *Wo he gongdang douzheng de huiyi*, 36.5–37.5.

82   Wakeman, *Spymaster*, 179–80.

83   Wakeman, *Spymaster*.

84   Geng Bing, "Chu shang jingtou de suxie" [Sketches before the camera], *Tiexue yuekan* 1, no. 5 (1933): 3–6; Ti Yue, "Weilai de huohua" [Sparks of the future], *Tiexue yuekan* 1, no. 5 (1933).

85   Zhongguo di'er lishi dang'an guan, ed., "Guomindang zhongyang zhixing wei-yuanhui wenhua shiye jihua weiyuanhui zuzhitiaolie," in *Zhonghua minguoshi dang'an ziliao huibian*, 1; Wu, "Kangzhan shiqi Zhongguo Guomindang de wenyi zhengce jiqi yunzuo," 49–57.

86   "Guomindang zhongyang xuanchuan weiyuanhui dianying shiye zhidao weiyua-nhui zuzhi dagang"; "Guomindang zhongyang guangbo shiye zhidao weiyuanhui zuzhi dagang," in Zhongguo di'er lishi dang'an guan, *Zhonghua minguoshi dang'an ziliao huibian*, 5–6.

87   "Guomindang zhongyang wenhua shiye jihua gangyao," in Zhongguo di'er lishi dang'an guan, *Zhonghua minguoshi dang'an ziliao huibian*, 28–30.

88   "Chen Guofu guanyu zhongyang wenhua shiye jihua weiyuanhui chengli yilai gongzuo zhuangkuang de baogao," in Zhongguo di'er lishi dang'an guan, *Zhong-hua minguoshi dang'an ziliao huibian*, 31.

89   Wakeman, *Spymaster*, 233–36.

90   Chung, *Élitist Fascism*, 223–38.

91   Boorman and Howard, *Biographical Dictionary of Republican China*, vol. 1, 205.

CONCLUSION

1   As in chapter 1, this is paraphrased from Buck-Morss, *Dreamworld and Catastro-phe*, 43.

2   Wakeman, "Confucian Fascism," 425.

3   Dikötter, *The Age of Openness*.

4   See the work of Reto Hofmann on the ways in which postwar discourses of Japa-nese ultranationalism worked to establish Japanese fascism as a distinct political formation. Hofmann, *The Fascist Effect*.

5   Oldstone-Moore, "The New Life Movement of Nationalist China," 217; Tozer, "Taiwan's 'Cultural Renaissance,'" 81–99.

6   Chun, "From Nationalism to Nationalizing," 57–58; in Oldstone-Moore, "The New Life Movement of Nationalist China," 220.

7   Tu, *Confucian Traditions in East Asian Modernity*. For a critical perspective on such discourse, see Dirlik, "Confucius in the Borderlands"; also Jayasuryia, "Understanding Asian Values as a Form of Reactionary Modernization."

8   See esp. Tsui, *China's Conservative Revolution*, on ties between GMD rightists, liberal intellectuals, and the Boy Scouts. Also Mulready-Stone, *Mobilizing Shanghai Youth*.

Alber, Charles J. *Enduring the Revolution: Ding Ling and the Politics of Literature in Guomindang China*. Westport, CT: Praeger, 2002.

Anderson, Benedict. *Imagined Communities: Reflections on the Origins and Spread of Nationalism*. New York: Verso, 1991.

Anderson, Marston. *The Limits of Realism: Chinese Fiction in the Revolutionary Period*. Berkeley: University of California Press, 1990.

Averill, Stephen C. "The New Life in Action: The Nationalists in South Jiangxi, 1934–1937." *China Quarterly*, no. 88 (1981): 594–628.

———. *Revolution in the Highlands: China's Jinggangshan Base Area*. Lanham, MD: Rowman and Littlefield, 2006.

Bai Chun. "Jiang Jieshi ruhua sanminzhuyi zhi pingxi" [On the train of thought and the essence of Chiang Kai-shek turning Sun Yat-sen's Three Principles of the People into Confucianism]. *Nanjing zhengzhi xueyuan xuebao* 19, no. 1 (2003): 76–79.

Balibar, Etienne, and Immanuel Wallerstein. *Race, Nation, Class: Ambiguous Identities*. New York: Verso, 1991.

Barlow, Tani E. "Debates over Colonial Modernity in East Asia and Another Alternative." *Cultural Studies* 26, no. 5 (2012): 617–44.

———, ed. *Formations of Colonial Modernity in East Asia*. Durham, NC: Duke University Press, 1997.

———. *The Question of Women in Chinese Feminism*. Durham, NC: Duke University Press, 2004.

Bauman, Zygmunt. *Modernity and the Holocaust*. Ithaca, NY: Cornell University Press, 2001.

Benjamin, Walter. *Illuminations*. Translated by Harry Zohn. New York: Schocken, 1988.

Bergère, Marie-Claire. *Sun Yat-sen*. Translated by Janet Lloyd. Stanford, CA: Stanford University Press, 1998.

Berke, Joseph H., Stella Pierides, Andrea Sabbadini, and Stanley Schneider, eds. *Even Paranoids Have Enemies: New Perspectives on Paranoia and Persecution*. New York: Routledge, 1998.

Berman, Marshall. *All That Is Solid Melts into Air: The Experience of Modernity*. New York: Penguin, 1988.

Bloch, Ernst. *Heritage of Our Times*. Translated by Neville and Stephen Plaice. Berkeley: University of California Press, 1990.

Bodenhorn, Terry D., ed. *Defining Modernity: Guomindang Rhetorics of a New China, 1920–1970*. Ann Arbor: University of Michigan Center for Chinese Studies, 2002.

Boorman, Howard L., and Richard C. Howard, eds. *Biographical Dictionary of Republican China*, vol. 1. New York: Columbia University Press, 1967.

———. *Biographical Dictionary of Republican China*, vol. 3. New York: Columbia University Press, 1970.

Brownell, Susan, Jeffrey Wasserstrom, and T. W. Laqueur, eds. *Chinese Femininities, Chinese Masculinities: A Reader*. Berkeley: University of California Press, 2002.

Buck-Morss, Susan. *Dreamworld and Catastrophe: The Passing of Mass Utopia in East and West*. Cambridge: MIT Press, 2000.

Chai Fu, ed. cc *Neimu* [The inside story of the cc Clique]. Beijing: Zhongguo wenshi chubanshe, 1988.

Chan, Ming K. *Historiography of the Chinese Labor Movement: A Critical Survey and Bibliography of Selected Chinese Source Materials at the Hoover Institution*. Stanford, CA: Hoover Institution Press, 1981.

———. "A Turning Point in the Modern Chinese Revolution: The Historical Significance of the Canton Decade, 1917–1927." In *Remapping China: Fissures in Historical Terrain*, edited by Gail Hershatter, Emily Honig, Jonathan Lipman, and Randall Stross. Stanford, CA: Stanford University Press, 1996.

Chan, Ming K., and Arif Dirlik. *Schools into Fields and Factories: Anarchists, the Guomindang, and the National Labor University in Shanghai, 1927–1932*. Durham, NC: Duke University Press, 1991.

Chang, Maria Hsia. *The Chinese Blue Shirt Society: Fascism and Developmental Nationalism*. Berkeley: Institute of East Asian Studies, University of California, 1985.

Chatterjee, Partha. *Nationalist Thought and the Colonial World: A Derivative Discourse*. Minneapolis: University of Minnesota Press, 1993.

———. *The Nation and Its Fragments: Colonial and Postcolonial Histories*. Princeton, NJ: Princeton University Press, 1993.

Cheek, Timothy, ed. *Mao Zedong and China's Revolutions: A Brief History with Documents*. New York: Palgrave, 2002.

Chen Feng. *Huangpu junxiao wanquan dang'an* [The complete archive of the Whampoa Military Academy]. Beijing: Jiuzhou chubanshe, 2011.

Chen, Guofu. *Chen Guofu xiansheng quanji. Di'er ce: Zhengzhi jingji* [The complete works of Mr. Chen Guofu, vol. 2: Politics and economics]. Taibei: Zhengzhong shuju, 1952.

Chen, Janet Y. *Guilty of Indigence: The Urban Poor in China, 1900–1953*. Princeton, NJ: Princeton University Press, 2012.

Chen, Jinxing. "The Rise and Fall of the China League for Civil Rights." *China Review* 6, no. 2 (2006): 121–47.

Chen Lifu [Chen Zuyan]. "Application of Mechanical and Electrical Devices to Coal Mining in China." Master's thesis, University of Pittsburgh, 1924.

———. *Chengbai zhi jian* [Reflections on success and failure]. Taibei: Zhengzhong shuju, 1994.

———. *The Storm Clouds Clear over China: The Memoir of Ch'en Li-fu, 1900–1993*. Compiled and edited by Sydney H. Chang and Ramon H. Myers. Stanford, CA: Hoover Institution Press, 1994.

———. *Zhongguo dianying shiye* [The Chinese film industry]. Shanghai: Chenbao she, 1933.

———. *Zhongguo wenhua jianshe xiehui gaikuang yilan* [A general survey of the Chinese Cultural Construction Association]. Shanghai: Zhongguo wenhua jianshe xiehui, 1934.

Chen Yongfa. *Zhongguo gongchan geming qishinian, shang* [Seventy years of the Chinese Communist Revolution, vol. 1]. Taibei: Lianjing, 2001.

Chen Youxin and Yang Ruilin. *Xinshenghuo yundong zhi lilun yu shiji; disanbian: Xinshenghuo yundong minglunji* [The New Life Movement in theory and practice, vol. 3: Prominent writers on the New Life Movement]. Nanjing: Jingguan gaodeng xuexiao, 1935.

Cheng, Pei-Kai, and Michael Leszt, eds. *The Search for Modern China: A Documentary Collection*. New York: W. W. Norton, 1999.

Chiang, Madame May-ling Soong [Madame Chiang Kai-shek]. *War Messages and Other Selections*. Hankow: China Information Committee, 1938.

Chow, Tse-tsung. *The May Fourth Movement: Intellectual Revolution in Modern China*. Cambridge, MA: Harvard University Press, 1960.

Chun, Allen. "From Nationalism to Nationalizing: Cultural Imagination and State Formation in Postwar Taiwan." *Australian Journal of Chinese Affairs* 31 (1994): 46–69.

Chung, Dooeum. *Élitist Fascism: Chiang Kaishek's Blueshirts in 1930s China*. Burlington, VT: Ashgate, 2000.

Chung, Jun-mei. *Ting Ling: Her Life and Her Work*. Taibei: National Chengchi University, 1978.

Clark, T. J. *Farewell to an Idea: Episodes from a History of Modernism*. New Haven, CT: Yale University Press, 1999.

Clements, Barbara Evans. "Emancipation through Communism: The Ideology of A. M. Kollontai." *Slavic Review* 32, no. 2 (1973): 323–88.

Clinton, Maggie. "Ends of the Universal: The League of Nations and Chinese Fascism on the Eve of World War II." *Modern Asian Studies* 48, no. 6 (2014): 1740–68.

Clinton, Margaret. "Fascism, Cultural Revolution, and National Sovereignty in 1930s China." PhD diss., New York University, 2009.

Coble, Parks M., Jr. *Facing Japan: Chinese Politics and Japanese Imperialism, 1931–1937*. Cambridge, MA: Harvard East Asian Monograph Series, 1991.

———. *The Shanghai Capitalists and the Nationalist Government, 1927–1937*, 2nd ed. Cambridge, MA: Harvard East Asian Monograph Series, 1986.

Cohn, Bernard. *Colonialism and Its Forms of Knowledge: The British in India.* Princeton, NJ: Princeton University Press, 1996.

Cowling, Mark, and James Martin, eds. *Marx's "Eighteenth Brumaire": (Post)Modern Interpretations.* Sterling, VA: Pluto, 2002.

Culp, Robert. "Rethinking Governmentality: Training, Cultivation, and Cultural Citizenship in Nationalist China." *Journal of Asian Studies* 65, no. 3 (2006): 529–54.

Dai Jinhua. *Cinema and Desire: Feminist Marxism and Cultural Politics in the Work of Dai Jinhua.* Edited by Jing Wang and Tani E. Barlow. New York: Verso, 2002.

Dai Jitao. *Sanminzhuyi zhi zhexue de jichu* [The philosophical foundations of the Three Principles of the People]. Beiping: Qingnian Shudian, 1945.

Danzker, Jo-Anne, Ken Lum, and Zheng Shengtian, eds. *Shanghai Modern, 1919–1945.* Munich: Hatje Kantz, 2004.

Davies, Gloria. *Lu Xun's Revolution: Writing in a Time of Violence.* Cambridge, MA: Harvard University Press, 2013.

De Bary, William T., W. Chan, and R. Lufrano, eds. *Sources of Chinese Tradition,* vol. 2: *From 1600 through the Twentieth Century.* New York: Columbia University Press, 2000.

Deng Wenyi, ed. *Lushan xunlian ji: Jiang Zhongzheng jiang* [A compilation of Lushan training materials: Speeches by Chiang Kai-shek]. Nanjing: Guofangbu xinwenju, 1947.

Deng Yuanzhong. *Guomindang hexin zhuzhi zhenxiang: Lixingshe, Fuxingshe, yu suowei "Lanyishe" de yanbian yu chengzhang* [The truth about the Guomindang's core organizations: The Forceful Action Society, the Renaissance Society, and the so-called "Blue Shirts"]. Taibei: Lianjing, 2000.

DesForges, Andrew. *Mediasphere Shanghai: The Aesthetics of Cultural Production.* Honolulu: University of Hawai'i Press, 2007.

Diamond, Norma. "Women under Kuomintang Rule: Variations on the Feminine Mystique." *Modern China* 1, no. 1 (1975): 3–45.

Dikötter, Frank. *The Age of Openness: China before Mao.* Berkeley: University of California Press, 2008.

———. *Crime, Punishment, and the Prison in Modern China.* New York: Columbia University Press, 2002.

Dirlik, Arif. *Anarchism in the Chinese Revolution.* Berkeley: University of California Press, 1991.

———. "Confucius in the Borderlands: Global Capitalism and the Reinvention of Confucianism." *boundary 2* 22, no. 3 (1995): 229–73.

———. "Ideological Foundations of the New Life Movement: A Study in Counterrevolution." *Journal of Asian Studies* 34, no. 4 (1975): 945–80.

———. *The Origins of Chinese Communism.* New York: Oxford University Press, 1989.

Dong, Madeleine Y. "Who Is Afraid of the Chinese Modern Girl?" In *The Modern Girl around the World: Consumption, Modernity, and Globalization,* edited by Alys

Eve Weinbaum, Lynn M. Thomas, Priti Ramamurthy, Uta G. Poiger, and Madeleine Yue Dong. Durham, NC: Duke University Press, 2008.

Duara, Prasenjit. *Rescuing History from the Nation: Questioning Narratives of Modern China*. Chicago: University of Chicago Press, 1995.

Duiker, William J. *Ho Chi Minh: A Life*. New York: Hyperion, 2000.

Durkheim, Émile. *The Rules of Sociological Method*. Edited by Steven Lukes. New York: Free Press, 1982.

Duus, Peter. *The Abacus and the Sword: The Japanese Penetration of Korea, 1895–1910*. Berkeley: University of California Press, 1998.

Eastman, Lloyd E. *The Abortive Revolution: China under Nationalist Rule, 1927–1937*. Cambridge, MA: Harvard University Press, 1974.

Eley, Geoff. *Nazism as Fascism: Violence, Ideology, and the Ground of Consent in Germany, 1930–1945*. New York: Routledge, 2013.

Esherick, Joseph W. "The Many Faces of Chiang Kai-shek." *Chinese Historical Review* 17, no. 1 (2010): 16–23.

Fan Yuansheng. "Nongmin de xinshenghuo" [New life for peasants]. Nanjing: Zhongzheng shuju, 1934.

Fanon, Frantz. *The Wretched of the Earth*. New York: Grove, 1964.

Feldman, Allen. *Formations of Violence: The Narrative of the Body and Political Terror in Northern Ireland*. Chicago: University of Chicago Press, 1991.

Ferlanti, Frederica. "The New Life Movement in Jiangxi Province, 1934–1938." *Modern Asian Studies* 44, no. 5 (2010): 961–1000.

Finnane, Antonia. "What Should Women Wear? A National Problem." *Modern China* 22, no. 2 (1996): 99–131.

Fitzgerald, John. *Awakening China: Politics, Culture, and Class in the Nationalist Revolution*. Stanford, CA: Stanford University Press, 1996.

Foucault, Michel. *Discipline and Punish: The Birth of the Prison*. New York: Vintage, 1995.

Fung, Edmund S. K. *The Intellectual Foundations of Chinese Modernity: Cultural and Political Thought in the Republican Era*. New York: Cambridge University Press, 2010.

———. "Nationalism and Modernity: The Politics of Cultural Conservatism in Republican China." *Modern Asian Studies* 43, no. 3 (2009): 777–813.

Furth, Charlotte. "Culture and Politics in Modern Chinese Conservatism." In *The Limits of Change: Essays on Conservative Alternatives in Republican China*, edited by Charlotte Furth. Cambridge, MA: Harvard University Press, 1976.

Gellately, Robert. *Backing Hitler: Consent and Coercion in Nazi Germany*. New York: Oxford University Press, 2001.

Gerth, H. H., and C. Wright Mills, eds. *From Max Weber: Essays in Sociology*. New York: Oxford University Press, 1958.

Gerth, Karl. *China Made: Consumer Culture and the Creation of the Nation*. Cambridge, MA: Harvard East Asian Monographs, 2003.

Gibson, Richard M., with Wenhua Chen. *The Secret Army: Chiang Kai-shek and the Drug Warlords of the Golden Triangle*. Singapore: John Wiley and Sons, 2011.

Gilmartin, Christina Kelley. *Engendering the Chinese Revolution: Radical Women, Communist Politics, and Mass Movements in the 1920s.* Berkeley: University of California Press, 1995.

Glosser, Susan. *Chinese Visions of Family and State, 1915–1953.* Berkeley: University of California Press, 2003.

Goodman, Bryna. "Things Unheard of East or West: Colonialism, Nationalism, and Cultural Contamination in Early Chinese Exchanges." In *Twentieth Century Colonialism and China: Localities, the Everyday, and the World,* edited by Bryna Goodman and David S. G. Goodman. New York: Routledge, 2012.

Goodman, Bryna, and Wendy Larson, eds. *Gender in Motion: Divisions of Labor and Cultural Change in Late Imperial and Modern China.* Langham, MD: Rowman and Littlefield, 2005.

Gramsci, Antonio. *Selections from the Prison Notebooks.* Translated by Quintin Hoare. New York: International Publishers, 1971.

Gregor, A. James. *A Place in the Sun: Marxism and Fascism in China's Long Revolution.* Boulder, CO: Westview, 2000.

Griffin, Roger. *Modernism and Fascism: The Sense of a Beginning under Mussolini and Hitler.* London: Palgrave MacMillan, 2007.

———. *The Nature of Fascism.* New York: Routledge, 1993.

Guan Zhigang. *Xinshenghuo yundong yanjiu* [Research on the New Life Movement]. Shenzhen: Haitian chubanshe, 1999.

Guha, Ranajit, and Gayatri Chakravorty Spivak, eds. *Selected Subaltern Studies.* New York: Oxford University Press, 1998.

Guo Qingyou, ed. *Zhonghua minguo shiqi junzheng zhiguan zhi, shang* [A record of military and civil officials during the Chinese Republican period, vol. 1]. Lanzhou: Gansu renmin chubanshe, 1990.

Harootunian, Harry. *History's Disquiet: Modernity, Cultural Practice, and the Question of Everyday Life.* New York: Columbia University Press, 2000.

———. *Overcome by Modernity: History, Culture, and Community in Interwar Japan.* Princeton, NJ: Princeton University Press, 2000.

Harrison, Henrietta. *The Making of the Republican Citizen: Political Ceremonies and Symbols in China, 1911–1929.* New York: Oxford University Press, 2000.

Harvey, David. *The Condition of Postmodernity: An Enquiry into the Origins of Cultural Change.* New York: Wiley-Blackwell, 1991.

———. *The New Imperialism.* New York: Oxford University Press, 2003.

He Zhonghan. *He Zhonghan xiansheng jiangshu xuanlu* [Selected speeches of Mr. He Zhonghan]. Edited by Ming Zhang. Nanjing: Tiba Shudian, 1933.

Herf, Jeffrey. *Reactionary Modernism: Technology, Culture, and Politics in Weimar and the Third Reich.* New York: Cambridge University Press, 1986.

Herzog, Dagmar. *Sex after Fascism: Memory and Morality in Twentieth-Century Germany.* Princeton, NJ: Princeton University Press, 2007.

Herzstein, Robert E. *Henry R. Luce, Time, and the American Crusade in Asia.* New York: Cambridge University Press, 2006.

Hevia, James L. *English Lessons: The Pedagogy of Imperialism in Nineteenth-Century China*. Durham, NC: Duke University Press, 2003.

He Zhonghan xiansheng zhisang weiyuanhui. *He Zhonghan xiansheng shilüe* [A biographical sketch of Mr. He Zhonghan]. Taibei: He Zhonghan xiansheng zhisang weiyuanhui, 1972.

Hobsbawm, Eric, and Terrence Ranger, eds. *The Invention of Tradition*. New York: Cambridge University Press, 1987.

Hofmann, Reto. *The Fascist Effect: Japan and Italy, 1915–1952*. Ithaca, NY: Cornell University Press, 2015.

Hong, Fan. "Blue Shirts, Nationalists, and Nationalism: Fascism in 1930s China." In *Superman Supreme: Fascist Body as Political Icon—Global Fascism*, edited by J. A. Mangan. London: Frank Cass, 2000.

Hu Jiafeng. *Ganzheng shinian: Xiong zhuxi zhiGan shizhounian jinian tekan* [A decade of Jiangxi administration: Special edition for the tenth anniversary of Governor Xiong Shihui's rule]. Nanchang: Jiangxi shengzhengfu Ganzheng shinian bianji weiyuanhui, 1941.

Hu Shuyi. "Ertong de Xinshenghuo" [New life for children]. Nanjing: Zhongzheng shuju, 1934.

Hung, Chang-tai. *Going to the People: Chinese Intellectuals and Folk Literature*. Cambridge, MA: Harvard East Asia Monographs, 1986.

———. *War and Popular Culture: Resistance in Modern China*. Berkeley: University of California Press, 1994.

Iwai Eiichi. *Ran'isha ni kansuru chōsa* [*Investigations into the Blue Shirts*]. English translation by the Federal Bureau of Investigation. U.S. State Department, Confidential Central Files, China, Internal Affairs, 1945–1949. 893.00/3-3045.

Jackson, Anna. "Art Deco in East Asia." In *Art Deco 1930–1939*, edited by Charlotte Benton, Tim Benton, and Ghislaine Wood. Boston: Bullfinch, 2003.

Jayasuryia, Kanishka. "Understanding Asian Values as a Form of Reactionary Modernization." *Contemporary Politics* 4, no. 1 (1998): 77–91.

Jeans, Roger B. *Democracy and Socialism in Republican China: The Politics of Zhang Junmai (Carsun Chang), 1906–1941*. Lanham, MD: Rowman and Littlefield, 1997.

Jensen, Lionel. *Manufacturing Confucianism: Chinese Traditions and Universal Civilization*. Durham, NC: Duke University Press, 1997.

Judd, Ellen R. "Revolutionary Drama and Song in the Jiangxi Soviet." *Modern China* 9, no. 1 (1983): 127–60.

Judge, Joan. *Print and Politics: "Shibao" and the Culture of Reform in Late Qing China*. Stanford, CA: Stanford University Press, 1996.

Karl, Rebecca E. *Staging the World: Chinese Nationalism at the Turn of the Twentieth Century*. Durham, NC: Duke University Press, 2002.

Khalili, Laleh. "Gendered Practices of Counterinsurgency." *Review of International Studies* 37, no. 4 (2011): 1471–91.

Kiangsi Rural Reconstruction Centers, Head Office. *Reconstruction in Rural Kiangsi*. Nanchang: National Economic Council, 1935.

Kiangsi Rural Welfare Centers, Head Office. *New Life Centers in Rural Kiangsi*. Nanchang: National Economic Council, 1936.

Kirby, William C. "Engineering China: Birth of the Developmental State, 1928–1937." In *Becoming Chinese: Passages to Modernity and Beyond*, edited by Wen-hsin Yeh. Berkeley: University of California Press, 2000.

———. *Germany and Republican China*. Stanford, CA: Stanford University Press, 1984.

———. "Images and Realities of Chinese Fascism." In *Fascism outside Europe: The European Impulse against Domestic Conditions in the Diffusion of Fascism*, edited by Stein Ugelvik Larsen. New York: Columbia University Press, 2001.

Ko, Dorothy. *Teachers of the Inner Chambers: Women and Culture in Seventeenth-Century China*. Stanford, CA: Stanford University Press, 1994.

Koonz, Claudia. *The Nazi Conscience*. Cambridge, MA: Belknap, 2003.

Ku, Hung-ting. "The Merchants versus Government: The Canton Merchants' Volunteer Corps Incident." *Asian Affairs* 9, no. 3 (1978): 309–18.

Kwan, Daniel Y. K. *Marxist Intellectuals and the Chinese Labor Movement: A Study of Deng Zhongxia, 1894–1933*. Seattle: University of Washington Press, 1997.

Lam, Tong. *A Passion for Facts: Social Surveys and the Construction of the Chinese Nation State, 1900–1949*. Berkeley: University of California Press, 2011.

Lanza, Fabio. *Behind the Gate: Inventing Students in Beijing*. New York: Columbia University Press, 2010.

Lean, Eugenia. *Public Passions: The Trial of Shi Jianqiao and the Rise of Popular Sympathy in Republican China*. Berkeley: University of California Press, 2007.

Lee, Leo Ou-fan. *Shanghai Modern: The Flowering of a New Urban Culture in China, 1930–1945*. Cambridge, MA: Harvard University Press, 1999.

Lenin, Vladimir. "Can the Bolsheviks Retain State Power?" In *Lenin's Collected Works*, vol. 26, 87–136. Moscow: Progress, 1972. https://www.marxists.org/archive/lenin/works/1917/oct/01.htm.

Levenson, Joseph R. *Confucian China and Its Modern Fate: A Trilogy*. Berkeley: University of California Press, 1968.

Li, Guannan. "Culture, Revolution, and Modernity in China: The Guomindang's Ideology and Enterprise of Reviving China, 1927–1937." PhD diss., University of Oregon, 2009.

———. "Reviving China: Urban Reconstruction in Nanchang and the Guomindang National Revival Movement, 1932–1937." *Frontiers of History in China* 7, no. 1 (2012): 106–13.

Li Haisheng and Zhang Min. *Minguo liang xiongdi: Chen Guofu yu Chen Lifu* [Two brothers of the republic: Chen Guofu and Chen Lifu]. Shanghai: Shanghai renmin chubanshe, 2011.

Li, Hsiao-ti. "Making a Name and a Culture for the Masses." *positions: east asia cultures critique* 9, no. 1 (2001): 29–68.

Li Yansheng. *Zhongguo baokan tushi* [A pictorial history of Chinese periodicals]. Wuhan: Hubei renmin chubanshe, 2005.

Lipkin, Zwia. *Useless to the State: "Social Problems" and Social Engineering in Nationalist Nanjing, 1927–1937*. Cambridge, MA: Harvard East Asia Monographs, 2006.

Liu Jianqun. *Fuxing Zhongguo geming zhi lu* [The path to reviving the Chinese revolution]. Beijing: Beijing zhongxian tuofang keji fazhan youxian gongsi, 2012.

Liu, Lydia H. *Translingual Practice: Literature, National Culture, and Translated Modernity—China, 1900–1937*. Stanford, CA: Stanford University Press, 1995.

Louie, Kam. *Theorising Chinese Masculinity: Society and Gender in China*. New York: Cambridge University Press, 2002.

Lu, Albert. "The Renaissance of Rural Kiangsi." *China Information Bulletin* 2, no. 2 (1936).

Lu Hsun [Lu Xun]. *Selected Works of Lu Hsun*, vols. 3 and 4. Edited and translated by Gladys Yang and Hsien-Yi Yang. Peking: Foreign Languages Press, 1960.

Lu Xun. *Lu Xun quanji*, vol. 6. Beijing: Beijing wenxue chubanshe, 2005.

Lu, Yan. *Re-understanding Japan: Chinese Perspectives, 1895–1945*. Honolulu: University of Hawai'i Press, 2004.

Luo, Zhitian. *Inheritance within Rupture: Culture and Scholarship in Early Twentieth Century China*. Translated by Lane Harris and Chun Mei. Leiden: Brill, 2015.

———. *Liebianzhong de chuancheng: Ershi shiji qianqi de Zhongguo wenhua yu xueshu*. Beijing: Zhonghua shuju, 2003.

Ma Fangruo, ed. *Zhongguo benwei wenhua jianshe taolunji* [A collection of debates about Chinese cultural construction]. Shanghai: Longwen Shudian, 1935.

Maffei, Nicolas P. "The Search for an American Design Aesthetic: From Art Deco to Streamlining." In *Art Deco 1930–1939*, edited by Charlotte Benton, Tim Benton, and Ghislaine Wood. Boston: Bullfinch, 2003.

Maier, Charles S. "Between Taylorism and Technocracy: European Ideologies and the Vision of Industrial Productivity in the 1920s." *Journal of Contemporary History* 5, no. 2 (1970): 27–61.

Malraux, André. *Man's Fate*. New York: Vintage, 1969.

Mann, Michael. *Fascists*. New York: Cambridge University Press, 2004.

Mao, Joyce. *Asia First: China and the Making of Modern American Conservatism*. Chicago: University of Chicago Press, 2015.

Marotti, William. "Japan 1968: The Performance of Violence and the Theater of Protest." *American Historical Review* 114, no. 3 (2009): 97–153.

Marx, Karl, and Friedrich Engels. *The Communist Manifesto: A Modern Edition*. New York: Verso, 1998.

Mast, Herman, III, and William G. Saywell. "Revolution out of Tradition: The Political Ideology of Tai Chi-t'ao." *Journal of Asian Studies* 34, no. 1 (1974): 73–98.

Mayer, Arno. *Dynamics of Counterrevolution in Europe, 1870–1956*. New York: Harper and Row, 1971.

———. *The Furies: Violence and Terror in the French and Russian Revolutions*. Princeton, NJ: Princeton University Press, 2000.

McClintock, Anne. *Imperial Leather: Race, Gender, and Sexuality in the Colonial Contest*. New York: Routledge, 1995.

Michaud, Eric. *The Cult of Art in Nazi Germany*. Translated by Janet Lloyd. Stanford, CA: Stanford University Press, 2004.

Minick, Scott, and Jiao Ping. *Chinese Graphic Design in the Twentieth Century.* London: Thames and Hudson, 2010.

Morris, Andrew D. *Marrow of the Nation: A History of Sport and Physical Culture in Republican China.* Berkeley: University of California Press, 2004.

Mosse, George L. *The Fascist Revolution: Towards a General Theory of Fascism.* New York: Howard Fertig, 2000.

Mulready-Stone, Kristin. *Mobilizing Shanghai Youth: CCP Internationalism, GMD Nationalism, and Japanese Collaboration.* New York: Routledge, 2015.

Murdock, Michael G. *Disarming the Allies of Imperialism: Agitation, Manipulation, and the State during China's Nationalist Revolution, 1922–1929.* Ithaca, NY: Cornell East Asia Series, 2006.

Musgrove, Charles D. *China's Contested Capital: Architecture, Ritual, and Response in Nanjing.* Honolulu: University of Hawai'i Press, 2013.

Nairn, Tom. *The Break-Up of Britain.* London: Verso, 2003.

Nedostup, Rebecca. *Superstitious Regimes: Religion and the Politics of Chinese Modernity.* Cambridge, MA: Harvard East Asian Monographs, 2010.

Neizhengbu nianjian bianzuan weiyuanhui. *Neizheng nianjian, di er ce* [Domestic Affairs Almanac, vol. 2]. Shanghai: Shangwu yinshuguan, 1936.

Neocleous, Mark. *Fascism.* Minneapolis: University of Minnesota Press, 1997.

Ni Wei. *"Minzu" xiangxiang yu guojia tongzhi: 1929–1949 nian Nanjing zhengfu de wenyi zhengce yu wenxue yundong* [The "national" imaginary and state control: Literary movements and art and literary policies of the Nanjing government, 1929–1949]. Shanghai: Shanghai jiaoyu chubanshe, 2003.

Oldstone-Moore, Jennifer Lee. "The New Life Movement of Nationalist China: Confucianism, State Authority and Moral Formation." PhD diss., University of Chicago Divinity School, 2000.

Osborne, Peter. *The Politics of Time: Modernity and Avant-Garde.* New York: Verso, 1995.

Osterhammel, Jurgen. "Semi-colonialism and Informal Empire in Twentieth-Century China: Towards a Framework of Analysis." In *Imperialism and After: Continuities and Discontinuities,* edited by Wolfgang Mommsen and Jurgen Osterhammel. London: Allen and Unwin, 1993.

Pan, Lynn. *Shanghai Style: Art and Design between the Wars.* San Francisco: Long River, 2008.

Peralta, Gabriel Aguilera. "Central America between Two Dragons: Relations with the Two Chinas." In *Latin America Facing China: South-South Relations beyond the Washington Consensus,* edited by Alex E. Fernandez Jilberto and Barbara Hogenbloom. New York: Berghahn, 2010.

Perry, Elizabeth J. *Shanghai on Strike: The Politics of Chinese Labor.* Stanford, CA: Stanford University Press, 1993.

———. "Social Banditry Revisited: The Case of Bai Lang, a Chinese Brigand." *Modern China* 9, no. 3 (1983): 355–82.

Pickowicz, Paul G., Kuiyi Shen, and Yingjin Zhang, eds. *Liangyou: Kaleidoscopic Modernity and the Shanghai Global Metropolis, 1926–1945.* Leiden: Brill, 2013.

Qu Qiubai. *Qu Qiubai xuanji* [Selected writings of Qu Qiubai]. Beijing: Renmin chu-banshe, 1984.

Qu Qiubai and Chen Duxiu. *Fan Dai Jitao de guomin geming guan* [Countering Dai Jitao's views on the people's revolution]. Shanghai: Xiangdao zhoubao she, 1925.

Rabinbach, Anson G. "The Aesthetics of Production in the Third Reich." *Journal of Contemporary History* 11, no. 4 (1976): 43–74.

———. *The Human Motor: Energy, Fatigue, and the Origins of Modernity*. Berkeley: University of California Press, 1992.

Reese, Roger R. *The Soviet Military Experience: A History of the Soviet Army, 1917–1991*. New York: Routledge, 2000.

Robin, Corey. *The Reactionary Mind: Conservatism from Edmund Burke to Sarah Palin*. New York: Oxford University Press, 2011.

Rogaski, Ruth. *Hygienic Modernity: Meanings of Health and Disease in Treaty Port China*. Berkeley: University of California Press, 2004.

Ross, Kristin. *May '68 and Its Afterlives*. Chicago: University of Chicago Press, 2002.

Roy, M. N. *Revolution and Counterrevolution in China*. Calcutta: Renaissance, 1946.

Sayer, Derek. *Capitalism and Modernity: An Excursus on Marx and Weber*. New York: Routledge, 1991.

Schmitter, Phillipe C. "Still the Century of Corporatism?" *Review of Politics* 36, no. 1 (1974).

Schnapp, Jeffrey T. *Staging Fascism: 18 BL and the Theater of Masses for Masses*. Stanford, CA: Stanford University Press, 1996.

Schoenhals, Michael, ed. *China's Cultural Revolution, 1966–1969: Not a Dinner Party*. Armonk, NY: M. E. Sharpe, 1996.

Schwarcz, Vera. *The Chinese Enlightenment: Intellectuals and the Legacy of the May Fourth Movement of 1919*. Berkeley: University of California Press, 1986.

———. "Ibsen's Nora: The Promise and the Trap." *Bulletin of Concerned Asian Scholars* 7, no. 1 (1975): 3–5.

Scott, James C. *Seeing Like a State: How Certain Schemes to Improve the Human Condition Have Failed*. New Haven, CT: Yale University Press, 1998.

Shahar, Meir. "Violence in Chinese Religious Traditions." In *The Oxford Handbook of Religion and Violence*, edited by Mark Juergensmeyer, Margo Kitts, and Michael Jerryson. New York: Oxford University Press, 2012.

Shih, Shu-mei. *The Lure of the Modern: Writing Modernism in Semicolonial China, 1917–1937*. Berkeley: University of California Press, 2001.

Silverberg, Miriam. *Erotic Grotesque Nonsense: The Mass Culture of Japanese Modern Times*. Berkeley: University of California Press, 2006.

So, Wai-chor. *The Kuomintang Left in the National Revolution, 1924–1931: The Leftist Alternative in Republican China*. New York: Oxford University Press, 1991.

Song Qingling. *Song Qingling xuanji* [Selected works of Song Qingling]. Jiulong: Zhonghua shuju, 1967.

Spackman, Barbara. *Fascist Virilities: Rhetoric, Ideology, and Social Fantasy in Italy*. Minneapolis: University of Minnesota Press, 1996.

Strauss, Julia C. *Strong Institutions in Weak Polities: State Building in Republican China, 1927–1940.* Oxford: Clarendon, 1998.

Sun Yat-sen. *The International Development of China.* New York: G. P. Putnam's Sons, 1929.

——— [Sun Zhongshan]. *Sanminzhuyi* [Three Principles of the People]. Beijing: Jiuzhou chubanshe, 2011.

Tang, Leang-li. *Chinas kampf gegen den Kommunismus* [China's struggle against Communism]. Shanghai: Verlag China United Press, 1935.

———. *Suppressing Communist Banditry in China.* Shanghai: China United Press, 1934.

Tang, Xiaobing. *Chinese Modern: The Heroic and the Quotidian.* Durham, NC: Duke University Press, 2000.

———. *Origins of the Chinese Avant-Garde: The Modern Woodcut Movement.* Berkeley: University of California Press, 2007.

Taylor, Frederic Winslow. *The Principles of Scientific Management.* New York: Cosimo Classics, 2006.

Taylor, Jay. *The Generalissimo: Chiang Kai-shek and the Struggle for Modern China.* Cambridge, MA: Belknap, 2011.

Thomas, Julia Adeney, and Geoff Eley, eds. "Visualizing Fascism in East Asia and Europe: Imagining, Displaying, Looking at Power." Unpublished manuscript, 2016.

Tien, Hung-Mao. *Government and Politics in Kuomintang China.* Stanford, CA: Stanford University Press, 1972.

Tozer, Ralph. "Taiwan's 'Cultural Renaissance': A Preliminary View." *China Quarterly,* no. 43 (1970): 81–99.

Trotsky, Leon. *Leon Trotsky on China.* Edited by Les Evans and Russell Block. New York: Pathfinder, 1976.

Tsin, Michael. *Nation, Governance, and Modernity in China: Canton, 1900–1927.* Stanford, CA: Stanford University Press, 2003.

Tsui, Brian Kai Hin. "China's Conservative Revolution: The Quest for a New Order, 1927–1949." Unpublished manuscript, 2016.

———. "China's Forgotten Revolution: Radical Conservatism in Action, 1927–1949." PhD diss., Columbia University, 2013.

Tu, Wei-ming. *Confucian Traditions in East Asian Modernity: Moral Education and Economic Culture in Japan and the Four Mini-Dragons.* Cambridge, MA: Harvard University Press, 1996.

van de Ven, Hans. *From Friend to Comrade: The Founding of the Chinese Communist Party, 1920–1927.* Berkeley: University of California Press, 1991.

———. *War and Nationalism in China, 1925–1945.* New York: Routledge Curzon, 2003.

Wakeman, Frederic E. *Policing Shanghai, 1927–1937.* Berkeley: University of California Press, 1995.

———. "A Revisionist View of the Nanjing Decade: Confucian Fascism." *China Quarterly,* no. 150 (1997): 295–432.

———. *Spymaster: Dai Li and the Chinese Secret Service.* Berkeley: University of California Press, 2003.

Wakeman, Frederic E., and Richard L. Edmonds, eds. *Reappraising Republican China.* New York: Oxford University Press, 2000.

Wan Renyuan et al., eds. *Zhongguo jindai zhencang tupianku: Jiang Jieshi yu guomin zhengfu, shang* [Treasures from modern China's pictorial archives: Chiang Kai-shek and the republican government, vol. 1]. Taibei: Taiwan shangwu yinshuguan, 1994.

Wang Hailong. "Dianyuan de xinshenghuo" [New life for shopkeepers]. Nanjing: Zhongzheng shuju, 1934.

Wang Qisheng. *Geming yu fangeming: Shehui wenhua shiyexia de minguo zhengfu* [Revolution and counterrevolution: The republican government in social and cultural perspective]. Beijing: Shehui kexue wenxian chubanshe, 2010.

Wang Xiaohua. *"Mofan" Nanchang: Xinshenghuo yundong ceyuandi* ["Emulate" Nanchang: The base of the New Life Movement]. Nanchang: Jiangxi meishu chubanshe, 2007.

Wang, Yiyan. "Mr. Butterfly in Defunct Capital: 'Soft' Masculinity and (Mis)engendering China." In *Asian Masculinities: The Meaning and Practice of Manhood in China and Japan*, edited by Kam Louie and Morris Low. New York: Routledge Curzon, 2003.

Wang, Zheng. *Women in the Chinese Enlightenment: Oral and Textual Histories*. Berkeley: University of California Press, 1999.

Ward, Max. "The Problem of 'Thought': Crisis, National Essence, and the Interwar Japanese State." PhD diss., New York University, 2011.

Wei, William. *Counterrevolution in China: The Nationalists in Jiangxi during the Soviet Period*. Ann Arbor: University of Michigan Press, 1985.

Wells, Audrey. *The Political Thought of Sun Yat-sen: Development and Impact*. New York: Palgrave Macmillan, 2001.

Wen Zuo and Yan Bi. "'Zuolian' shiqi Guomindang wenyi qikan qiantan" [A brief discussion of Guomindang art and literary periodicals during the "League of Left-Wing Writers" period]. *Zhongguo wenxue yanjiu*, no. 1 (2006): 68–73.

Wilbur, C. Martin, and Julia Lien-ying How. *Missionaries of Revolution: Soviet Advisers in Nationalist China, 1920–1927*. Cambridge, MA: Harvard University Press, 1989.

Wilson, David A. "Principles and Profits: Standard Oil Responds to Chinese Nationalism, 1925–1927." *Pacific Historical Review* 46, no. 4 (1977): 625–47.

Wu Jie, ed. *Zhongwen qikan dacidian* [A dictionary of Chinese periodicals]. Beijing: Beijing daxue chubanshe, 2000.

Wu Yiping. "Kangzhan shiqi Zhongguo Guomindang de wenyi zhengce jiqi yunzuo" [The literature and art policy of the Kuomintang, 1937–1945]. PhD diss., National Chengchi University, 2009.

———. "Wenhua tongzhi yu guojia suzao: Guomindang zhongyang wenhua shiye jihua weiyuanhui, 1936–1937" [Cultural control and national formation: The Guomindang Central Cultural Enterprise Planning Committee, 1936–1937]. Paper presented at the Dijiujie liang'an sandi yanjiusheng lunwen fabiaohui, Hong Kong, Chu Hai College of Higher Education, September 2008.

Wyatt, Don J. "Confucian Ethical Action and the Boundaries of Peace and War." In *The Blackwell Companion to Religion and Violence*, edited by Andrew R. Murphy. New York: Wiley Blackwell, 2011.

Xiao Jizong, ed. *Xinshenghuo yundong shiliao* [Historical materials on the New Life Movement]. Taibei: Zhongguo Guomindang dangshi weiyuan hui, Jingxiaochu zhongyang wenwu gongyingshe, 1975.

Xiao Youmei. "Yinyuejia de xinshenghuo" [New life for musicians]. Nanjing: Zhong-zheng shuju, 1934.

Xiao, Zhiwei. "Anti-imperialism and Film Censorship during the Nanjing Decade." In *Transnational Chinese Cinemas: Identity, Nationhood, Gender*, edited by Sheldon Lu. Honolulu: University of Hawai'i Press, 1997.

Xiong Yuansheng. *Nanchang xingying* [The Nanchang field headquarters]. Nanchang: Jiangxi meishu chubanshe, 2007.

Xu Enceng. *Wo he gongdang douzheng de huiyi* [A memoir of my struggles with the Communist Party]. N.p., 1953.

Xu Youwei. "1930 niandai Lixingshe yanzhong de Yidali faxisizhuyi" [Italian fascism as seen by the Vigorous Action Society during the 1930s]. In *Yijiusanlingniandai de Zhongguo*, vol. 1, edited by Zhongguo shehui kexueyuan jindaishi yanjiusuo Min-guoshi yanjiu shi. Beijing: Shehui kexue wenxian chubanshe, 2006.

Yan Fu and Ye Chucang, eds. "Funü de xinshenghuo" [New life for women]. Nanjing: Zhongzheng shuju, 1935.

Yang Kuisong. *Guomindang de "liangong" yu "fangong"* [Kuomintang: Unity with Communists and anti-Communism]. Beijing: Shehuikexue wenxian chubanshe, 2008.

Yang Tianshi. *Jiang Jieshi yu Nanjing guomin zhengfu* [Chiang Kai-shek and the Nanjing republican government]. Beijing: Zhongguo renmin daxue chubanshe, 2007.

Yao, Xinzhong. *An Introduction to Confucianism*. New York: Cambridge University Press, 2000.

Ye Chucang and Pan Gongzhan, eds. "Xuesheng de xinshenghuo" [New life for students]. Nanjing: Zhongzheng shuju, 1935.

Yeh, Wen-hsin, ed. *Becoming Chinese: Passages to Modernity and Beyond*. Berkeley: University of California Press, 2000.

Yen, Hsiao-pei. "Body Politics, Modernity and National Salvation: The Modern Girl and the New Life Movement." *Asian Studies Review* 29, no. 2 (2005): 165–86.

Yergin, Daniel. *The Prize: The Epic Quest for Money, Oil, and Power*. New York: Free Press, 2008.

Young, Clarence Kuangson. *Vers la fin du communisme et du banditisme en Chine*. Paris: Agence Chekiai, 1934.

Young, C. W. H. [Hanming Chen]. *New Life for Kiangsi*. Shanghai: China Publishing, 1935.

Yu, Ying-shih. "Sun Yat-sen's Doctrine and Traditional Chinese Culture." In *Sun Yat-sen's Doctrine in the Modern World*, edited by Chu-yuan Cheng. Boulder, CO: Westview, 1989.

Zanasi, Margherita. *Saving the Nation: Economic Modernity in Republican China*. Chicago: University of Chicago Press, 2006.

Zarrow, Peter. *China in War and Revolution, 1895–1949*. New York: Routledge, 2005.

Zhang Daming. *Guomindang wenyi sichao: Sanminzhuyi wenyi yu minzuzhuyi wenyi* [Trends of Guomindang literary and artistic thought: Three Principles of the People literature and art and nationalist literature and art]. Taibei: Showwe Information, 2009.

Zhang Gongyuan. "Yinhangyuan de xinshenghuo" [New life for bank clerks]. Nanjing: Zhongzheng shuju, 1934.

Zhang Junmai. "Ruijin zhan zai jingshenshang fanggong diyi xian" [Ruijin stands on the spiritual front line of anti-Communism]. In *Youke hua Jiangxi* [Visitors' accounts of Jiangxi], 11–16. Shanghai: Hanxue Shudian, 1937.

Zhang Xianwen, Fang Qingqiu, and Huang Meizhen, eds. *Zhonghua minguoshi dacidian* [A dictionary of the Republic of China's history]. Nanjing: Jiangsu guji chubanshe, 2001.

Zhang, Yingjin, ed. *Cinema and Urban Culture in Shanghai, 1922–1943*. Stanford, CA: Stanford University Press, 1999.

Zhongguo di'er lishi dang'an guan. *Guomindang zhengfu zhengzhi zhidu dang'an shiliao xuanbian (shang ce)* [An anthology of historical materials on the Guomindang political system, volume 1]. Hefei: Anhui jiaoyu chubanshe, 1994.

———, ed. *Zhonghua minguoshi dang'an ziliao huibian, diwuji, diyibian, wenhua (yi)* [A compilation of Chinese Republican history archival documents; series 5, volume 1, culture part 1]. Nanjing: Fenghuang chubanshe, 1994.

Zhou Daiyin. "Jingcha de xinshenghuo" [New life for police]. Nanjing: Zhongzheng shuju, 1934.

Zhu, Qian. "The Politics of Everyday Life: Non-party Leftists in Republican China, 1919–1937." PhD diss., New York University, 2011.

Zito, Angela. *Of Body and Brush: Grand Sacrifice as Text/Performance in Eighteenth-Century China*. Chicago: University of Chicago Press, 1997.

Žižek, Slavoj. *Organs without Bodies: On Deleuze and Consequences*. New York: Routledge, 2012.

PERIODICALS

Donglu yuekan [East route monthly] 1, nos. 1–4 (1934). Gan Yue Min Xiang E jiaofeijun donglu zongsilingbu bianji weiyuanhui.

Funü xinshenghuo yuekan [New Life women's monthly] 1, nos. 1–8 (1936–37). Nanjing: Xinshenghuo yundong cujin zonghui funü zhidao weiyuanhui.

Ganzai huikan [Jiangxi catastrophe newsletter]. 1 vol. (1930). Yangzhou: Ganzai shanhou xiejinhui.

Hanxue zhoukan [Sweat and blood weekly]. 6 vols. (1933–37). Shanghai: Hanxue shudian.

Jingcheng yuekan [Absolute sincerity monthly]. 1 vol., 5 nos. (1933). Nanchang: Zhongguo Guomindang di bashisan shi tebie dangbu jingcheng yuekan bianweihui.

North China Herald, and Supreme Court and Consular Gazette (1870–1941). Shanghai.

Qiantu [The future]. 5 vols. (1933–37). Shanghai: Qiantu zazhi she.

Saodang huabao [Mopping up pictorial]. 1 vol., 6 nos. (1933). Nanchang: Guomindang junshi weiyuanhui zhengzhi xunlianchu.

Saodang xunkan [Mopping up thrice monthly]. 37 nos. (1933–34). Nanchang: Guomindang junshi weiyuanhui zhengzhi xunlianchu.

Shehui xinwen [Society mercury]. 13 vols. (1933–36). Shanghai: Xinguang shuju.

Shehuizhuyi yuekan [Socialism monthly]. 1 vol. (1934). Shanghai: Shehuizhuyi yuekan she.

Shidai gonglun [Era public opinion]. 156 nos. (1932–35). Nanjing: Shidai gonglun she.

Tiexue yuekan [Iron and blood monthly]. 5 nos. (1934). Nanchang: Lujun di shisi shi tebie dangbu.

Wenhua jianshe [Cultural construction]. 3 vols. (1934–37). Shanghai: Wenhua jianshe she.

Xinshenghuo yundong cujin zonghui huikan [Periodical of the New Life Movement Promotion Association]. 33 nos. (1934–36).

Xinshengming [New life]. 3 vols. (1928–31). Shanghai: Xinshengming yuekanshe.

Zhongguo wenhua [Chinese culture]. 1, no. 1 (1930). Nanjing: Zhongguo wenhua she.

Zhongguo wenhua jianshe xiehui huibao [Periodical of the Chinese Culture Construction Association]. 2 vols. (1934–35). Shanghai: Zhongguo wenhua jianshe xiehui.

Chiang Wei-kuo, 113, 208n44

China: ancient and mythical emperors of, 79, 81, 89; art and architecture of, 45, 48, 60, 90, 195; cities of, 4, 9, 87; coal industry of, 32; coastal, 14; colonial control of, 206n8; cosmopolitanism of, 74; diversity of, 18, 71; dynastic past of, 10, 19, 45, 48, 65, 66–67, 87, 95, 96, 135, 141, 159, 192, 195; ethnic minorities in, 5, 199; as friend of Germany, 208n38; future of, 5–10; Japan invades, 13, 14; missionaries in, 129, 209n58; natural resources of, 41; northern, 35; rural interior of, 4, 25, 87, 191; secret societies in, 36; as "sick man of Asia," 86; Society of the Oppressed Peoples of Asia and, 205n2; southern, 1–2, 39

China Film Studio, 52

China League for Civil Rights (Zhongguo minquan baozhang tongmeng), 7, 165, 181, 182, 184–85

China's One Day (Zhongguo de yi ri) investigations, 229n21

Chinese Communist Party. See CCP

Chinese Cultural Construction Association (Zhongguo wenhua jianshe xiehui), 44; journal of, 45, 92

Chinese Cultural Renaissance Movement (Zhongguo wenhua fuxing yundong), 198

Chinese Culture Study Society (Zhongguo wenhua xuehui), 44, 215n123

Chinese Educational Film Association, 49, 235n44

Chinese Nationalist Party. See GMD

Chinese Revolutionary Party, 79

Chinese Young Comrades Association, 37

Chow, Tse-tsung, 217n21

Christianity, Christians, 20, 209n58, 218n29

Chu Minyi, 224n22

Chung, Dooeum, 38, 206n18

Churchill, Winston, 215n120

class, classes: conflict between, 7, 11, 13, 33, 72–75, 76, 80, 81, 97, 99, 126, 207n25, 207n26, 212n53; GMD right rejects, 71; harmony and cooperation between, 9, 72–75, 79, 82, 129, 193; hierarchies of, 65; identity of, 33; metropolitan, 26; national collective vs., 10. See also names of classes

Cold War, 16, 100, 126, 197, 198

colonialism, 2, 4, 13, 100; anti-, 4, 15–16, 17, 18, 27; colonial modernity and, 205–6n8;

colonization and, 39, 74, 219n56; concessions and, 27, 34, 43, 78, 113, 115–16, 185; post-, 17, 140; semi-, 62, 80–81, 133, 193, 205–6n8; violence of, 70. See also imperialism, imperialists; and names of colonizing nations

combatants: cultivation of, 104–12; definition of, 102

Comintern (Third Communist International), 1, 24–25, 70–71, 74, 192; agents of, 11, 114–15

Communism, 1–2, 20, 21, 69, 81, 194; in Cold War, 16, 197; fascism vs., 3, 25, 205–6n8; internationalism of, 10, 70, 103, 192. See also CCP; Marxism, Marxists

Confucianism, 22, 66, 132, 140, 198, 217n21; anti-, 65, 69; Chen Lifu and, 32, 33; classics of, 32–33; Confucius, 19, 66, 89, 209n58; GMD rightists and, 10–11, 17–18, 19, 65, 68, 70, 73, 88–89, 193–94, 229n15; industrial modernity and, 71–79, 196; interpersonal obligations of, 80; martial traditions of, 107; modernization and, 3, 4, 14, 67; as "national spirit," 5, 42, 83, 92; national unity and, 63, 74, 80, 192; neo-, 84, 145, 146; New Culture Movement repudiates, 68, 79; NLM and, 130, 131–32, 148, 158; paternalism of, 41; principles and values of, 16, 21, 22, 49, 68, 71, 73–74, 79, 87, 97, 108, 112, 136, 139, 141, 157–58, 192; reform and, 218n30; scholarly ideals of, 5; self-reflection and, 120; social harmony and hierarchy in, 11, 22, 68, 75, 81, 97, 99, 100, 142–48, 198, 218n29, 230–31n50; Sun and, 14, 67, 71–79, 97, 218n29, 218n30; texts of, 69, 78–79, 93, 107, 145; as true agent of revolution, 26, 196. See also li, yi, lian, and chi

Congress of the Toilers of the East (Moscow, 1922), 39, 69

conservatism, conservatives, 25, 63, 67, 95, 141, 194, 211n22, 216n5; context of, 216–17n6; GMD and, 65, 197

corporatism, 13, 29–30, 34, 63, 81, 196

counterinsurgency, 21, 197; MAC responsible for, 37, 40; Nationalists' campaigns of, 97, 121; nativist prose of, 98–127

counterrevolution, 12, 22, 80–81, 196; Communists and, 10, 28; fascism and, 4, 11, 13, 24–25, 62, 97; of GMD rightists, 24, 97; of Nationalists, 21, 28, 99; revolution and, 9, 80, 81–82, 196; violence of, 62, 99

feminism, feminists, 2, 24, 100, 115, 192, 199
feudalism, 14, 21, 65, 77, 84, 92, 129, 157; Confucianism and, 63, 67, 86, 143, 194, 198; remnants of, 85, 87, 88
film and cinema, 21, 22, 158, 171–75; Blue Shirts and, 42, 44; CC Clique and, 42, 44, 49; Chen Lifu on, 49, 164–65, 172–75; Chinese, 49, 172–73, 184, 235n44; foreign, 173, 234n41; Hollywood, 165, 166, 172, 181; as immoral, 136, 167, 173; movie theaters and, 134, 156, 157, 229n27, 234n41; newsreels, 173, 174; propaganda use of, 164, 171, 175; as weapon, 52, 171
Five Martyrs, 162, 166, 181
Forceful Action Society (Lixingshe), 36–37, 40
Ford, Henry, 14, 26, 81; factories of, 72, 75; Fordism and, 79
Foucault, Michel, 35
France, French, 192, 209n49, 227n96; Shanghai Concession of, 27, 34, 78
French Revolution, 80
Frunze Military Academy, 39, 40
fugu, 67, 217n13
Fung, Edmund S. K., 65, 216–17n6
Funü xinshenghuo yuekan (*New Life Women's Monthly*), 152, 154, 155
fuxing, 67, 217n13
fuxing fei fugu, 67, 217n13

Gandhi, Mohandas K., 26
Geming daobao (Revolutionary guide) (Shanghai), 220n67
gender, 11, 101, 232n79; CCP and, 98, 99, 223n10; of combatants, 102–3; hierarchies of, 65, 68, 113; identities of, 113, 140. *See also* women
General Left-Wing Cultural Alliance, 183
George, Henry, 14, 81
Germany, Germans, 7, 62, 113, 123–24, 159, 192, 227n96; Beauty of Labor organization in, 172; Blue Shirts and, 38; Chiang on, 144–45; China and, 208n38; fascists in, 13, 104, 206n13, 216n129; League of Nations and, 104; moral map of, 84; trains military officers, 104. *See also* Nazism, Nazis
Gerth, Karl, 136, 230n34
Gilroy, Paul, 65
GMD (Guomindang) (Chinese Nationalist Party), 17, 35, 62, 89, 101, 227n96, 229n15; anti-Communism of, 11, 20–21, 147; as

anti-imperialist, 74; Bureau of Investigation of, 31; in Canton, 68–69; Central Executive Committee of, 31, 208n42; Central News Agency of, 208n42; Central Propaganda Bureau, 167; Chiang and, 20; Cold War and, 16; Comintern and, 1; Confucianism and, 17, 65, 70, 88–89; corruption and incompetence of, 26; counterrevolutionary violence of, 99; coup of, 207n25; Dai Jitao and, 80, 208n42; as developmental nationalists, 193, 207n33; dynamic politics of, 13; Examination Branch of, 27; Executive Branch of, 103, 224n22; extreme nationalism of, 208n38; factionalism in, 29–30, 103, 191, 192, 211n22; fascism of, 28, 53, 63, 96; Fifth Party Congress of (1935), 31, 43; flees Nanjing, 212n60; founders of, 67; justice system of, 185; literature and art of, 162–63, 167; May Fourth Movement and, 67–83; militant, 196; military counterinsurgency campaigns of, 21; militia of, 105; modernization and, 46, 163; Nanjing Decade and, 4, 17, 196; nationalist project of, 2, 18; New Culture Movement ideas and, 68; new hegemony of, 233n6; NLM and, 21–22, 67–83; officers of, 39; Organization Department of, 31; Pan and, 235n44; predecessors to, 79; propaganda and, 123, 132, 223n10, 225–26n61; purge of, 34, 222n1; radiates conservatism, 197; reorganization of, 26, 72; revolution and, 24, 94, 106, 208n37, 211n21; right wing of, 8, 10, 14, 15, 67, 69–70, 71, 73, 83, 146, 193–94; self-image of, 45; Soviet Union and, 69, 72; splits with CCP, 3, 10, 80; star of, 85, 105; Sun and, 2, 67, 106; Sun thought and, 4, 11–13, 79; Sun Yat-senism Study Society and, 220n65; Third Party Congress of (1929), 30; Three Parts Military Seven Parts Politics approach of, 102; training and, 224n32; unions and, 29, 189; violence of, 111; White Terror and, 24, 28–29, 162, 165, 182, 184–87, 207n25; as *xianzhixianjue*, 77; young, 73, 192, 193
Goebbels, Joseph, 161–62, 174
Göring, Hermann, on postcards, 161
GPCR (Great Proletarian Cultural Revolution), 101, 197–98
Gramsci, Antonio, 219n39, 234n37
Great Leap Forward (1958–59), 197
Great Wall, 45, *48*, 195

Jinggang Mountains, 222n1

jingshen (spirit), 89, 91, 94, 226n76. *See also* "national spirit"; "native culture"

Jiujiang, Jiangxi Province, 123

Kaifeng, 221n81

Kang Ze, 52

Kapelle, A., 124, 227n96

kidnapping, 22; of Ding Ling, 181, 185–86; of literary figures, 162, 181

Kirby, William C., 208n38, 215n120, 216n129

Kissinger, Henry, 114

Kollontai, Alexandra, 100, 223n7

Koonz, Claudia, 83–84

Korea, 86, 205n2

Kuomintang, 228n4

labor, laborers, 27, 139, 151, 219n39, 226n72; division of, 77, 138, 141, 146, 148

labor, organized, 33, 115; anti-, 24, 29, 149, 192; in Shanghai, 34, 211n21; strikes by, 1, 2, 33, 220n65; subjugation of, 115, 212n53

Lam, Tong, 71

Lan-i-she Society, 35. *See also* Blue Shirts

League of Chinese Military Youth, 82

League of Left-Wing Writers (Zuoyi zuojia lianmeng), 162, 171; attacks on, 165, 186; CCP and, 165, 181, 183; *Mass Literature and Arts* journal, 167

League of Nations, 36, 104, 192

League of Young Chinese Revolutionary Soldiers, 37

Lean, Eugenia, *Public Passions*, 228n3, 233n96

Le Corbusier, 26

leftists, 69, 87, 152, 160, 194, 229n21, 233n6; publications of, 53, 58, 183

Left-Wing Playwrights Association, 183

Lenin, Vladimir, 26, 78, 223n7, 235n72; Leninism and, 66, 171

Levenson, Joseph R., 17, 66

Li, Guannan, 31, 96, 132, 207n27, 220n70; on Sun and Confucianism, 72, 218n30

li, yi, lian, and *chi* (propriety, righteousness, integrity, and humility), 130, 133, 151, 156; Chiang on, 85–86, 143–44; He on, 145–46; significance of, 145. *See also* ritual

Liang Qichao, 42, 182

Liang Shuming, 65

Liangyou (*The Young Companion*), 49, 53, 195

liberalism, liberals, 11, 25, 28, 79, 87, 88, 194; flaws and weakness of, 138, 192

Li Dazhao, 39, 88

Lipkin, Zwia, 118

literacy and illiteracy, 106, 170, 172, 188

literature, 161–90; avant-garde, 176; Blue Shirt publications, 5, 6, 7–9, 36, 37, 49, 52–53, 54–57, 60, 61, 84, 168, 170, 176, 188, 206n18; CC Clique publications, 8, 22, 13, 26, 44, 45–46, 48, 49, 60, 84, 85, 168, 188; collective voice in, 166–81; historical stories, 168–69, 174; mass (*dazhong*) literature, 165, 167, 171; as mass education, 162, 170, 174–75, 188; nationalist, 170, 171, 176–81, 190; national spirit and, 165, 175; novels, 162; organizations, 183; overproduction of, 164; power and purpose of, 163–64, 168, 169, 171, 181, 188–89; proletarian, 166, 167; as reactionary, 132, 175; realism, 169–70; romanticism, 170; science fiction, 163; suppression and censorship of, 165, 167, 181, 182–87; Three Principles of the People in, 167, 188. *See also* League of Left-Wing Writers; magazines; propaganda

Liu Bingli, 134, 215n121

Liu Daxing, 52

Liu Jianqun, 36

Liu, Lydia, 16

liuxianxing (streamlined style), 46, *51*

Long March, 222n1

Longwen Press, 96

Lu, Yan, 113, 208n43

Luce, Henry, 20

Luo Jialun, 169

Luo Zhitian, 17

Lushan, Jiangxi Province, 104, 108, 223n20

Lushan Officers' Training Conference (Lushan junguan xunliantuan), 104, 108–9, 223n20

Lu Xun (Lu Hsun), 7, 70, 120, 152, 182, 183, 226n76; "Diary of a Madman," 68; on GMD, 162–63, 190, 184; *Literature* and, 53; "The Present Condition of Art in Darkest China," 233n5

Lyon, Frederick E., 35

magazines, 152, 195, 214n98, 215n125; Blue Shirts and, 44, 60, 99–100, 105, 111, 188; CC Clique and, 44, 60, 99–100, 188

Manchu Dynasty, 74

Nanjing Decade and Regime (*continued*)
Economic Council, 119, 223n17; Railway
Development Bureau, 79; NLM and, 129,
228n1; popular rule and, 210n12; propaganda and, 43; reorganization of, 37; revolutionary nativism during, 83–95; Special
Services Group, 114; state activity during,
226n72; Sun's widow spurns, 27; Supreme
National Defense Council, 189; weakness of
GMD during, 29, 191; White Terror during,
7–8, 24; women during, 230n34; Xu Enceng
and, 114–15
Nanking Times (CC Clique newspaper), 117–18
nation, 45, 66, 94, 108, 129, 219n56; Blue
Shirt view of, 60, 62; GMD vision of, 19, 101;
military productivity of, 132–41; nativist
conception of, 13–14; self-sacrifice for, 137,
145; unity and, 72, 96, 171, 192. *See also*
national culture; nationalism; "national
spirit"; state, the
national culture, 16, 18, 67, 71, 81, 192.
See also Confucianism; culture; New Culture Movement
nationalism, 12, 33, 38, 44, 49, 68, 87, 91, 197,
208n38, 218n30, 233n6; affect and, 17, 96;
of anticolonial elites, 70, 197; anti-Japanese,
104; as concurrently backward and forward
looking, 5, 19, 64, 84; fascism and, 4–5, 9,
13, 20, 64–65, 88, 207n22, 210n65; Sun and,
13. See also *minzu jingshen*; *minzu wenyi*;
minzuzhuyi
National Revolutionary Army, 15, 111
"national spirit" (*minzu jingshen*): ancient,
10, 19, 67, 84, 193, 194; CC Clique and, 93,
108; Communism and, 21, 110; Confucianism and, 5, 19, 21, 42, 83, 84, 88, 92, 110,
194; in fascist discourse, 85–89; loss and
regeneration of, 44, 88, 127; soldiers and,
107
"native culture" (*guyou wenhua*) , 3, 22, 45, 63,
71, 81, 86, 88, 97; native spirit and, 19, 89.
See also Confucianism
nativism, 13–14, 99; revolutionary, 83–95, 108,
192; Sun's thought and, 79, 82, 208n43
Nazism, Nazis, 7, 24–25, 60, 104, 134, 139,
147, 159, 210n3, 210n65; Blue Shirts and CC
Clique admire, 88, 184, 216n129; concentration camps and, 124; Jews and Holocaust
and, 40, 83, 147; propaganda of, 83–84,
161–62, 172; racism of, 13, 232n83

Neizheng nianjian (*Domestic Affairs Almanac*),
214n98, 215n123
New Culture Movement, 3, 10, 66, 67, 74, 84,
87, 114, 193, 209n50; condemns Confucian
traditions, 16, 63, 65, 68, 72, 79, 142; ethos
of, 21; Nationalists' response to, 67–83, 114;
origins of, 67–68; Sun and, 72, 73
newspapers, 105, 214n98; Blue Shirt, 42, 44,
52, 105, 206n18; CC Clique and, 42, 44,
117–18
Ni Wei, 166, 233n6
NLM (New Life Movement), 21–22, 53, 120,
123, 127, 130, 147, 198; as backlash, 148–49;
Blue Shirts and, 119, 228n4; CC Clique and,
119; celebrations by, 128–29, 132; Chiang
and, 135, 143–45, 151; Confucian traditionalism of, 130, 131–32, 140; core ideas and
purposes of, 128, 130, 131; everyday life and,
131, 133; fashion and, 156, 230n49; in *Future*,
134–35, 139; GMD and, 217n13; ideology of,
228n3, 230–31n50; launch of, 128–29, 158,
194–95; society as machine and, 137–41;
Song Qingling criticizes, 142–43; Taylorized
modernity and, 128–60; women and, 136,
140
Northern Expedition, 15
Noulens, Hilaire, 115

Opium War, 14
Osborne, Peter, 143, 206n13

pacification, 100, 101, 103
patriarchy and paternalism, 68, 234n37; of
Confucianism, 26, 41, 82, 100, 108. *See also*
family
peasantry, peasants, 3, 41, 80, 100, 118, 234n37;
idleness and, 99, 117; organization of, 114,
205n2
Peking University, 220n67
Peng Pai, 114
people, the, 18, 71, 231n50. *See also* masses
People's News Agency, 69
People's Republic of China (PRC), 12, 199
Perry, Elizabeth J., 34, 211n21
political prisoners, 122, 123
productivism, 137–41
Proletarian Poetry Alliance, 183
proletariat, 3, 80, 88, 116, 163
propaganda: Blue Shirt, 206n18; Central
Propaganda Bureau, 167; Dai Jitao and, 79,

Taylor, Frederick J., 33, 134; *The Principles of Scientific Management* (1911), 219n39

Taylor, Jay, 209–10n65

Taylorism, 33, 66, 159; NLM and, 128–60

technology, 195; ancient Chinese, 92; communications, 49, 91; in *Cultural Construction* magazine, 46, 51; engineering and, 29, 31, 32, 45, 69, 114, 132; fascism and, 206n13; GMD right and, 23, 24, 60, 71; of mechanical reproduction, 42; social dislocation and, 65; military and, 40, 41; training and, 66, 192. *See also* industry and industrialization; science

Temple of Heaven, 45, *48*, 195

Teng Jie, 36, 40

Ten Professors, "Manifesto for the Construction of Culture on a Chinese Basis," 96

"Three Principles of the People" (Sun Yat-sen's 1924 lectures), 19, 25, 43, 44, 72–73, 74, 78–79, 92, 107, 129, 130, 132, 133, 146, 218n29, 233n6; CC Clique and, 44; Chiang on, 89, 145; cultural revolution and, 92; Dai Jitao and, 79–83; fascists and, 84; fifth lecture, 78; first lecture, 72, 75; in literature and arts, 167, 188; sixth lecture, 73; state in, 25

Three Principles of the People Forceful Action Society (Sanminzhuyi lixingshe), 36

Three Principles of the People Youth Corps, 189

Tianjin, 105, 130; Beiyang University in, 32, 69

Tiba Shudian, 215n115

Tien, Hung-Mao, 30, 38, 211n21, 213n70

Tiexue yuekan (*Iron and Blood Monthly*), 52, 105

ti-yong (substance-function) debates, 93

Tokyo, 40

Tongmenghui, 32

totalitarianism, 12

Trotsky, Leon, 15

Tsui, Brian, 14, 79, 208n37

Turkey, 144–45, 216n129

United Front (First), 1, 2, 11, 14, 20–21, 25, 66, 70, 74, 80; Canton during, 15, 16, 21, 67, 83, 94, 192, 193; Chen Lifu in, 30, 33, 69; Chiang during, 15; Comintern and, 1, 70–71; Dai Jitao and, 27, 80, 82, 94, 208n42; rhetoric and propaganda and, 9, 10; split of, 3, 15, 23, 83; Sun and, 72. *See also* Second United Front

United Mine Workers, 33

United States, 11, 20, 33, 113, 233n5; anti-Communism in, 100; Chen Lifu in, 15, 32–33; Chinese exclusion laws in, 32, 33; Cold War and, 197; control of China and, 206n8; culture in, 92; FBI in, 31, 35; Ford factories in, 75; liberalism in, 88; Nationalist strategists trained in, 3, 13, 31, 114, 193; Song Meiling and, 129; Sun's view of, 76; Union Pacific trains in, 46, *51*

universities, 11, 15, 32, 70, 114. *See also names of specific universities*

University of Pittsburgh, 15, 32, 70

"unknown unknowns," 102, 127

USSR (Union of Soviet Socialist Republics), 98, 192; Blue Shirts and, 38; CCP and, 88, 111; Cheka in, 31; Chiang's coup and, 15–16; Chinese fascists in 13, 38; GMD and, 208n42; Nationalist strategists trained in, 3, 39, 69, 193; publications in, 45; United Front and, 1, 10, 23, 26; Whampoa Military Academy and, 2, 11, 15, 82, 213n82, 220n65

vanguard, vanguardism, 52, 76, 158; Blue Shirts and CC Clique as, 8, 9, 30; GMD fascists as, 18, 21, 26, 28, 66, 88–89; Sun's views on, 78. See also *xianzhixianjue*

Versailles Treaty, 68

Vietnam, 86, 192

violence, 1, 43, 97, 197, 230n49, 233n96; of CC Clique and Blue Shirts, 4, 35–36, 108; against Communists, 99, 106, 108; counterrevolutionary, 62, 99; against dissent, 8, 9, 104, 140; fascist, 9, 97, 134, 141; of GMD, 3, 14, 111; of imperialism, 5, 70, 206n8, 218n25; by state, 28–29; threat of, 130, 132; torture and, 120; against women, 149, 230n49

Wakeman, Frederic, 185, 194, 215n115

Wang Jingwei, 119, 223n20, 227–28n96; Executive Branch headed by, 37, 103; left-wing faction of, 29–30, 103, 213n69, 223n17

Wang Xiaohua, 215n123, 229n24

Wang Yangming, 146

Wang, Zheng, 68

warlords, 2, 15, 192

Weber, Max, 35

Wenhua jianshe (*Cultural Construction*) (CC Clique monthly), 45, 93–94, 96, 156, 188; GMD modernization and, 46, 92–93; illustrations in, *48, 50, 51, 53, 59, 60*

Wenhua jianshe xiehui huikan (*Periodical of the Chinese Cultural Construction Association*), 92, 96, 138–39

Wenxue (*Literature*), 53, 58

West, the, 9, 41, 75, 93, 96, 198, 205n2; affirmation of culture of, 67–68, 93; attacks on culture of, 93, 230n49; class warfare in, 7; Communism and Communists and, 113, 116; fashions of, 133, 156; knowledge of, 93, 216n5; Sun influenced by, 72, 208n43, 218n29

Whampoa Military Academy, 27, 39, 80; alumni of, 84, 85, 101; Blue Shirts and, 30, 35, 36, 38, 62, 85, 211n21; cadets of, 80, 82; Chiang and, 15, 32, 82; Soviets and, 2, 213n82; Sun Yat-senism Study Societies in, 11, 15, 69, 82–83

White Terror, 8–9, 23, 31, 149, 207n25; assassinations and murders during, 7–8, 15, 182–87; Blue Shirts and CC Clique and, 21, 24, 62; Communists and, 28–29

women, 27, 108, 135, 230n34; as after-knowers, 151; as athletes, 53, 55, 149; as bandits, 122; Blue Shirts' attitude toward, 149, *150*, 151; Communist, 22, 113; domestic role of, 136, 149, *150*, 232n79; fashion and, 116, 149, *150*, 151; magazines for, 152, 155; modern femininity and, 152; as Modern Girls, 152, 230n49, 232n85; NLM and, 102, 151, 152; in politics, 224–25n33; portrayals of, *117*, *150*, *153*, *154*, 167; rights of, 149; subordination of, 159; violence against, 149, 230n49; as widows, 27–28

workers, 29, 75

World War I, 104

World War II, 13, 135, 196, 197, 199, 209n63

Wuchang, 39, 69

Wuhan, 221n81

Wu Tiecheng, 45

Wuxing, 31, 32

Xia Hanhua, 155–56

Xiang Ziyu, 135, 170; "Establishing a Nationalist Literature," 169, 174

xianzhixianjue (foreknowers), Sun on, 76–77

Xiao, Zhiwei, 234n41, 235n44

xinling (mind-spirit), denied by Communists, 98

Xin qingnian (*New Youth*), 67

Xinshengming (*New Life*) (CC Clique monthly magazine), 44, *46*, 85

Xiong Shihui, 215n123

Xu Enceng, 22, 31, 32, 182–83, 116; on Communist immorality, 100, 114–15, 223n7; on kidnapping of Ding Ling, 185–86; memoir of, 222n6; zishou zixin and, 121

xunlian (training), 224n32

Xu Zexiang, 138–39

Yang Tianshi, 19

Yang Xingfo (Yang Quan), 184; assassination of, 7, 181, 182, 185, 187

Yangzi delta, 38, 43, 192

Ye Chucang, 167

Ye Fawu, 91

yi, shi, zhu, xing (clothing, food, shelter, transportation), 78

yibeishuizhuyi (glass-of-water-ism), 100, 223n7

Yihua Film Company, 184

Young, C. W. H., 123, 124

Young Vanguards, 115

Youth Service Society, 69

Yue Fei, 168–69

Zanasi, Margherita, 12, 29–30

Zarrow, Peter, 207n25, 209n50

Zhang Daming, 166, 233n6

Zhang Junmai, 98–99, 101

Zhejiang Province, 15, 30, 31, 32

Zhejiang Society of Revolutionary Comrades, 30

zhengqihuayi (to make uniform), 130, 139

Zhongguo ribao (*China Daily*), 52

Zhongguo wenhua (*Chinese Culture*), 85

Zhongyong (*Doctrine of the Mean*), 93

Zhou Dynasty, 5, 89

Zhu De, 99

zishou zixin ("giving oneself up to the law and making a fresh start"), 121